JAGGERMEN'S BRIDGES ON PACKHORSE TRAILS

Picture on front cover:
Cromwell's Bridge, near Clitheroe, Lancashire.

Pictures on rear cover:
Beggar's Bridge, Glaisdale, North York Moors.
Wycoller Clam Bridge, Colne, Lancashire.
Thorns Gill Bridge, Gearstones, Ribblesdale, North Yorkshire.

Published by Sledgehammer Engineering Press Ltd, World From Rough Stones House, Farling Top, Cowling, Keighley, West Yorkshire, BD22 0NW, England,
Telephone: 01535 637153
Email: { HYPERLINK "mailto:lankyboilermaker@btconnect.com" }
Website: www.sledgehammerengineeringpress.co.uk

All distribution enquiries should be addressed to the publisher.

Also by Sledgehammer Engineering Press Limited:

Chronicles of a Lancastrian Boilermaker	**1998, ISBN: 978-0-9532725-0-8**
Fred Dibnah's Chimney Drops	**2008, ISBN: 978-0-9532725-1-8**
Historic Steam Boiler Explosions	**2009, ISBN: 978-0-9532725-2-5**
Jaggermen's Bridges on Packhorse Trails	**2010, ISBN: 978-0-9532725-3-2**

Forthcoming new titles:

Smokestacks – An Illustrated History Of Industrial Chimneys In Northern England And The Industries They Served - 2011.

The Scrapmetal Moguls – The Rags To Riches Stories Of Britain's Dismantling And Metal Recycling Wizards – Late 2011.

Printed by Amadeus Press, Ezra House, West 26 Business Park, Cleckheaton, West Yorkshire, BD19 4TQ
Telephone: 01274 863210: Fax: 01274 863211: Email: info@ amadeuspress.co.uk Website: wwwamadeuspress.co.uk

DEDICATED TO ALAN McEWEN

With special thanks to my husband Alan, for without him this book would have remained a dream. In my previous life as a Business Secretary and P.A. the idea of researching and studying, prior to writing a book was simply just a wild dream. However, with Alan's guidance, which opened up for me a whole new world that is Britain's Industrial Heritage, I thank him.

ACKNOWLEDGEMENTS

Angie Simpson, Richmond Library; Carol Scott, Northumberland Museum and Archives; Caroline Furey, Bolton Museum and Archive Service; Community History Department, Central Library, Burnley; Debbie Allen, Dales Countryside Museum, Hawes; Duncan Armstrong, Burnley; Gerald Schofield, Blackburn; Jean and Martin Norgate, Lake District Images; Jean, Chorley Library; Kate Holliday, Cumbria Record Office, Kendal; Lynn Watkinson, Leyburn Library; Margaret Ford, Pudsey Civic Society; Melanie Whitehead, Briercliffe Society; Peter Iles, Lancashire Record Office, Preston; Stephen Ralph, North Yorkshire County Council; Theresa Dixon, Newcastle City Library.

WITH SPECIAL THANKS TO:

Robin Sharples, Artist, Cowpe, Rossendale; David Ford, Artist; Oldham; Dorothy Macleod, Lancashire Record Office, Preston; Helen Mason, Ryedale Folk Museum; John Fletcher, O.B.E. Chairman - Manchester Bolton & Bury Canal Society; Paul Kabrna, Craven & Pendle Geological Society (1998); Robert White, Yorkshire Dales National Park Authority.

My heartiest apologies to anyone I may have forgotten.

BIBLIOGRAPHY

Barnes, Bernard, *Passage Through Time, Saddleworth Historical Society, 1981.*
Bray, Robin, *Walking on Bridges, Hayloft 2009*
Goldthorpe, Ian, *Further Rossendale Rambles, Rossendale Groundwork Trust.*
Hartley, Marie, Wharfedale, J.M. Dent & Sons Ltd., 1938.
Hartwell, Michael, *An Illustrated Guide to The Packhorse Bridges of the Lake District, Ernest Press 1994.*
Hinchlifffe, Ernest, *A Guide to the Packhorse Bridges of England, A Cicerone Guide.*
Jervoise, E. *The Ancient Bridges of the North of England, The Architectural Press, 1931.*
Mee, Arthur, *The King's England, Yorkshire West Riding, Hodder & Stoughton Ltd, 1950.*
Morrison John, and Speakman, Lydia, *Pennine Rails and Trails, Leading Edge Press and Publishing 1990.*
Patchett, Arnold N, *Some Yorkshire Bridges of Beauty and Romance, The Pentland Press Ltd., 1992.*
Raistrick, Arthur, *Green Tracks on the Pennines, The Dalesman Publishing Co. Ltd., 1962.*
Slack, Margaret, *The Bridges of Lancashire and Yorkshire, Robert Hale Ltd., 1986.*
Thornber, Titus, *Seen on the Packhorse Tracks, South Pennine Packhorse Trails Trust.*
Wood, G. Bernard, *Bridges in Britain, Cassell & Co. Ltd., 1970.*
Wright, Geoffrey N, *Roads and Trackways of The Yorkshire Dales, Billings & Sons Ltd., 1985.*

JAGGERMEN'S BRIDGES ON PACKHORSE TRAILS

CONTENTS
****

JAGGERMEN'S BRIDGES ON PACKHORSE TRAILS

INTRODUCTION

On a Jack Frost freezing cold Sunday morning in December 2003 whilst out rambling with my husband Alan along the cinder towpath of the Leeds and Liverpool Canal in the Weavers' Triangle, Burnley, Lancashire, taking in the sad, forlorn vistas of the old tumbled-down, grey-stone cotton mills with their countless sightless windows, ruinous stubby chimneys, and with us both firing off shot upon shot with our cameras of the surrounding derelict, but nonetheless, fascinating industrial ruination, I found myself becoming more and more fascinated with Alan's regular highly descriptive accounts regarding the Lancashire cotton industry, the Leeds and Liverpool Canal, and also the ancillary or in Alan's words, the 'piggy-back' industries that these now crumbling mill buildings once proudly served.

It was this highly atmospherical journey through these canyons of once prestigious Lancashire cotton mills that became the spring-board to one of the most fascinating of past-times I have ever enjoyed. Since that period I have come to thoroughly enjoy our regular forays all over Northern England researching and photographing Britain's Industrial Heritage, which has, at an alarming rate over the last 20 years, virtually disappeared.

During the Christmas holiday of 2004, Alan enthusiastically introduced me to two local sites in East Lancashire where there were what Alan described as being 'packhorse bridges'. My very first sighting of a packhorse bridge was Higherford Old Bridge at Barrowford which I enjoyed immensely. Alan informed me that in certain parts of Lancashire and Yorkshire packhorse bridges were sometimes known as 'Jaggermen's bridges', the name being derived from a breed of packhorses, the 'Jaeger' imported from Germany. We then explored the once abandoned eighteenth century weavers' hamlet of Wycoller near Colne which boasts a splendid, picturesque, medieval twin-arched stone packhorse bridge. With rising excitement of seeing this bridge, Alan then pointed out another equally fascinating bridge situated a little further upstream. This bridge built of huge slabs of local sandstone is known as a clapper bridge. On walking further upstream and past the beautifully and authentically restored huge Tithe barn set in delightful Pennine surroundings, Alan then showed me the third of Wycoller's interesting old bridges. This bridge consists of one massively hewn block of Millstone Grit which is mounted on huge boulders at either end and spans the moorland-draining beck in one gigantic leap.

During the four mile journey back to Cowling I found myself becoming so fascinated with these fabulous little bridges that I made the immediate decision to seek out, to research and to photograph as many other of the old packhorse bridges that Alan said were scattered all over the mountainous areas of Northern England: the Pennines, the North Yorkshire Moors, the Lake District and County Durham.

With boundless fascination for my subject I then delved more deeply into researching the specific localities of surviving northern packhorse bridges. I also realised that it would indeed be very worthwhile to visit these bridges, to individually record and photograph these historic, enigmatic, and often beautiful little structures.

So in the Spring of 2005, Alan and I commenced with, what some of my friends have described as - 'a pilgrimage' - to visit every surviving packhorse bridge in the North of England. A truly massive yet profoundly interesting endeavour!

And so it came about during the late spring and early summer of 2005 as a consequence of me seeking out quite a goodly number of locally situated packhorse bridges such as the Donkey Bridge at Oxenhope, Beckfoot Bridge at Bingley and Bronte Bridge at Haworth, the concept of me actually writing a book on packhorse bridges: a sort of illustrated guide and gazetteer of these amazing, historical structures was then put into practice. Within the following few weeks the idea of me writing the packhorse bridge book became a sort of burning ambition, and so I found myself spending most of my free time in gleaning information from books, libraries, industrial museums and of course the internet. Alan with his deep knowledge of industrial history and his intimate knowledge of the Pennines, the Yorkshire Dales, the Lake District and other upland areas of Northern England where packhorse bridges were located, the majority being in wild but fantastically beautiful countryside, was of great assistance to me.

During the second half of 2004 I had two articles published in Yorkshire Ridings Magazine and Lancashire Magazine which encouraged me to commence writing this book.

Jaggermen's Bridges on packhorse Trails chronicles my adventures in searching out and finding packhorse bridges all over Northern England. I do not claim to be an expert on packhorse bridges and any mistakes found herein will be my own, as this is my first attempt at book writing!

A SHORT HISTORY OF THE JAGGERMEN'S BRIDGES OF NORTHERN ENGLAND

Ever since ancient times man has been required to traverse the bleak mountainous regions of the North of England to barter or sell his wares, his animals; cattle, oxen, sheep and goats. Man has also moved his cattle on to better pastures, for the well-being of himself and his family depended on the milk, meat, hides and bones. Therefore, to enable him to live more profitably, man constructed bridges across the numerous fast flowing mountain streams and becks. Many of the pathways over the mountains and hills of Northern England had been trod by ancient Britons and also Roman soldiers.

All over the North of England where the Jaggermen's trails came down from the tops of the hills to the many rivers and becks, these water courses would be crossed by old wooden bridges or by ancient fords. However, where the banks were too steep, then a steeply humped, single-arched bridge would be constructed. Many of these specifically designed bridges were built particularly in the seventeenth and eighteenth centuries, the accentuated curvature of the arches allowing high levels of flood water to flow beneath. The majority of these packhorse bridges when first built either had no parapets or had extremely low ones to allow the heavily ladened Jaggermen's packhorse trains to pass over without hindrance.

By around 1800, numerous Scottish cattle dealers known as 'Drovers' drove huge herds of cattle on packhorse tracks over the Lakeland mountains and the Pennine dales en route to the burgeoning towns and cities with large hungry populations further to the south. Many of these narrow packhorse bridges which spanned treacherous, fast-flowing, deep mountain becks, were of course too narrow to accommodate this bovine traffic, therefore, significant numbers of them were consequently widened, or rebuilt to include parapets from the middle to the end of the nineteenth century.

CUMBRIA AND THE LAKE DISTRICT

The majority of the surviving packhorse bridges of Northern England are to be found in the wilds of Cumbria, North Yorkshire, particularly in the Dales, and the South Pennine regions of West Yorkshire and East Lancashire.

Until the advent of the turnpikes in the eighteenth century and the coming of the railways in the nineteenth century, the lonely, high altitude passes of Cumbria and the Pennines were exceedingly difficult to negotiate by wheeled vehicles.

The Lake District's packhorse bridges undoubtedly rank alongside the finest of these diminutive structures found anywhere in Britain, and are usually located in breathtakingly beautiful surroundings.

Virtually anywhere in Northern England where there is a packhorse bridge, on a delicious warm mid-summer's morning, or perhaps in the depths of winter when a thick carpet of snow covers the high moorland and fells, to rest a while by one of these delightful packhorse bridges along with your thoughts, allowing the surrounding wild grandeur, majesty, peace and tranquillity to flush out your demons and everyday worries is a fantastic experience; to enjoy the silence, disturbed only perchance by a hidden grouse or pheasant's crying, or the rustle of the reeds as a sleepy rabbit forages for food; or the melodious babbling of the laughing, dancing, sparkling mountain torrent which was born a short time back as a raindrop cascading onto the summits of the lonely mountains. This is the magic of Britain's great outdoors.

THE LAKE DISTRICT

Within the outstanding beautiful and majestic setting of the Lake District National Park, there are a goodly number of delightful stone-built packhorse bridges. Two of these distinctive and most attractive diminutive bridges: High Sweden Bridge and Sosgill Bridge are annually crossed by countless thousands of fell walkers, backpackers and ramblers as they tramp their way up the surrounding fells and mountains.

Kendal, the attractive, bustling market town on the south-eastern edge of Lakeland was once an extremely busy crossroads for the packhorse trains which left the town on a weekly basis hauling all manner of goods to Appleby-in-Westmorland, Barnard Castle, County Durham, Wigan in Lancashire, Settle in the West Riding of Yorkshire and further still to far off London and Glasgow.

WHAT DID THE PACKHORSES CARRY?

Kendal and the surrounding Lakeland villages were renowned for knitting stockings. By the closing decades of the eighteenth century Kendal produced and exported over 30,000 dozen pairs of woollen stockings all over Britain, the vast majority being transported by packhorses.

During medieval times a dozen important monasteries and abbeys had become well established in the Lake District. Furness Abbey, which was Cistercian, was the largest and wealthiest, whose monks were expert wool producers and traders in local commodities. The Furness monks were adept at trading the rich Furness and West Cumberland haematite iron ores, and together with a variety of other merchandise, were shipped all over Britain on the backs of packhorses.

In the late sixteenth century, the Society for the Mines Royal was set up in Keswick to exploit the locally mined copper, lead and silver which was extracted from the fells to the west of Derwentwater and also in the Newlands Valley. Vast quantities of these rich metallic ores were conveyed by packhorse trains to Copperheap Bay, on the lake shore, where it was then transhipped to the smelt mill at Brigham, a short distance north-east of Keswick.

Celia Fiennes travelling through Lakeland in 1698 gave a lucid description of the local packhorses:

"..........they use horses on which they have a sort of pannyers some close, some open that they strew full of hay, turf and lime and dung and everything they would use, and the reason is plaine from the narrowness of the lanes."

To make the journey over the high Lakeland passes easier for the packhorse trains, zig-zag routes were hewn through the stoney sides of the fells, thereby easing the severe gradients. A number of these zig-zags can still be seen, two examples being the Kentmere side of the Nan Bield pass and the Langdale side of Stake Pass. Wrynose Pass and Hard Knott Pass were the last routes in England to be regularly travelled by packhorses.

BAD WEATHER

Inclement weather, snow, ice or severe frost could cause many of the packhorse tracks passing over the hills impassable. Heavy, persistent rain, so typical of the Lake District and other exposed areas of North Western England quickly turned the tracks into quagmires with small rivulets of water running down the sides. In the summer when the tracks were much drier conditions were much improved.

PACKHORSE CHARGES

Around the start of the nineteenth century packhorse charges were about a shilling per ton carried per mile, which some carriers slightly reduced if conveying commodities lengthy distances. Some manufacturers and merchants entered into contracts with the packhorse carriers for periods of say six months or maybe a year.

Carriage costs in 1770 would average eleven pence per ton per mile which added around two per cent to the final selling price of the goods when sold. The packhorse journey from Kirkby Stephen down to London took fourteen days which they regularly carried out, notwithstanding the prolonged heavy snows of the winter months.

To carry a pack of knitted wool stockings from Kirkby Stephen to London was still profitable for the stockings manufacturer, for in 1784 the cost to carry 938 pairs of special Guards Hose to London amounted to £2. 11s. 0d. which, on reaching the capital sold for above £100. During the late 1700s, about one thousand dozen pairs of woollen stockings were conveyed by packhorse to London, usually in wrapped packs of fifty dozen pairs weighing 322 lbs. The typical value of the consignment would be between £30 and £60.

Packhorse carrying costs varied between summer and winter, resulting from the difference in travelling conditions, the condition of the tracks, the weather and the length of daylight hours. During extensive journeys for example over perhaps fifty miles, overnight stopping places were required that would allow the horses to feed, drink and rest. A number of wayside inns and remote farmhouses would provide stabling for the horses and refreshment for the carriers.

THE YORKSHIRE DALES

The Pennine Dales of North Yorkshire are blessed with their own indigenous character, symbolized by the wonderful landscape of grassy, high limestone fells dotted with countless sheep, the fast flowing, laughing, dancing rivers and the miles of drystone walls that climb up the vertical sides of the hills; and the numerous stone field barns.

Here too, as elsewhere, the Cistercian monks were superbly dominant in the Dales prior to the Dissolution of the Monasteries. In the wild limestone Craven countryside, a million acres of the finest pastures were owned by Fountains Abbey who grazed the lush grasslands with large flocks of sheep. Woollen fleeces and mutton were despatched vast distances by packhorses.

JAGGERMEN'S BRIDGES ON PACKHORSE TRAILS

Particularly around Skipton and Grassington, prodigious quantities of limestone have been quarried and then burnt in the once abundant coal-fired lime kilns, the finished product lime being spread to sweeten the pastures of acid-rich, sour moorland soils. Lime was also commonly used to make lime mortar for the construction of buildings right through until well into the twentieth century.

Stone for the construction of farmsteads, dwellings, barns, mills and for the erection of the miles of drystone walls was quarried on small and large sites all over the Dales.

On the high Gritstone fells and also in the banks of the becks, thin seams of coal have been won from medieval times until the middle twentieth century.

For centuries, many of the Dales have witnessed significant mining activity, resulting in ores of lead, zinc, calamine, copper and to a lesser extent iron being extracted. For over two hundred years, two extensive areas of the Dales were mined for lead, lead mining being the most important industry. In the northern lead mining districts, of Swaledale and Arkengarthdale, together with some areas of the north side of Wensleydale, the mining of lead and the smelting of the ore was the principle occupation. The other significant lead mining areas extended from Ashfoldside Gill, high above Pateley Bridge in Nidderdale, westwardly across the high peaty moorland of Greenhow Hill and Appletreewick, thence into Hebden, Grassington and Kettlewell in Wharfedale and extending also over the watershed to the southern slopes of the Wensleydale fells close to West Burton.

There were considerably more lead mines than the Smelt Mills to which the dressed lead ore was delivered to be smelted for the production of lead. Jefferey's map dated 1771 shows only four Smelt Mills: Marrick in Swaledale; Braithwaite, also called Burton Mill in Wensleydale; Heathfield near to Pateley Bridge in Nidderdale; and Grassington Low Mill in Wharfedale.

Packhorses conveyed the finished lead to the lead markets. The lead produced in the northern districts was carried to Richmond, Stockton-on-Tees or to Yarm. The lead produced in Nidderdale as well as from Grassington and other mines in Wharfedale was carried by packhorse trains to Boroughbridge.

In Bastow Wood near Grassington a number of small, neatly drystone-walled enclosed crofts were constructed by Wharfedale lead miners for the cultivation of vegetables, corn etc, in return for them looking after the numerous pack ponies which were vital to the lead mining industry.

Packhorses were extensively employed throughout the length and breadth of the Yorkshire Dales to carry prodigious yearly tonnages of the commodities produced.

Typical set of packhorse bells used by Jaggermen on the packhorses.

By courtesy of the Dales Countryside Museum, Hawes.

An artist's impression of Jaggermen and their horses.

JAGGERMEN'S PACKHORSES

Packhorse trains which could consist of twelve to around thirty horses would be heralded by the jingling of the bell collar worn by the lead horse. This cacophony would undoubtedly notify the Jaggerman leading his packhorse train from the opposite direction, and would act as a safety measure, particularly if both packhorse trains had to pass each other as they were making their way through high, narrow rocky passes, typical of the Pennines or Lakeland mountains.

The Jaggermen would lead the horses at a brisk walking pace of say three miles per hour. Therefore, during an eight hour day, the packhorse trains would usually cover twenty four miles.

When setting out on their journey, perhaps at first light, the Jaggermen would allow their horses to eat the surrounding grass. Once satisfied that their animals had had sufficient food, the Jaggermen would then fit muzzles onto each of their horses enabling the packhorse train to proceed until around mid-day when the men would stop their horses, remove the muzzles and then allow the horses to freely graze.

In the lead-mining areas of Northern England packhorses annually carried huge quantities of lead-ore. As the horses slowly trotted along, small quantities of lead-ore dust would be shaken from the panniers and drop onto the track. This lead-adulterated, highly toxic dust would contaminate the grass and other plants growing alongside the trackways. This is the reason why the Jaggermen would muzzle their horses, as the muzzling stopped the animals from eating the lead-contaminated grass, which could probably induce serious poisoning of the horses, or worse, death.

Regarding the loading of the packhorse's panniers, the Jaggermen had to be mindful of loading each of the twin panniers with about 125 lbs; - the maximum weight of the two panniers therefore, amounting to around 250 lbs, - and also to ensure the loads were balanced evenly. Above this weight and the horses would struggle to handle the loads.

A typical packhorse train of perhaps fifteen to thirty horses probably travelled in head-to-tail fashion and not tied together. This was known as 'loose-headed', and the string of packhorses would cover the allotted day's mileage in this manner. At the end of the day when the train reached their destination, perhaps a large village or a town, the Jaggermen would then rope all of the pack train together as a means of ensuring that all of his charges were secure. Generally, particularly in good weather conditions this was good and safe practice. However, in rain, sleet or in a combination of both, parts of the often rocky, twisting tracks, many having vertiginous drops on one side could become deadly to negotiate for the packhorses and Jaggermen alike. In situations like this the Jaggermen much preferred to keep their horses untied.

Trackways could become dangerous for the horses due to rain-washed loose stones covering the surfaces, so leaving the horses untied was probably much safer than having between fifteen and twenty, sweating, tired animals become restless due to the uneveness of the paths. Should a horse have faltered resulting in it falling off the track, if the animal was loose it would not therefore, pull any of the others down also. Alternatively, should all of the horses been tied together, then perhaps several horse would have also fallen resulting perhaps in serious injury and the loss of the goods in the panniers.

Should even a single packhorse fall down a rocky hillside, then the Jaggermen would have to not only clamber down to the unfortunate, frightened and perhaps injured horse, but he would also have to unload the 250 lbs weight of goods from the panniers. This situation would be bad enough in fine weather, but in harsh wintry weather involving driving snow or in a rainstorm, the job of unburdening the poor horse would be even more difficult due to the leather strapping becoming wet.

A number of seventeenth century packhorse trails were troubled by highwaymen and robbers. The 'Galloway Gate', the drove road and packhorse track which connected south-west Scotland with Shap in Cumbria was regularly frequented by mounted highwaymen, particularly where a number of the cattle drove roads and packhorse tracks met within the remoteness of the Lune Gorge. The name 'Galloway Gate' was derived from the employment of Galloway packhorses that travelled the track.

To see a string of fifteen to thirty, dusty, sweating, heavily ladened, packhorses travelling in a single file working their way down a steep stony track, that zig-zagged down a mountain-side, the leading horse, known as the 'bell mare', due to the set of polished brass bells hanging from the centre of her collar and perhaps three or four smaller bells hanging each side, would have created a truly memorable picture.

Walking slightly to the side of the leading horse, would be a tall, well-muscled Jaggerman, perhaps sporting a heavy unkempt beard and a bushy moustache.

These hardy individuals lived a tough, yet free life, caring for their horses and despite weather conditions eating their meals and sleeping roughly up on the fells and often after walking more than twenty miles up and over remote, rocky passes either in the Pennines or in the Lakeland mountains.

LOADING THE PACKHORSE PANNIERS

Special knowledge and care was required by the Jaggermen when loading the panniers or packs. The fully laden packs, one either side of the horse had to be evenly balanced within a couple of pounds, or else the loaded pannier would slide and unbalance the load as soon as the animal commenced walking.

A small packhorse train of around ten horses travelling perhaps a dozen miles or so would be handled by just one Jaggerman, but for longer journeys involving perhaps a team of around thirty horses, one Jaggerman would be responsible for looking after four horses. Alternatively, a team of maybe ten packhorses leading a heavy load of lead-ore from a lead mine to the Lead Smelt Mill, a distance of perhaps ten miles, would sometimes be handled by two Jaggermen and a lad.

Packhorse panniers would come in a considerable variety of shapes and sizes and would be made from stout canvas, leather or wood. For the carrying of coal or metaliferous ores, limestone etc; the packs or panniers comprised a rectangular bag-like shape which had a lid made from canvas and also a strongly-braced bottom door hinged and secured by pins. To unload, the Jaggermen would pull out the securing pins which released the loose materials. The removal of the pins had to be done simultaneously at each side of the horse, to enable the unloading to be carried out evenly.

AILSE O'FUSSARS
LAST OF THE ROCHDALE 'LIME GAL' PACKHORSE DRIVERS

In the mountainous area known as the Rossendale Fells that thrust upwards between Rochdale and Burnley, for many decades of the late seventeenth, the eighteenth and up to around the mid-nineteenth centuries there were numerous Jaggermen, locally known as 'Lime Gal' drivers – this colloquialism being derived from the Galloway breed of packhorses and the lime they carried – from the Burnley lime-kilns, or further north from Clitheroe over the hills and down to the Rochdale district.

The last of these 'Lime Gal' packhorse drivers, was a rather strange-looking woman, whose name was Mary Alice Hartley, but was known far and wide as 'Ailse O'Fussars'. She was obviously an expert Jaggerwoman, who had taken over her father's packhorse carrying business, on his death.

Ailse owned a small stone-built hill farm called, Holough which was perched on the edge of the high, bleak, windswept moorland above the hamlet of Shawforth close to the top of the Whitworth Valley between Rochdale and Bacup. She had been born in the Whitworth Valley around 1812, and was unfortunate for she was no beauty. Physically, she was short in height and extremely rotund, and her facial characteristics appeared masculine.

In nineteenth century Pennine Lancashire characters were plentiful, but Ailse's rather grotesque and mannish appearance could be considered somewhat unusual, even for the times, for it was her daily habit to be dressed in a man's heavy woollen topcoat and on her head she wore a battered 'Jim Crow' hat which was secured in place by a handkerchief passing over the top of the hat and tied in a knot beneath her chin. She was very plump and walked with a pronounced gait of a stout middle-aged man, and in her hand she always carried with her a long blackthorn shepherd's crook.

Ailse owned around twenty Galloway packhorses which she operated daily carrying coal from a small pit known as Land, near Shawforth, to users all down the Whitworth Valley, to the weaving villages of Littleborough and Wardle, and also to Rochdale and beyond.

Ailse O'Fussars
© Rochdale Boroughwide Cultural Trust

Alternatively, she would occasionally lead her packhorses loaded with lime from the lime-burners kilns near Burnley, or further north, from the lime-burners near Clitheroe in the Ribble Valley up and over the bleak extensive wastes of the Rossendale Fells and then down through the Whitworth Valley thence to Rochdale, where, the lime would be despatched to mortar-makers or to farms for sweetening the acid soils of the moorland pastures.

The mountainous route she would take, treacherous in winter, would be from Clitheroe to Burnley, then the stiff climb up to Deerplay; then downhill through Weir and Broadclough, where she would pass a number of bustling, busy coal pits. On reaching Bacup which lies in a bowl-like depression at the head of the Rossendale Valley, she would take the steep incline of the Rochdale Road and climb to the summit at Britannia, where she would then take the ancient packhorse track that passed to the east of the villages of Shawforth and Whitworth; thence she would lead her string of packhorses in a circuitous route around the bottom of the bulk of the large hill, Brown Wardle and then proceed downhill through Cronkeyshaw and finally onwards to Rochdale.

Despite Ailse's bizarre, and masculine appearance, surprisingly she had been courted for some time by Thomas Walton, a young hill-farmer who resided with his parents at Hursted Nook, close to the hamlet known as Pottery. Ailse and Thomas were considered by the locals to be indiscreet lovers, and in April 1838 the bizarre-looking female Jaggerwoman gave birth to a boy, whom the couple named Reuben. Reuben was baptised at Whitworth Church on the 21st of April 1838, but tragically died shortly after. The infant was buried at the church on the 6th of May 1838, and Ailse herself stubbornly carried the tiny wooden coffin up the steep hillside to the grave.

Ailse O'Fussars, or to give her real name, Mary Alice Hartley ran her string of 'Lime Gals' carrying lime, coal, and probably other goods until the end of the packhorse era. Towards the end of her life, Ailse, lived in a humble, stone cottage at Potovens, a tiny hamlet built on an 'intake' on the moorland edge, above Shawforth. Despite her advancing years she was still extremely active and regularly delivered bagged coal fastened onto the back of a donkey to customers all over the Whitworth Valley. Ailse named the donkey 'Jerry', which lived in her cottage and was nightly fastened to her bedpost!

Ailse O'Fussars, the last of the 'Lime Gal' drivers died in 1879 and was buried in the churchyard at Whitworth, a short distance from the packhorse track that she regularly used.

JAGGERMEN SAMUEL AND EDMUND LORD

Another interesting insight into Packhorse lore, is published in a book by William Robertson: *From: Rochdale & the Vale of Whitworth, William Robertson, 1897.*

"Samuel Lord, of High Wardle Farm, and Edmund, his brother, up to about fifty years ago, kept sixteen Galloways. They conveyed lime from Towneley, near Burnley, and also from Clitheroe, along the moor to Rochdale. On these long journeys in the summer time, if persons in charge of 'Lime Gals' could not get to their destination before nightfall, they unloaded the animals and let them brouse (sic) the moors. Then the drivers would have their evening meal, and, after carolling the quaint old songs, would rehearse old stories.

"And often, when no cause appeared,
The mountain ponies pricked their ears."

"The drivers at last feeling drowsy would get into sacks and sleep on the heather renewing their journey the next morning.

There was another packhorse road, which branched off at the foot of Brown Wardle to the right, skirted the moor above Watergrove and came out at Walsden, or by travelling another branch to the left, the traveller arrived at Todmorden. It is called 'The Lang Causey' and just above Marlearth (Marld Earth) (at Rough Hill End), near Wardle, a portion of it at the present time is flagged, as are other parts of the route. The flags were placed on those parts of the track which were boggy to prevent the ponies sinking knee-deep into the earth. As soon as the crest of the hill is reached there is a beautiful panorama view of the valley and hills which stretch into Yorkshire. These packhorse roads are discernable, and they are still traversed by persons on business, as well as those intent on recreation or relaxation. There is some poetry left among us yet; some love for the simple beauties of nature in ...... each hill and dale, each deepening glen and wold."

CHRISTOPHER DUCKWORTH
A MEMORABLE ROSSENDALE JAGGERMAN
(1744 – 1800)

Christopher Duckworth's Gravestone in Haslingden Parish Churchyard.

© *Christine McEwen Collection*

Christopher Duckworth began working for Richard Lonsdale as a packhorse driver or Jaggerman at what we in our modern times would consider to be the rather tender age of ten.

But of course, the employment of young children in eighteenth and nineteenth century Britain was universally accepted.

JAGGERMEN'S BRIDGES ON PACKHORSE TRAILS

Richard Lonsdale was a wealthy Haslingden corn chandler or merchant who supplied corn, oats and similar merchandise to farmers, ostlers, bakers and so on, all over the Rossendale Fells; and daily he would despatch young Duckworth with his loaded string of packhorses to delivery his merchandise. From that first day of his chosen occupation until his last when he died, he was held in high esteem by all who knew him, and particularly his employers, the Lonsdale family.

The first day that Christopher Duckworth set off with his packhorses to trot over the high, wild Rossendale hills; to ford the numerous raging torrents in the bottoms of the deep, dangerous cloughs to deliver Lonsdale's corn and oats, he became renowned for his cheerful disposition, his honesty, and for being a dependable, hard working Jaggerman.

For fifty years, until his death on the 18th of June 1800, aged 66, Duckworth cheerfully daily tramped along the many diverse packhorse trackways holding the bridle of his lead horse, whilst puffing on his favourite clay tobacco pipe. Many of the gritty, hill farmers remembered him as being a most cheerful character and even when the Pennine drizzle fell relentlessly from dark brooding skies causing dense moorland fogs, Duckworth's approach down the vertiginous slopes of the fells was heralded by the sweet sounds of the many brass bells that was festooned over the collar of his faithful lead packhorse.

On his death, the ever grateful Lonsdale family had Duckworth's coffin buried next to their own family graves in Haslingden Parish Churchyard, and they also paid for a stonemason to inscribe the Jaggerman's gravestone with what is, undoubtedly, a most wonderful poetic tribute to all Jaggermen:

UNDERNEATH
This stone are deposited, the Remains of Christopher Duck--worth; who (in the capacity of Servant, to Mr. Richard Lonsdale and his son Mr. Daniel Lonsdale of Haslin--den) followed a gang of pack--horses upwards of half a cen--tury and died on the 18th Day Of June 1800 Aged 66 years.

**'Fifty six years he inoffensive Drove,
(Loving his horses, by his horses Lov'd,)
In faithful servitude the Roads Along,
And seldom said and seldom did he Wrong.
His faithful services have due Regard,
His Masters Honor high heavens Reward,
Where long prov'd worth and honesty Combined
T'illume his spirit with a ray Devine.
A grateful Master, whom he lov'd and Fear'd,
With tearful eye, this stone memorial Reard.
Reader repose in Christ the Lord thy Truth,
Like honest Christopher, be true and Just.**

Further down Duckworth's gravestone was the following inscription:

**Here resteth the Body of
Richard Thextone, who died
the 24th Day of May 1802.
Aged 14 years**

Perhaps young Richard Thextone was either a close relative of Duckworth's or a well regarded person who looked after the packhorses.

Albeit rather neglected, Duckworth's gravestone can still be seen in Haslingden Parish Churchyard.

NORTH YORK MOORS

The North York Moors in area is smaller than either the Lake District or the Yorkshire Dales, is less mountainous, the highest summits of the moorland not quite reaching the fifteen hundred foot contour; however, the wide open spaces of the undulating moorland is without a doubt one of Britain's most stunning and beguiling landscapes. Hereabouts, you can experience the vastness of the moorland scenery that appears to be never ending, you can listen to the calls of the upland birds: Red grouse, the 'pee-wit, pee-wit' call of the lapwing, or the familiar whistling 'curlee, curlee' sounds of the long-beaked Curlew.

All year round the vast moorland reaches are a sea of all dominating heather, which from early July bathes these uplands with colour, the distinctive bell-like flowers nodding their scented heads in the moorland breeze. From about the middle of August, the moorland transforms into a vast ocean of vibrant purple as the more common heather flowers.

The backbone of the North York Moors are the Cleveland Hills that run from the Hambleton Hills in the west for around forty miles and across the broad acres of North Yorkshire to the rugged east coast.

ALUM

Alum used for hundreds of years in the manufacture of vegetable dyes for the dyeing industry was extensively quarried and mined in the cliffs to the north and south of Whitby which caused significant deep scarring of the terrain.

Alum was a Royal Monopoly of the Stuart Kings in the mid-seventeenth century. The mineral occurs in crystal formation in its natural state, and was essential to a number of early industries, particularly the woollen trade – (medieval England's primary industry) – where it significantly improved the manufacture of natural dyes used in the dyeing of woollen cloths.

Prior to the seventeenth century, the primary sources of alum were overseas: the Middle East and the Papal States, north of Rome. These suppliers, however, were unreliable being susceptible to internacine wars. During the sixteenth century, the English Crown financed anyone attempting to prospect for alum in Britain. However, despite a considerable amount of geological exploration, no alum was discovered. Later at the beginning of the seventeenth century, Britain's luck changed when Jurassic Upper Lias shales discovered on cliffs around Whitby were found to contain aluminium-sulphate, the vital ingredient of alum.

The discovery of alum was so significantly important that in 1604 the first alum processing works which proved to be successful, was established at Belman Bank, near Guisborough. A number of other alum processing works were subsequently built, and over two hundred years later in the 1820s the alum trade, by now, a major

North Yorkshire industry was recorded to be employing over six hundred people, and in 1822, the six alum mines cumulative output amounted to some 3,200 tons of the mineral.

During the two and a half centuries that the production of English alum was concentrated in the Whitby area, the trade stimulated the development of other diverse industries and played a significant role in Britain's rapidly expanding industrial revolution. By the nineteenth century however, new techniques involving the chemical treatment of waste shale from collieries to produce alum took hold, and this together with the introduction of aniline dyes, caused a massive decline in the industry. The remaining alum mines located at Sandsend, near Whitby closed down in 1871.

PACKHORSE TRAINS

On the North York Moors, packhorses were called 'Pannier Ponies' and the stone-paved causeways which they trod were called 'Pannerways'. The packhorse goods commonly carried peculiar to the North York Moors was alum, the transportation of the mineral being regularly carried out by scores of packhorse trains who conveyed this profoundly important commodity across the wide expanse of the North York Moors on ancient stone causeways laid into the wet peat; these products of the Whitby area alum industry were journeyed south-west to numerous dye houses in the West Riding and over the Pennines into distant Lancashire.

STONE TROUGHS FOR PACKHORSES ON THE NORTH YORK MOORS

Along many of the old packhorse tracks which criss-cross the North York Moors, stone drinking troughs, especially provided for the packhorses, packmen and their dogs, were once a common feature. The troughs were hewn by stone masons out of huge blocks of local sandstone.

Several of these troughs are still to be seen at the side of tracks, especially where natural springs are found. Opposite Broom Hill House on the Western Daleside Road in Farndale is a huge six-tiered, stone trough positioned by a drystone wall. The troughs are fed from a moorland spring. There are two other stone troughs set beside the Blackey Ridge road between Castleton and Hutton-le-Hole; one is a three-tiered trough.

THE SALT ROAD AND SALT BOX AT GLAISDALE

From earliest times salt was a profoundly valuable commodity. The Saltersgate Inn was the start of the old unpaved track called the Salt Road, used by the packhorse trains to carry salt from the coastal salt pans. Until the removal of the salt tax in 1825, salt was smuggled from Robin Hood's Bay via Lilla Cross to Saltersgate, to avoid paying the tax. When the salt arrived to the household it had to be kept dry as the old dwellings were usually very damp. To store the salt, a stone salt box was embedded into the thickness of the wall next to the kitchen fire to keep dry.

The salt box was made of local stone of which there is an abundant supply on the North York Moors, and comprised a basestone surmounted with a left and a right- hand six inch thick squared stone blocks, which left a six inch wide gap forming the entrance. The salt box was finished with a large stone cap.

An oak frame was wedged into this six inch square space, and a leather flap acting as a door, kept out the damp. The salt boxes found around the moorland communities are unique, their size varies from 21 inches across to 31 inches.

There is no exact date as to when salt boxes first came into use. Perhaps in the seventeenth century when stone dressing traditions developed in the area? They were still being made as late as the early part of the eighteenth century.

A Guide Stone at Lilla Cross. The route the smugglers would have used to take salt from Robin Hood's Bay to Saltersgate.

© Ryedale Folk Museum

NORTH YORK MOORS FEATHERBED LANE PAVED CAUSEWAY OR PACKHORSE TRACK

In former times, the fascinatingly named Featherbed Lane was famously renowned for it being the most fortuitously narrow upland road in the whole of England, although I am certain there were more than a few others just as narrow that traversed the high ground of Northern England.

Whitby's monks travelling down to York via Aislaby, trod down Featherbed Lane whilst wending their way to the moorland hamlets of Briggswath and Sleights. In 1600, the 'trod' or 'causeway' was licensed as one of the Kings Highways which formed part of the highroad between Whitby and Kirkbymoorside. The causeway snakes its way steeply downhill from Aislaby - once an important moorland village with a substantial church and hall - to Briggswath.

Featherbed Lane's – (no records of where the intriguing name sprung from) - existing causey stones survive the whole length of this little 'trod', except for where they have been removed where the modern A169 road crosses the ancient track at Sleights.

CAUSEWAYS OR PACKHORSE TRODS

Running across the high ground of the wide expanse of the North York Moors are over one hundred and fifty miles of stone paved causeways similar in construction to Featherbed Lane, many dating back into the medieval era. Cistercian monks, who were extremely accomplished farmers and producers of livestock regularly journeyed on these causeways whilst travelling between their Abbeys, Priories and Granges. The stone-surfaced causeways provided a solid, dry route across the often rain-soaked peaty ground for the numerous sizeable, heavily laden packhorse trains travelling in single file. A significant number of these stone causeways used by the packhorse trains were constructed in the eighteenth and nineteenth centuries to also serve the increasing numbers of travellers crossing the moors between the villages and hamlets. Occasionally, huge, locally quarried, thick flagstones, were laid down to form lines and if a small beck or stream was encountered then one, massive lengthy stone slab would be laid spanning the watercourse acting as a bridge-stone.

A Causeway or Packhorse Trod.

A 'Hand' Guide Post showing the road to Pickering and Malton.

© Ryedale Folk Museum

OLD LIME KILNS FOUND ON THE NORTH YORK MOORS

Ever since the mid-seventeenth century lime has been used to sweeten the acid soil on the fields and meadowland won from the sour moorland of the North York Moors. As man continued to reclaim land for agricultural use, lime was spread evenly on the surface, then ploughed and worked into the acidic soil to encourage the growing of a wide range of grassland crops as well as arable produce: a variety of vegetables, swedes, potatoes etc. Lime was in demand also for flux used in iron smelting and also for the manufacture of lime mortar used in the many buildings of the North York Moors.

Old lime kilns built of local stone are fortunately still to be seen in a variety of places all over the North York Moors, with quite a few interesting examples to be found on or near farms. The kilns were employed to calcine lumps of broken limestone into powder. The firing process involved loading the limestone into the top of the kiln with successive layers of coal or peat and dry heather and then lit. After several hours of the fire burning, the rising temperature would cause the limestone to break down into powder. As the burning progressed more limestone and fuel would be continually added until the required quantity of lime was produced. Upon reaching the conclusion of the kiln operations, the lime would be shovelled out from the bottom. Around one ton of coal would be required to reduce approximately four tons of limestone rubble into the finished lime product.

At the foot of Cropton Bank, limestone was quarried for over two hundred years and burnt for lime manufacture in the once numerous local kilns, the burnt lime product being bartered all over Rosedale in exchange for coal that had been mined from the many outcroppings up on the moorlands.

Close to Old Byland, there is an interesting row of four listed nineteenth century lime kilns built of large limestone blocks. The kiln at the western end of the site is in the best condition and has been restored in recent years.

From the eighteenth century large quantities of limestone rubble was quarried on the south-facing escarpments of the Corallian limestone beds north of the Vale of Pickering. Huge horse-drawn wagon loads of the limestone could be seen halting for well earned refreshments at moorland inns: Saltersgate Inn, Blakey Inn, Hamer Inn, Chequers Inn and Limekiln House. The North York Moors limestone trade eventually entered a rapid decline when cheaper produced limestone was imported by ships into nearby Whitby.

A Typical lime kiln used in the North York Moors.

© Christine McEwen Collection

NORTH YORK MOORS
TROUGH HOUSE, ON CUT ROAD PACKHORSE TRACK, DANBY HIGH MOOR

Lying just to the side of the ancient packhorse track called Cut Road stands a small building of sandstone known as Trough House. The name 'Trough' is mentioned in a document dated 1223 as 'Troch' which alludes to the area surrounding Trough House. The Cut Road meets with the ancient George Gap Causeway renowned for originally being the longest paved causeway or 'pannierway' on the North York moorlands from Fryup Head to Rosedale Head. For hundreds of years packmen leading packhorse trains loaded with coal from pits known as 'day holes' on Danby High Moor would stop on reaching Trough House to rest, feed and water the horses and slake their thirst with the ironstone miners.

Incidentally, Rosedale Ironstone was once described as – **'the richest iron ore in the North Riding',** over three quarters of a million tons annually were extracted during the peak of mining operations, the majority of the ore going to Consett, Co. Durham where it was smelted.

Trough House is also associated with the famous preacher John Wesley for in June 1772 whilst preaching in Castleton, he apparently converted two men, John Ross and John Plews to Methodism. Consequently, the two men set to preach the gospel all over the district which resulted in a large gathering of worshippers from Westerdale, Farndale and Danby meeting at Ralph's Cross every Sunday. During inclement weather the gathering would meet at Trough House illuminating their way over the pitch black of the moors with horn-panelled lanterns; the early Methodists became known as the Lantern Saints.

Jaggermen and their packhorses en route with their panniers laden with goods.

© Christine McEwen Collection

NORTH YORK MOORS
GUIDE POSTS OR STOOPS – LOCALLY KNOWN AS 'HANDSTONES'

Undoubtedly, the oldest tracks extending in all directions across the moors were the ridgeways generally on the firm ground of the summits. In the days of the packhorse trains working their way across the moorlands, the Jaggermen would often have to find their way in heavy rain, through dense fogs blown inland from the North Sea or on the darkest of nights. Despite the stone causeway underfoot to act as a guide, should the packhorse trains have veered off, they would find themselves in squelchy wet peat or up to the forelocks in cloying porridgey mud.

On the 2nd of October 1711, the Justices at Northallerton Court ordered that guideposts should be erected throughout the North Riding. As the Court directed the guideposts were hewn from huge pieces of stone and set up in locations where roads, footpaths and trackways, used by the numerous packhorse trains crossed. Most of these guideposts or 'stoops' were relatively plain four-sided upright stone slabs with the names of villages roughly inscribed on the four faces. Several guideposts were curiously roughly carved with a human hand indicating the way. The names of the hamlets and villages were often mis-spelt or varied from stone to stone and the stonemasons, probably illiterate, often experienced difficulty in setting out the wording prior to actually chiselling the lettering of the place names and did not always fit it on one side of the stone.

Despite being well-weathered, fortunately there are a number of surviving examples of these enigmatic old stoop stones still to be seen on the North York Moors. The best known example stands on Blakey Ridge two miles north of Hutton-le-Hole. This intriguing stoop stone probably placed here in 1712, displays three human hands, deeply carved onto the faces of the guidepost; one pointing rather mysteriously up into the sky! There is another interesting example which is found on remote Urra Moor near Round Hill. On the north face are carved the words: THIS IS THE WAY TO STOXLA, together with the pointing hand, and on the south face: THIS IS THE WAY TO KIRBIE and a hand. The whole condition of the stone is poor, the surface eroded by severe winter weather. There are three more 'handstones'. One is on Ingleby Moor close by the old ridgeway 'track' known as Thirklesti; it displays two pointing hands together with the date, 1757. A short hop from the Castleton to Westerdale old road junction, there is a most attractive handstone, which has only one hand carved upon it; and set beside the road from Commondale to Kildale is the third handstone which displays two carved hands, one with the thumb above and the other with the thumb below.

The Hand Stone on Urra Moor.

© Ryedale Folk Museum

BEGGARS BRIDGE, EGTON, NORTH YORK MOORS

Beggars Bridge, built 1621 that spans the beautiful River Esk at Egton. May 2005.

© Christine McEwen Collection.

The intriguingly titled Beggar's Bridge at Egton spans the often fast flowing River Esk in one high, graceful leap of fifty-four feet, and was evidently constructed circa 1621 by Thomas Ferris, the son of a desperately poor moorland farmer.

It is located about half a mile below attractive Glaisdale village, once the home of the miners who worked in the local iron-stone industry. From hereabouts an ancient Jaggermen's trail constructed of stone slabs – 'trods' – locally known as a 'Pannier Way' climbs up the hillside through Arncliffe Woods.

The bridge is built of local random sandstone with massively hewn and well dressed voussoir stones forming the arch. The cobbled track across the bridge is six feet, six inches wide and there are stone parapets twelve inches high on each side. Sometime probably in the nineteenth century a large upright slab of stone was placed in the centre of the trackway to stop heavily ladened waggons and carts from traversing the bridge and damaging the structure.

It was originally known as Ferris' Bridge and Thomas Ferris' initials and the date of construction: 1621 are carved into the stonework. There is a wonderful romantic almost forgotten story attached to the history of this beautiful, stone packhorse bridge.

Locally born, Thomas Ferris, a dis-inherited farmer's son made a sparse living wandering across the North York moorlands carrying out small jobs in the hamlets and farmsteads. His appearance was that of a beggar, but underneath the muck and the grime and ragged clothes he was in fact a good looking young man.

The raggedly dressed young Thomas had fallen deeply in love with a beautiful young lass Agnes, the daughter of one of Egton's wealthiest landowners. Agnes's father however, did not relish the prospect of his lovely blond-haired daughter courting a beggar-like moorland farmer's son and therefore, forbade her from seeing Thomas.

JAGGERMEN'S BRIDGES ON PACKHORSE TRAILS

One freezing February morning Thomas, desperate to see his lovely sweetheart was in the throes of attempting to cross the cold, fast-flowing River Esk on partly submerged stepping stones when he slipped and fell into the river which was in full flood. After being swept someway down stream by the violent current and almost drowned, Thomas struggled to safety onto the opposite bank, whereupon he met his sweetheart, the comely Agnes and despite him being soaked, the deeply in-love young couple kissed and passionately embraced.

Unfortunately, Agnes's irate father suddenly emerged from the midst of some nearby dense bushes where he had been concealed, watching his daughter and the young man, Thomas Ferris, who attired in his wet, mud-splattered and ragged clothes resembled a poor down-and-out moorland beggar. The extremely angry father then banished a distraught Agnes to his mansion and threatened Thomas with a dire warning should the hapless young chap attempt to see Agnes again.

With a heavy heart whilst making his way home through the thickly-wooded rising ground above the Esk, Thomas stopped, looked down and on viewing the flooded river, swore to himself two oaths: one, that he would endeavour to make himself wealthy and thus win the hand of Agnes, and two: that he would one day build a stout stone bridge for the convenience of future travellers on the spot where he fell into the Esk.

The following day he bid Egton goodbye and set off walking the considerable distance to Hull where he intended to become a merchant seaman and to seek his fortune sailing the world's seas and oceans.

Several years passed by, and after experiencing a great many swash-buckling adventures sailing the oceans far and wide, Thomas Ferris by now immensely wealthy, returned to Egton on the North York moors, and after finding favour with Agnes's father, eventually married his sweetheart.

His earlier pledge he had made to himself was also shortly fulfilled when the bridge spanning the Esk was subsequently built with him providing the money. The bridge used perhaps for around two hundred and fifty years by the Jaggermen's packhorses became known as Beggars Bridge, the name alluding to Thomas Ferris' poor circumstances when young.

Whether this romantic, historic tale is true, no-one appears to know.

On the glorious spring day that I made this image I could almost imaging the Jaggermen of old leading a string of Galloway packhorses over this delightful stone bridge. The large vertical stone block in the centre of the cobbled pathway was set into the surface to stop heavily ladened waggons and carts passing over and damaging the bridge's parapets. May 2005

© Christine McEwen Collection

DUCK BRIDGE, DANBY, NORTH YORK MOORS

Duck Bridge depicting the accentuated graceful hump and the attractive parapets. To the left is a massively constructed buttress of huge stone blocks, probably built to strengthen the bridge during the regular high flood levels of the River Esk during the winter. In the centre of the parapet is the carved stone arms of the Neville family, custodians of Danby Castle in the late fourteenth century. July 2005.

© Christine McEwen Collection

Duck Bridge is a striking and beautiful specimen of a medieval segmental packhorse bridge and was constructed from local stone circa 1386. The accentuated hump of the bridge is relatively high.

This ancient packhorse bridge spans the River Esk at Danby in a giant leap of forty five feet, with the width of the cobbled trackway – (now tarmaced) - between the parapets built of long stone slabs, being six feet, six inches. The parapets that appear to have been heightened are themselves forty-three inches in height with nicely worked coping stones fastened together with wrought-iron staples.

There is evidence of deep scratches and indentations on the inside surfaces of the parapets, possibly caused by vehicular traffic.

Acting as a splendid example of a keystone in the centre of the parapets is a large piece of stone carved with the arms of the Neville family who evidently took residence of Danby Castle in the late fourteenth century.

The bridge originally called Danby Castle Bridge until the structure was extensively repaired

by a Danby stone mason, George Duck early in the eighteenth century, consequently, thereafter, became known as Duck Bridge.

Close-up of the Neville family arms. July 2005.
© Christine McEwen Collection.

HUNTER'S STY BRIDGE, WESTERDALE, NORTH YORK MOORS

Owing to the encroaching, almost invasive Sycamores, Alders and Ash trees in all their leafy glory, photography of this remarkable, ancient packhorse bridge was difficult, nevertheless the verdant surroundings all add atmosphere and character to Hunter's Sty Bridge. July 2005.

© Christine McEwen Collection.

Numerous small becks that drain the north facing slopes of the Cleveland Hills, which thrust upwards to a height of almost fifteen hundred feet, come together as the infant River Esk, which then flows due east through a deep, glacial valley: beautiful Eskdale.

Near to the River Esk's source is the small, attractive ancient moorland village of Westerdale, and here a most attractive thirteenth century packhorse bridge known as Hunter's Sty Bridge spans the often turbulent waters of the river.

This beautiful, ornamented and rather enigmatic, stone-built packhorse bridge is undoubtedly the best one out of the three packhorse bridges that span the Esk, but is different from the others because of its prominent medieval semi-circular ribbed arch. The large stone slabs that form the trackway over the bridge are severely worn similarly to the stone 'trods' that form the packhorse tracks criss-crossing the moors. The span of the semi-circular, high hump-back arch is eighteen feet

with a width of nine feet, six inches. The curiously, decorative carved stone plaque in the centre of the upstream parapet displays the coat of arms of the Duncomb family who fully restored the bridge in 1874. On the opposite parapet are the incised words:

'THIS ANCIENT BRIDGE WAS RESTORED BY COLONEL, THE HONOURABLE G. DUNCOMB A.D. 1874.'

Whether Colonel Duncomb just restored the parapets, or carried out extensive work to the rest of the structure is debatable, but a number of bridge historians have considered that the bridge had been over restored by the good Colonel in 1874.

The intriguing name for the bridge: Hunter's Sty is probably derived from the ancient local word 'sty' meaning path or track.

There is rumour that the bridge was possibly constructed by stonemasons belonging to the Order of Knights Templar, who had been granted agricultural land and a hall hereabouts by Guido de Bovingcourt in the early twelfth century.

Close-up of the carved stone plaque of the Duncomb coat of arms incorporated into the stone-work of the upstream parapet . July 2005.

© Christine McEwen Collection

To make this photograph, I returned during the January of 2006 and I could clearly see that the large stone slabs that form the trackway over the bridge were severely worn probably due to the passage over the centuries of countless, horses hooves and human feet. This wear is very similar to the badly eroded stone 'trods' on some of the packhorse tracks that criss-cross the North York Moors.

© Christine McEwen Collection

ROMANBY BRIDGE, NORTHALLERTON, NORTH YORK MOORS

Two views of Romanby Bridge showing the hump of the arch and the massive single slab stones that form the parapets. February 2008.

© Christine McEwen Collection.

Despite this bonny little packhorse bridge lying several miles out of the North York Moors National Park, I have, nevertheless, grouped it within this section of the book together with the other historic packhorse bridge near Thirsk.

Situated a cockstride from Northallerton, the old county town of the North Riding, this segmental arch bridge, known as Romanby Bridge leaps across the Brompton Beck, a small tributary of the River Swale, and close by a quiet country road running from Romanby to Yafforth.

The span of twenty-one feet is achieved with a pronounced hump. The width of the trackway is fifty eight inches within the eighteen inch high parapets, which are constructed from large stone slabs stapled together with wrought-iron.

The records of the Sessions for October 1620 mention that the sum of £22 15s 0d. was granted to complete repairs to Romanby Bridge. However, the appearance of the current bridge possibly suggests the construction being slightly later, perhaps late seventeenth century.

STOKESLEY BRIDGE, CLEVELAND, ON THE EDGE OF THE NORTH YORK MOORS

We reached this handsome seventeenth century Stokesley Bridge via a path at the side of the Post Office and we then spent an enjoyable hour or so with tape measure, pens and cameras recording the details. The underside of the arch is clearly silhouetted in the waters of the River Leven.
July 2005

© Christine McEwen Collection.

The elegantly designed, ancient town of Stokesley sits astride the River Leven at the foot of the Cleveland Hills about two miles from the northern boundary of the North York Moors National Park.

Stokesley was granted a charter to hold fairs in 1223 by Henry III, and there are several excellent Georgian and Regency buildings grouped along the wide cobbled High Street. In 1086, the Domesday Book records a corn mill powered by the River Leven.

Stokesley's industrial past includes printing and publishing and the weaving of woollen goods. Another important local industry, linen was carried out during the eighteenth century in a number of small stone-built mills, powered by the waters of the Leven; a later linen mill constructed by Thomas Mease was worked by a steam engine.

The River Leven upon leaving Stokesley flows to Yarm, where it joins the mighty River Tees. In the centre of the town, the Leven is spanned by a most attractive stone, packhorse bridge constructed in the seventeenth century. This quaint historic bridge spans the Leven in a leap of thirty six feet by a handsome segmental arch. The width between the thirty six inch high wrought-iron stapled parapets measures thirty two inches. The path over the bridge has retained its splendid stone cobbles.

Some of Stokesley's elder town's folk know it as 'Taylorson's Bridge' presumably because the stone mason was called by this surname. It is recorded that the bridge was extensively repaired in 1638 – possibly due to floodwater damage. Stokesley Bridge sits on an ancient packhorse track running from Great Ayton south-westwardly where it probably converged with the renowned 'Hambleton Drove Road'.

Stokesley Bridge July 2005
I was thrilled on seeing the historic and attractive stone cobbles of the trackway over the bridge.

© Christine McEwen Collection.

WORLD'S END BRIDGE, NEAR THE NORTH YORK MOORS

Worlds End Bridge with the Cod Beck in flood. February 2008

© Christine McEwen Collection

The rather intriguing name of this fine stone packhorse bridge which in a throw of thirty three feet spans the Cod Beck in the village of Sowerby near Thirsk, is associated with the local, long-closed Worlds End Inn.

The bridge was built circa 1672 by the inn's landlord. Apparently, the inn received its unusual name, due to the all too regular severe flooding of the Cod Beck, which rises in the Cleveland Hills and is one of the many tributaries of the River Swale. When the Cod Beck was in flood, the villagers could not get to the inn. By the same token, should anyone be quaffing the ale or taking the spirits in the hostelry prior to the sudden rising of the beck, then unfortunately, these folk too, would be stranded, cut-off in World's End Inn. The bridge is also called, Town End Bridge.

The width of the bridge's trackway between the thirty-inch high parapets is some sixty-five inches. The parapets appear to have been additionally heightened by six inches, and the coping stones are stapled together along the top and also to the stonework beneath with wrought-iron.

Until 1929, any travellers approaching Sowerby village from the south were forced to cross the Cod Beck by the bridge, or should the river be flowing gently, via the ford.

Near the southern end of Sowerby is the curiously named, Pudding Pie Hill, which is a Bronze Age burial mound, but was evidently re-used for burials in the early Saxon period. During excavations on the summit of the hill in 1855, three human skeletons, several cremation urns, weaponry and other pre-Christian era artefacts were discovered. Hereabouts, the good local folk of Sowerby whisper that Pudding Pie Hill is the haunt of fairies.

What a delightful interesting location, and what a truly super packhorse bridge!

THE YORKSHIRE DALES
NIDDERDALE PACKHORSE TRAINS
AND LEAD SMELT MILLS

In Nidderdale, the Abbots of Fountains Abbey operated a Lead Smelt Mill near Brimham where they smelted lead ore mined around bleak Greenhow Hill, the ore being carried down through Pateley Bridge and onwards to Brimham in leather side panniers hung over the backs of **'strings of Jagger horses'**.

Situated on the southern bank of the River Nidd below Pateley Bridge is a dense wood of Oak, Birch and Alder known hereabouts as Lead House Ing. Within this woodland, lies a jumble of thought-inspiring, roughly squared sandstone blocks, considered to be evidence of an early Lead Smelt Mill.

A typical Pennine Lead Smelt Mill.

BIRSTWITH NEW BRIDGE, NIDDERDALE

The beautiful and graceful Birstwith New Bridge which spans the River Nidd in a gigantic leap of seventy feet. January 2004.

© Christine McEwen Collection.

Birstwith 'New Bridge' was constructed in 1822 as a significantly stronger replacement for the original, late sixteenth century timber bridge frequented by packhorse trains carrying Nidderdale lead, limestone and flax out of the dale to Ilkley in Wharfedale or north-east to Ripon and beyond.

The turbulent waters of the River Nidd, have an infamous reputation for severe flooding therefore, the 'new bridge' was constructed from huge blocks of the local Millstone Grit. This remarkable Georgian packhorse bridge spans the Nidd in one gigantic leap of seventy feet, which took account of the propensity of the river to

rapidly flood. The width of the trackway which has still retained some of the stone cobbled surface is six feet between the delightful, curvaceous stone parapets.

Birstwith New Bridge was one of the very first packhorse bridges I had ever seen, and on the icy-cold, overcast, New Year's Day of 2004 when Alan and I viewed this incredible bridge in its lonely, but beautiful location, my interest was aroused which consequently encouraged me to research, and then to visit well over a hundred of these amazing historic structures all over the North of England.

The snow-covered trackway of the bridge with the parapets built of huge stone slabs. Note the two large vertical stones set inside the parapets, purposely placed to restrict wide farm carts and merchants waggons which could cause damage to the structure of the bridge.
January 2004.

© Christine McEwen Collection.

HAMPSTHWAITE BRIDGE, NIDDERDALE

**The handsome triple-arched Hampsthwaite Bridge built circa 1640.
1st January 2004.**

© Christine McEwen Collection.

Similarly to numerous other place names in the Yorkshire Dales, the name Hampsthwaite which means, - 'thwaite' or meadow belonging to Ham or Hammall is derived from Old Norse.

The historic village of Hampsthwaite sits astride the River Nidd close to where the Roman road from Aldborough to Ilkley crossed the river. Hampsthwaite was known as a Royal village, its geographical spread including the surrounding land, belonging to the King's Forest of Knaresborough during the reign of King William the Conqueror. Because of its important location, the village was granted its fair and market charter by Edward I around 1304.

In the Medieval period through to the Georgian era, the village, and especially the hamlet of Clint across the Nidd, specialised in the making of spurs, which were marketed at Ripon.

Beside the Medieval church, dedicated to the brutally murdered Archbishop of Canterbury, Thomas a' Becket, is the seventeenth century constructed stone bridge that spans the River Nidd, which for centuries carried the important road linking York and Lancaster. Interestingly, hereabouts, until the mid-nineteenth century stood an ancient inn, known as - 'The Lamb in Hampsthwaite' – which was a haunt of the Jaggermen and their strings of packhorses whilst carrying lead-ore, burnt lime, woollens and linen between York, and Skipton lying to the west over Blubberhouses Moor.

The old road possibly an early packhorse track linking Hampsthwaite to the hamlet of Clint crosses the River Nidd by the handsome Hampsthwaite Bridge comprising of three stone, segmental arches. This splendid structure was built at a cost of £400 circa 1640. Fortunately, the bridge itself has not suffered from being widened to accommodate motor traffic, but the trackway across the top has been moderately increased in width, achieved by supporting the heavy rectangular stones forming the parapets on a row of round-nosed corbels. The three arches, the two robustly-built triangular cutwaters which actually strengthen the structure, and the distinctive corbelling all add to the charm of this splendid Nidderdale bridge, which although not specifically built as a packhorse bridge, was most definitely regularly used by the Jaggermen's packhorse trains.

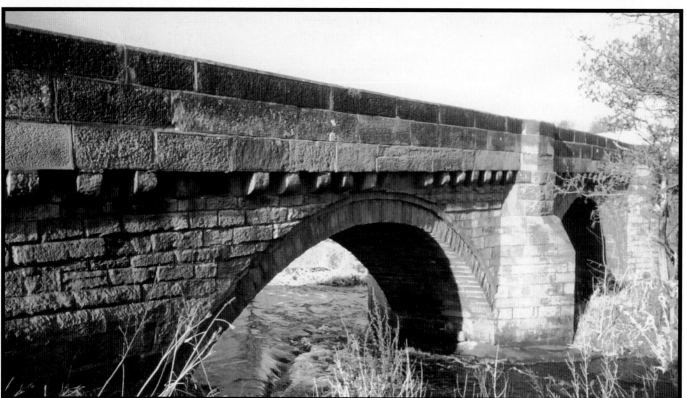

Hampsthwaite Bridge 1st January 2004.
Both photographs depict the bridge's interesting architectural details: the triangular cutwaters which also act to strengthen the structure during flooding and the row of round-nosed corbelling supporting the parapets built of large rectangular stone slabs.

© Christine McEwen Collection.

COCKHILL BECK PACKHORSE BRIDGE, HAMPSTHWAITE, NIDDERDALE

Cockhill Beck Packhorse Bridge displaying the semi-circular arch and the random stone parapets.

© Christine McEwen Collection.

Close by the middle of the old road in Hampsthwaite there is a pleasant typically Dales, village green harking back centuries, probably being created around 1304, when King Edward I, granted Hampsthwaite a charter for operating a fair and market.

Running from the centre of the village green, there is a well-trodden footpath which goes a short distance until the Cockhill Beck is reached. Spanning this small, almost insignificant watercourse is a most striking specimen of a small narrow packhorse bridge constructed from gritstone rubble. The bridge consists of one high semi-circular arch with a span of around twelve feet; the trackway between the twenty-six inch high parapets, locked together with square-section staples of wrought-iron, and also built of random stone is about fifty-four inches in width.

Near to the Cockhill Packhorse Bridge are a bewildering number of old, inter-connecting trackways – (possibly ancient packhorse tracks) - that lead south-eastwards from Hampsthwaite village the handful of miles to Oak Beck near Killinghall, where an intriguing track crosses the Knox or Spruisty packhorse bridge near this small watercourse's confluence with the River Nidd.

THORNTHWAITE BRIDGE, NIDDERDALE

**Thornthwaite Bridge in its snow-covered tranquil setting over the Padside Beck.
1st January 2004.**

© Christine McEwen Collection.

This most enigmatic, crudely constructed yet highly photogenic little sixteenth century packhorse bridge spans the narrow Padside Beck a few yards from a ford on the twisting, minor road that threads its way through the historic, stone-built, tranquil hamlet of Thornthwaite.

This bonny diminutive semi-circular – 'high humped' – arched-bridge spans the Padside Beck in a throw of thirteen feet, and is constructed from locally quarried Millstone Grit.

The well-trodden stone slabs forming the trackway over the bridge are three foot wide. The stone parapets which follow the pleasing contours of the arch, are fastened together with staples of wrought-iron.

Thornthwaite Bridge lies on an historic packhorse track between Ilkley in neighbouring Wharfedale and Ripon.

This was one of the Nidderdale packhorse bridges I had immense pleasure seeing during our visit on the New Year's Day of 2004.

**The narrowness of the trackway between the Gritstone parapets.
1st January 2004.**

© Christine McEwen Collection.

WATH BRIDGE, NIDDERDALE

**The fine segmental arched Wath Bridge that spans the River Nidd in a leap of fifty-one feet.
1st January 2004**

© Christine McEwen Collection

The small grey stone hamlet of Wath whose intriguing name comes from Old Norse meaning a ford, is located in the wild, mountainous upper reaches of Nidderdale. There are the remains of a ford probably dating back to pre-Medieval times across the often fast flowing River Nidd that rushes down through Wath. During the Middle Ages a wooden bridge was built creating all-weather access to both banks of the river. This wooden bridge which probably suffered regular damage during the frequent flooding of the Nidd, was replaced in the sixteenth century by the construction of a packhorse bridge of random stone.

The bridge, which was widened at the end of the nineteenth century, spans the Nidd in a jump of fifty-one feet comprising of one arch and an overflow arch, incorporated to deal with severe flooding. The current width of the trackway is eight feet, six inches and harks back to 1890 when the original width of the trackway across was only five feet obviously causing difficulty during the passing over of farm carts and waggons. (The five feet width was the correct measurement for a sixteenth century packhorse bridge).

It is probable that the packhorse bridge was built for the benefit of the farmsteads on the west bank of the River Nidd as a more convenient means of sending their produce by packhorse to the markets of Kirkby Malzeard and Ripon. There was also a great amount of lead-ore mined in nearby Ashfoldside Gill and locally produced flax-linen that used the packhorse trains to carry these products to the Lead Smelt Mills and Cloth Halls.

Prior to the widening of the bridge in 1890, local farmers and merchants needing to cross the narrow packhorse bridge with their carts and waggons, evidently had to endure the trouble-some task involving the removal of one set of wheels and to role the axle stubs along the top of the coping stones on one side of the bridge parapet to enable them to cross. A time consuming and dangerous job!

THE YORKSHIRE DALES
CALAMINE OR ZINC ORE

During the last decade of the eighteenth century massive deposits of Calamine, or zinc ore were discovered deep in an ancient system of natural caverns under Pikedaw Hill, near Malham.

To reach the rich veins of Calamine, or 'Smithsonite' and also several veins of quartz, copper minerals and galena, - 'lead-ore' - a seventy-five feet shaft was sunk from the summit of the thirteen hundred feet high Pikedaw Hill, which lies close to the Mid-Craven Fault.

Calamine, was in demand due to the mineral being required in the manufacture of copper alloys such as brass and bronze required by the ever-expanding Steam Engine Makers supplying the power to drive Britain's Industrial Revolution; brass and bronze were used for bearings, steam valves and other components; the processes having been discovered around the mid-1750s. Calamine was also used as an important ingredient during the manufacture of certain paints.

When John Houseman journeyed from Malham to Settle in 1800, his description written in his journal, mentions the Pikedaw Hill Calamine Mine: *'...........the road – when it can be called such – leads us over a wild, hilly country and extensive tracks of moors .... there are several Calamine Pits close to the road.'*

The 'road' Houseman was travelling along, would be a stony track which climbed out of Malham up the steep fellsides of Pikedaw Hill before dramatically descending down to Settle, the nearest town.

The Calamine ore once extracted from the bowels of the deep caverns was washed close by the mines to remove dirt and other loose material. The ore was then carried by packhorses or horse-drawn carts to the Smelt Mill near Lower Trenhouse, on Malham Moor where it was calcined or roasted in coke-fired furnaces, the old Lead Smelt Mill being specifically modified for this procedure. The Smelt Mill chimney still survives, it being totally restored in the 1980s by Craven mining enthusiasts.

The coal for processing into the coke required for heating the Calamine ore in the roasting furnaces was extracted from pits high up on the breezy heights of Fountains Fell.

Coke was used because it was a less heavier material to transport than coal, the fuel also had considerably fewer impurities than coal and would therefore, not adulterate the zinc metal produced in the calcining process.

The area of the coal-pits on Fountains Fell was originally established by Lord Ribblesdale in 1807. For the production of coke specifically for the Calamine industry, a Beehive coke oven was constructed in the close vicinity of the coal mines. The oven was built of coursed sandstone and in plan, approximately thirteen feet square by a maximum height of around seven feet. The oven had a hemispherical top or dome closely resembling a Beehive and an arched entrance led into the internal hearth where the coal was converted into coke.

Hereabouts, there are a number of surviving packhorse tracks that run from the site of each of the now disused coal pits to the Beehive oven.

Subsequent to 1815, coke produced in the Beehive oven was used for the smelting of lead extracted from a number of workings on Malham Moor. The coal mines and the coke oven were evidently still operating around 1830, but later fell into disuse.

The coke once produced, was carried by packhorses along an ancient trail known as 'the Coal Road', then being used for the transportation of the Fountains Fell mined coal to Malham Lead Smelt Mill, and from here it was then carried along another trackway leading to the Calamine House, the specifically constructed building containing the Calamine-ore roasting hearths, situated close to the Calamine pits.

Due to ever-increasing demand for Calamine, a new, much larger Calamine calcining building was built at the north end of Malham village, the Calamine ore and the coke for firing the hearths were carried down the wider Settle to Malham road.

PACKHORSE TRAINS

Upon completion, the calcined Calamine ores were transported by packhorse train the 120 miles down to Cheadle, Staffordshire where the metal was used in a number of local industries, particularly for the manufacture of brass and bronze.

Later, following the completion of the western extension of the Leeds and Liverpool Canal over the Pennines, Pikedaw Calamine was carried in special wooden casks mounted on the backs of packhorses who conveyed the valuable metal from Malham to Airton and to the canal wharf at Gargrave where it was then loaded onto barges.

THE YORKSHIRE DALES
THE COAL ROADS OF THE YORKSHIRE DALES

The earliest documented evidence of coal mining in the Yorkshire Dales was at the end of the thirteenth century, when coal was won from pits sunk in the 'new forest' in Arkengarthdale, which belonged to the Lords of Richmond Castle. The fuel was used domestically and also by Blacksmiths and Armourers. Subsequently, until around the first decade of the twentieth century apart from domestic use it went to fuel the Smelting Mills of the Lead Mining Industry.

A number of small scattered collieries around Tan Hill were supplying coal to Richmond Castle in the late fourteenth century, and from the start of the seventeenth century to Appleby-in-Westmorland, Brough, Kirkby Stephen, Penrith, Hawes, most of Upper Wensleydale and Swaledale.

Easily mined coal seams could be readily discovered at the base of the Millstone Grit which caps the higher fells, with smaller, thinner seams wedged within the rocks of the Yoredale Series. Generally, from around 1760 to the mid-nineteenth century quality coal was sold to the dwellings and cottages in the towns and villages all over the Dales. The poorer quality coal - usually extracted from the Yoredale Series - was often supplied to the Lead Smelt Mills and also to many local Lime Kilns. There were large numbers of local coal mines that just supplied the local villages and farmsteads.

PACKHORSE TRAINS

Many of the larger coal pits were served with packhorse tracks along which the coal could be transported by the packhorse trains considerable distances all over Northern England.

Commencing from around the middle of the seventeenth century strings of packhorses were regularly used to carry coal from the numerous small collieries and pits scattered all over the high, remote fell sides to the Lead Smelt Mills and also to farmsteads and sundry domestic users.

In Dentdale, Sedgewick, on regularly seeing horse-drawn carts piled high with huge loads of coal working their way through the twisting, narrow cobbled streets of Dent Village, writing as late as 1868, bemoaned that, *'Dent has lost the picturesque effect of its trains of packhorses.'*

Dentdale's coal was supplied by the extensive Garsdale Collieries at Cowgill Head, the workings extending over around one square mile. Even today there are many old abandoned and dangerous shafts lying scattered over the high moorland on both sides of the Galloway Gate, joined together by short lengths of packhorse tracks.

FOUNTAINS FELL COAL

Located between Malham and the head of scenic Littondale is the 2,192 feet bulk of Fountains Fell with its massive cap of Millstone Grit. The strata lying beneath this cap has been pierced with numerous coal-pits, the majority having been extensively worked at the end of the eighteenth century. Considerable amounts of coal were conveyed to Malham Lead Smelt Mill, while some coal was converted into coke in a Beehive oven for the Calamine industry – (See Calamine and Zinc Ore).

During the 1790s scattered all around the summit plateau of Fountains Fell a great many shafts were sunk and much coal was won, the highly productive pits combined annual tonnage of coal raised around this period amounted to between 900 and 1000 tons.

When loaded onto the packhorse trains, the total annual loads of coal ranged from a massive 8,000 to a staggering 11,000 which were carried down the road specifically constructed in 1810 between the grouping of collieries on Fountains Fell and the Malham to Arncliffe road on New Pasture.

From this location the 'Coal Road' proceeds south-westwards over the misty heights of Knowe Fell, then runs for around a mile before the track heads off to the south, eventually crossing another minor track lying north of Higher Tren House and then heads along the Malham Road, south-eastwards and past the restored Malham Lead Smelt Mill chimney.

The cylindrical chimney constructed of limestone rubble was for drawing the furnaces for the smelting of the lead, extracted from the local mines. The Lead Smelt Mill used coal won from the Fountains Fell pits delivered by packhorses, but closed in 1910.

TAN HILL COAL

The extensive seam of coal mined in numerous small pits around the 1,732 feet summit of Tan Hill where the three Northern English counties of North Yorkshire, Durham and Cumbria all meet, produced *'dirty, dusty Crow coal'* out of narrow straggly workings, the thickest seam being around three feet, six inches.

JAGGERMEN'S BRIDGES ON PACKHORSE TRAILS

The Tan Hill coal due to its poor calorific value and its dusty, crumbly nature was unsuitable for firing locomotives and other steam engines. It was however, widely favoured for domestic fires by countless Dales farmers' wives who mixed it with peat which made it burn well, and they would bank up their fires with it at night.

The remote Tan Hill Inn, reputedly the highest in England was built during the seventeenth century on the site of a much older ale house or inn. During the early nineteenth century, the inn must have enjoyed good trade due to the numerous thirsty Colliers and Packhorse drovers, otherwise known as Jaggermen, who were regular customers.

Indeed, the inn was probably built to serve the Tan Hill coal miners and the scores of Jaggermen leading their packhorse trains across the high, remote moorland tracks that converged hereabouts. For Tan Hill was a busy crossroads for the strings of packhorses carrying the locally-mined coal northwards over the mass of Stainmore to Arkengarthdale and Swaledale to fuel the hearths of the cottages and farms in these Dales; or due west across the wild peat hag-covered mountainous watershed to deliver the fuel to farms and cottages down into the Eden valley in Westmorland.

There are six surviving trackways that radiate out from Tan Hill, all of which would have been travelled daily by strings of packhorses with their bursting panniers chock-full of Tan Hill coal, setting off to make their deliveries of the fuel to the remote hamlets and villages scattered all over the surrounding high fells. One of these old trackways that leads south-westwardly to Raven-seat and Birkdale starts from around two hundred and fifty yards down the Tan Hill to Keld Road, but after a short distance the once well used track is now lost in the thick peaty ground, but can be re-discovered as it climbs the south-facing slope of Thomas Gill; from where the track gradually descends past a copse of deciduous trees before arriving in the wind-blown hamlet of Ravenseat. Nearby, leaping over the foaming, peaty fast flowing-waters of the Whitsundale Beck is a distinctive stone packhorse bridge, whose stony surface in times gone by would ring to the clatter of countless packhorse hooves thundering over the bridge, the packhorses' panniers fully laden with coal, lead-ore or other merchandise, being on their way to Kirkby Stephen and other points North.

The trackway leading from this attractive packhorse bridge, known locally for decades, as the *'Jagger Road'*, leads west to climb the high fells above Friar Side. In 1790, the Quarter Sessions records that the sum of fifty pounds was spent on repairs to this trackway – *'a certain common and ancient highway leading from the market town of Kirkby Stephen ...... towards the hamlet of Ravenseat'*. The trackway was described as being – *'.....a pack and prime way from Kirkby Stephen to Barnard Castle'*; its route would then proceed towards Tan Hill and join the Sleightholme trackway over mountainous Stainmore towards the direction of Bowes.

This ancient packhorse trackway now lies beneath a modern topping of tarmacadam and is part of the modern highway running through Ravenseat and then Birkdale, and eventually to the North Yorkshire – Cumbria county border at Hollow Mill Cross. Despite the mention of the word cross in its intriguing title, unfortunately there are no surviving marker stones or stoops at this crossroads. Although back in 1664, an horrendous murder was committed hereabouts. John Smith, a Swaledale Jaggerman was leading a string of packhorses, their panniers bulging with blue-dyed, knitted woollen stockings being carried from Kirkby Stephen to Swaledale, when he was set upon and brutally murdered by one or more men. Poor Smith's badly beaten corpse was later discovered deeply jammed down one of the abundant naturally occurring 'shakeholes' in the surrounding limestone rock to the north of the packhorse trackway. Even today, these grykes or shakeholes are locally known as Blue John Holes, as a grisly reminder of John Smith's terrible, brutal death, the reference to Blue John indicating the blue colour of the knitted woollen stockings that the Jaggerman's horses were carrying. Regrettably, due to lack of evidence no one was brought to trial for Smith's murder.

Let us imagine, that in the early nineteenth century on the Tan Hill to Keld packhorse trackway, the stony track would have been alive with the cacophony of thundering hooves, snorting, heavily sweating horses, and the tinkling of the bells fastened to the leading horses, as the thirty bustling packhorses thundered along, whilst passing the many local working coal-pits on either side of the trackway. Today this trackway has become part of the Pennine Way over Tan Hill Moss, Lad Gill Hill and Low Frith. Packhorses once delivered Tan Hill coal into Keld up a steeply rising hillside, now a holloway, and adopted as the route of the Pennine Way.

The countless regular strings of pack-horses carrying coal for the fiery furnaces at Beldi Hill Lead Smelt Mill located about a mile to the east of Keld, would travel on a trackway situated north of the river which they would cross via East Gill Bridge.

They would then proceed by keeping onto the trackway curving around and above the deep gorge of the Swale.

At Stony Hill, the main packhorse trackway to Beldi Hill branched to climb up to Crackpot Hill, and thence on to Swinnergill, which had another minor trackway which led to the Gunnerside Gill Lead Smelt Mill.

Domestic coal for the cottages and dwellings in Swaledale would be carried on the backs of packhorses who would travel down the east side of the Dale to Calvert Houses opposite Muker.

Approximately one hundred and fifty yards to the east of Tan Hill Inn is the packhorse road to Arkengarthdale, known as the Long Causeway: a poorly defined track now classified as a green road which runs in a south easterly direction to King's Pit Colliery, which in the seventeenth century supplied large quantities of coal to Lord Wharton's Lead Smelt Mills in lower Swaledale. Later, this productive pit also sent packhorse trains loaded with coal to Old Gang Lead Smelt Mill. Situated to the north of King's Pit Colliery another packhorse trackway runs across Mirk Fell Edge and continues on to the site of an abandoned coal mine at William Gill Houses, before heading up the eastern side of William Gill.

Many of the coal pits dotted around the summit of Tan Hill were extensively worked for decades. The coal seams produced significant quantities of Crow coal won from the pits on the south-facing flank of Great Shunner Fell.

OTHER COAL ROADS IN THE DALES

Cotterdale and Fossdale lying north-west of Hawes – also had a number of collieries. The Cotterdale collieries transported coal by packhorses down a trackway to Hardraw, then beyond into Wensleydale. Over in Fossdale, '**the Hearne Coal Road**' – itself a packhorse trackway was used for carrying coal by packhorses, and later right into the early twentieth century by horse-drawn colliery waggons.

There were a scattering of several other coal-pits located south of Wensleydale, perched on the elevated, long ridge of moorland between Walden Head and Coverdale. One such coal mine was Fleensop which supplied much coal to the dwellings, cottages and farmhouses of Coverdale. Today, evidence of the long abandoned coal-pit shafts and adits of Fleensop are still to be seen, lying to the south-west of this extremely remote hamlet which sits upon the ancient packhorse trackway linking Walden Head and Horsehouse-in-Coverdale. As well as coal, lead was also won from the rocky terrain of Fleensop Moor from the seventeenth to the nineteenth centuries. The packhorse trackway from Walden would have been used by countless strings of packhorses to convey the Fleensop lead ore and coal to West Burton Lead Smelt Mill.

During the 1850s, there was an inn at Braidley, which catered for the coal and lead ore packhorse traffic that crossed daily over the high fells from Walden Head, as well as the many packhorse trains negotiating the mountainous trackway steeply zig-zagging up the vertiginous Park Rash out of Kettlewell in Wharfedale.

One of the most extensive areas of coal mining in the Yorkshire Dales and which covers almost three square miles of the lower-level moorland is the coal-seam rich land lying between Wensleydale and Swaledale: the area bounded by the triangle formed by the Redmire to Grinton, the Redmire to Bellerby and the Grinton to Bellerby roads. Indeed, this whole area of early coal mining activity is marked on Jeffery's maps as '*Coal Pit Moor*'. Hideously pock-marking the landscape within the triangle are hundreds of bellpits and ruinous mine shafts, many extremely dangerous on Grinton Moor, Redmire Moor, Preston Moor and Bellerby Moor. Excepting the Grinton coal mines, all of the other collieries were within the Royalties of Castle Bolton Estates, who hold coal mining records dating back to the mid-sixteenth century.

Particularly within the first half of the seventeenth century, enormous quantities of coal were carried by packhorse trains from these collieries to the Alum refining works at Guisborough in Cleveland, and during the late eighteenth century, a number of the Bolton Estates collieries were leased by the more significant lead mine owners from Grassington in Wharfedale.

For centuries, coal was extensively mined all over the mountainous uplands of the Yorkshire Dales, many of the collieries keeping working until the late nineteenth century, when the development of the North Eastern Railway then replaced the last few working packhorses and also the lumbering horse-drawn coal waggons with steam locomotives. From this period the railway introduced the better quality Durham mined coal into Richmond and Wensleydale, and further south, the Midland Railway transported quality South Yorkshire coal into Airedale, Wharfedale and Ribblesdale. The days of strings of thirty packhorses working the coal roads of the Yorkshire Dales were finally over.

HUBBERHOLME BRIDGE, UPPER WHARFEDALE

In a mighty leap Hubberholme Bridge spans the River Wharfe.

July 2004.

© Christine McEwen Collection.

Whilst exploring the historic bridges of Upper Wharfedale, a visit to historic Hubberholme Bridge which spans the River Wharfe to link one of the most beautiful of Dales' churches, St. Michael and All Angels with the delightful, white-washed ancient George Inn is a must.

There has evidently been a stone-built single arched bridge spanning the river at Hubberholme for many hundreds of years. In 1693, the Quarter Sessions recorded that the structure of the bridge as being in *"great ruyne and decay",* resulting in the necessity of frequent repairs being carried out. Flood damage and bad weather caused massive deterioration of the structure which was completely rebuilt in 1734, a significant amount of the earlier structure being incorporated into the bridge as we see it today.

Historically, Hubberholme Bridge was obviously extremely important due to its location on *"the high roadeway leadinge between the markett towne of Lancaster in the countie of Lancaster, and the markett towne of Newcastle-upon-Tyne and other places in the countie of Northumberland".* The road would probably run from Lancaster via Clapham, Helwith Bridge, Greenfield then over the fells to Hubberholme; the trackway then carrying on over the Kidstone Pass into Bishopdale, Wensleydale, Richmond, Durham and finally Newcastle-upon-Tyne.

The actual structure of Hubberholme Bridge appears quite unusual due to the stones that form the arch being laid vertically. Never-theless, this would probably enhance the struc-tural strength of the arch. The parapets con-structed from coursed gritstone, laid horizontally rise to an approximate height of three feet from the trackway and the well-dressed, neatly laid coping stones run uphill from the ends of the bridge to the centre of the arch.

YOCKENTHWAITE BRIDGE, LANGSTROTHDALE

Yockenthwaite's strikingly prominent stone packhorse bridge spans the River Wharfe in a gigantic leap of fifty-four feet. Nowadays, the bridge is used only for pedestrian and farm vehicles. July 2004

© Christine McEwen Collection.

Just a pleasant saunter of perhaps a mile and a half up the River Wharfe from Hubberholme brings you to the secretive and ancient hamlet of Yockenthwaite ---- its thought-inspiring name comes from Norse-Irish and means: 'Clearing of Eogan'. Most probably, Eogan was the leader of a group of early Norse-Irish settlers who established a 'thwaite' - a settlement, in the dense forest that covered the surrounding fells. During the Norman period the Dale was part of Langstrothdale Chase - land set aside for the King for hunting.

Surrounded by the high bleak fells: Horse Head Gate to the south-west rises to about nineteen hundred and fifty feet above sea level, the most striking feature at Yockenthwaite is the old packhorse bridge of stone that in a gigantic leap of fifty-four feet gracefully spans the River Wharfe that hereabouts, meanders down the Dale over massive water-worn beds of limestone. The width between the stone parapets that partially follows the curved line of the arch is seven feet, six inches. Yockenthwaite Bridge possibly dating from the sixteenth century is constructed from random limestone. The oblong-shaped voussoir stones forming the arch are set vertically into the structure, similarly to the stones used to form the arch in Hubberholme Bridge.

Yockenthwaite lies on the ancient packhorse trackway from Wensleydale to Ribblesdale. The Jaggermen would lead their packhorses carrying coal, iron, lead-pigs, salt, woollens and diverse other goods through Yockenthwaite on a south-heading up the steep fell side at nearby Raisgill, then over the almost two thousand feet contour of Horse Head Moor and down into Halton Gill and Foxup in Littondale; thence to Horton-in-Ribblesdale.

Whilst visiting delightful Yockenthwaite with its wonderful Jaggermen's bridge, it is worth seeing the nearby rather enigmatic stone circle, believed to date from the Middle Bronze Age – (1600 B.C. to 1000 B.C.) - which stands about three feet high with a diameter of around twenty-five feet. Currently, experts suggest that the stubby standing stones originally formed the kerb of a burial cairn. This intriguing, ancient stone circle stands on a slight rise alongside the Wharfe at the foot of the precipitous Yockenthwaite Moor.

CROOK GILL PACKHORSE BRIDGE, CRAY, NEAR BUCKDEN, UPPER WHARFEDALE

Crook Gill Packhorse Bridge, January 2008

This fantastic hidden gem of an ancient packhorse bridge appears almost to be a natural occurrence in the surrounding limestone. We discovered the bridge was built of un-mortared, roughly-hewn sections of limestone. The shallow segmental arch spans Crook Gill in a throw of around thirteen feet, six inches. The keystone and other stones forming the arch are all crudely fashioned from limestone slabs which give a primitive feel to the whole structure.

© Christine McEwen Collection.

Heading from the rear of the remote, old drover's hostelry, the early seventeenth century White Lion Inn, at Cray on the ancient road that climbs over the Kidstones Pass, a steep rocky track meanders down into the depths of Cray Gill, where the air is filled with the melodious sounds of a multitude of laughing, chattering, dancing waterfalls as they tumble over bizarrely-sculptured boulders to cascade into deep, dark, water-filled pools, gouged out of the limestone bed over several millennia.

The Cray Beck's journey down the beautiful gill ends when this lovely little watercourse meets the River Wharfe between Buckden and Hubberholme. However, before the Cray Beck reaches the mighty Wharfe, another small beck that rushes headlong down Crook Gill merges amid a cluster of large water-rounded limestone boulders, ancient gnarled Hawthorns and dense shrubby Willows.

Spanning rocky Crook Gill, and virtually hidden by the Hawthorn and Willows, is an absolute gem of a diminutive bridge – to my mind clearly built for packhorses. Crook Gill Beck flows down the rocky fellside and crosses an ancient Jaggermen's trail that links Upper Wharfedale over the Kidstones Pass with Bishopdale and Wensleydale.

JAGGERMEN'S BRIDGES ON PACKHORSE TRAILS

During one Jack-Frost cold yet beautiful sunny morning in the early January of 2008, both Alan and I were delighted to discover this small, rather primitive-looking bridge. Three quarters of an hour earlier we had set off walking up Cray Gill from the direction of Hubberholme with the scantiest information regarding the whereabouts of this bridge. Alan, full of enthusiastic zeal as ever for historic structures of all kinds, was perhaps fifty yards in front of me when he suddenly excitedly shouted, *"It's here Christine, and what a good un".*

Breathlessly, I raced along the hard cold ground and catching up to Alan noticed for myself the bridge which was bathed in dappled wintry sunshine due to the surrounding dense shrubby trees. We both excitedly commenced an exploration of the bridge. *"When do you think this quaint little bridge was built, and who built it?"* Alan questioned. We both agreed, it was, despite its primitive construction, a definite packhorse bridge.

We discovered the bridge was constructed from roughly-hewn limestone without mortar - similar to dry stone walls. There was a shallow segmental arch spanning the narrow beck running down Crook Gill by a throw of around thirteen feet, six inches. The width of the roughly laid track over the arch was just six feet and there were no parapets. On the downstream side of the arch, a huge chunk of roughly shaped limestone, about three feet high by around ten inches in thickness which penetrated deep into the arch's structure, acted as a keystone. The other stones either side of the keystone forming the segments of the arch were just as crudely shaped, and were much smaller in size; several of them projected upwards through the track-bed, which was also crudely laid with limestone pebbles; probably originally sourced from the water-course.

After closely examining the bridge's structure, I jotted down the dimensions and other pertinent details in my dog-eared notebook. Alan, who was sat upon a large mossy boulder deep in thought suddenly said, *"Just imagine the bridge builders back in the sixteenth or perhaps the early seventeenth century struggling to dig out and prepare the foundations for the bridge; gather the stones, and then with maybe nothing more than a Blacksmith-fashioned hammer and a chisel or two cut and dress the hard random pieces of limestone; then actually build the bridge without mortar".* We finished what had been a truly delightful 'packhorse bridge-spotting morning', by quaffing a pint of the Skipton-brewed beer in the White Lion.

The crudely laid trackway over the arch consists of a mixture of limestone pebbles and jagged edged stones forming the arch that have penetrated upwards.

© Christine McEwen Collection.

CRAY HIGH BRIDGE, CRAY, UPPER WHARFEDALE

© Christine McEwen Collection.

A cockstride up the road from the White Lion Inn spanning the narrow Cray Beck that for millennia has gouged deeply into the limestone, is what appears to be a strongly constructed segmental-arched bridge built of uncoursed gritstone.

The span of the arch is around ten feet, and the trackway across measures around ten feet in width. The round-topped parapets range in height from about fifteen inches in the centre of the arch, to around twenty-six inches at the ends. On the downstream parapet there is a curiously-shaped stone tablet, well-weathered and in-scribed with intriguing but indecipherable hiero-glyphics – (to me that is!).

My earnest attempt to gather more information regarding this historic little bridge, which scant records suggest was used by packhorses to cross Cray Beck have to date, unfortunately, been fruitless.

I will of course be delighted to hear from anyone who can furnish me with more details.

LINTON-IN-CRAVEN BRIDGE, WHARFEDALE

The sixteenth century Linton-in-Craven packhorse bridge across the Eller Beck. The stony ford is situated to the front of the bridge. October 2003.

© Christine McEwen Collection.

Linton-in-Craven historically famous for wool-spinning is without doubt one of the most delightful, pretty little villages in the Yorkshire Dales.

The crystal clear waters of the Eller Beck babbles at the foot of the sloping village green which is overlooked by a quaint, yet appealing cluster of small limestone constructed cottages, and the historic pub, the Fountaine Inn. Dominating the village is the elaborate and ornamented stone Fountaine's Hospital with its opulent cupola and impressive side wings, built circa 1721 by Richard Fountaine as alms-houses.

Eller Beck is crossed in five different ways: a most beautiful late seventeenth century packhorse bridge; a clapper bridge (possibly early medieval); a late nineteenth century stone-built road bridge; a line of attractive stepping stones and, a stony ford.

Although I am certain that Jaggermen's packhorses crossed Eller Beck by trotting over both the packhorse bridge and the attractive clapper bridge, because this book does not include road bridges, I beg my readers' pardon to exclude a description.

This splendid, striking-looking bridge built of large gritstone blocks spans the beck by one massive, yet shallow segmental arch in a leap of sixty feet; there is also at one end a considerably smaller arched opening which acts as an overflow when the beck is in flood. The locals hereabouts, affectionately know the bridge as 'Redmayne's Bridge', because a native of Linton, a Mrs. Elizabeth Redmayne evidently provided the necessary finance to erect the structure circa 1690; the stonemasons probably using the foundations and perhaps some of the stone from the original fourteenth century packhorse bridge that had suffered regular severe structural flood damage. Mrs. Redmayne who died in 1718 was locally highly regarded and there is a brass memorial plate in Linton Church in her name for her benevolent act.

There is however, another old tale relating to finance provided for the re-building of Linton's old packhorse bridge, which I feel should be included. Local legend mentions that during the sixteenth century, two well-healed Linton women, every winter, regularly and vehemently pestered local farmers and other prominent villagers to provide money to finance the re-building of the ancient, flood water-ruined arched packhorse bridge across the Eller Beck. A re-structured bridge would enable them and other villagers to safely cross the often flooded waters to visit Linton Church on the other side. Despite, much haranguing of Linton's menfolk, the women's pleas fell on deaf ears. Therefore, failing to obtain the required financial backing these two strong-willed Yorkshire women themselves provided the money. The old packhorse bridge was then reconstructed by expert stone masons whose specific instructions from the women included that the trackway over the arch had to be built very narrow, thereby restricting access over the bridge for carts and wagons belonging to the local miserly farmers.

There is of course no surviving record of the women's names, so whether this tale rings true or not, we may never know.

© Christine McEwen Collection.

LI'LE EMILY'S OR EMILY NORTON'S BRIDGE, LINTON-IN-CRAVEN, WHARFEDALE

Set close to the spectacular Linton Falls this fourteenth century-built packhorse bridge presents an amazing spectacle. Note the time-worn stone step in front of the two stone posts. Li'le Emily's Bridge, August 2005

© Christine McEwen Collection

A short hop downstream from Linton village centre, is yet another fascinating, diminutive, stone bridge with the curious title of Li'le Emily's Bridge. In the old Craven vernacular, the dialect word 'li'le' translates to little, and particularly so in centuries past. Li'le could also be used as a term of endearment.

This intriguing little bridge is set amidst a group of limestone cottages closeby the delightful Linton Falls. So why was this beautiful little bridge, that spans the stream near the confluence of the Eller Beck and the Threshfield Beck be so titled? Behind the bridge's long history lies a charming tale:

Emily was the daughter of one of the Norton family of nearby Rylstone, and during the period of the infamous, ill-fated 'Rising of the North' in 1569, the whole Norton family found themselves in dire trouble for they were relentlessly hunted all over Craven. Emily's family members, Thomas and Christopher

Norton, when eventually captured paid a heavy price for their part in the insurrection, for they were duly executed.

Although history has not recorded her age, we can only assume that Emily was no more than a young lass, hence her endearing name, Li'le Emily. With her being a member of the outlawed Norton family Emily's life was in danger, but a local miller came to her rescue, and kept her well hidden in his cottage until the hue and cry for Norton blood-letting passed.

It was while she was being led to the sanctuary of the friendly miller's home, that Emily Norton had to cross the beck by the extremely narrow stone bridge, which thereafter became known as Li'le Emily's Bridge. The name of Emily Norton is also associated with Wordsworth's poem, 'The White Doe of Rylstone', who apparently credited the doe as the young girl's companion.

49

JAGGERMEN'S BRIDGES ON PACKHORSE TRAILS

Li'le Emily's or Emily Norton's Bridge was evidently constructed as a packhorse bridge in the fourteenth century. The construction is of local random gritstone, with the span of the single segmental arch being of around fifteen feet; the trackway over the moderately curved arch is about thirty inches in width, and is topped with twelve inch parapets fashioned from huge rectangular gritstone slabs. Inserted into the trackway at one end of the bridge to arrest the passage of wheeled carts are two roughly-hewn stone posts, one of which leans at a drunken angle.

When viewed from this perspective the bridge's structure presents a truly fascinating spectacle.

© Christine McEwen Collection

MALHAM BRIDGES, MALHAMDALE

New Bridge originally called Monk Bridge takes the form of a single segmental stone arch built of undressed limestone with parapets of around three feet in height. The span of the arch is around twelve feet. A former packhorse bridge which was considerably strengthened and widened during the eighteenth and early nineteenth century.   Spring 2006

© Christine McEwen Collection.

The infant River Aire rises at the base of the three hundred feet sheer limestone face of Malham Cove. Centuries ago, a massive waterfall plunged over the cliff, but nowadays the beck up on Malham Moor disappears deep into the limestone pavements to later emerge at the foot of the cliff.

Malham lends its name to the small valley of Malhamdale which is a tributary of Airedale. It is an exceedingly pretty village of ancient whitewashed limestone cottages and with its little beck which later becomes the River Aire, that tumbles down over limestone beds, together with the famous geological wonders of Malham Cove and Gordale Scar, make it one of the most entrancing and beautiful locations in the Yorkshire Dales. The village is divided by the beck which is spanned by a former packhorse bridge and a primitive-looking but highly attractive clapper bridge.

MONK BRIDGE OR NEW BRIDGE

New Bridge, Malham's main road bridge across Malham Beck was originally known as Monk Bridge, and was a clapper bridge over the ford built by monks; the design probably similar to Moon Bridge. From earliest times, the bridge was used regularly by the many packhorse trains that came through the village. In 1636, local worthy, one William Preston who lived at Hill Top bequeathed in his will the sum of six pounds to finance the construction of a new single high-arched bridge of robust construction which would withstand the flooding of the beck. When first built in the early seventeenth century the new bridge was a single-arched, narrow, typical packhorse bridge. During the eighteenth and early nineteenth century the structure was rebuilt and widened to allow waggons and farm carts unrestricted passage over. Today, the bridge is known as New Bridge and carries a considerable volume of traffic across its ancient stone structure.

Ancient Moon Bridge, a clapper bridge spanning Malham Beck. In former times it was also known Wash Dub Bridge. August 2005.

© Christine McEwen Collection.

MOON BRIDGE

I first had the pleasure one warm, sunny August afternoon of viewing Moon Bridge that spans Malham Beck and is located in a beautiful leafy glade of mature trees and shrubs. Moon Bridge is a delightful ancient clapper bridge, so named after the man who ordered it to be constructed - the last Prior of Bolton Priory, Prior Moon. To many of the older Malham residents the bridge is also known as Wash Dub Bridge due to its position on the beck, which in former times was used by the local shepherds who would wash the wool-grease from the fleeces of their flocks of hardy Dales sheep.

Constructed from massive thick slabs of much-weathered, deeply fissured, limestone supported on crudely-built low piers of random stone, this clapper bridge was built to carry a monastic trackway across Malham Beck that ran eastwards from Malham village, up past Gordale; Bordley – thence into Wharfedale. In the opposite direction the trackway went steeply uphill to join Straight Lane, thence over the fells and down into Settle.

In recent years to safeguard the countless holidaymakers and sightseers that annually flock to savour Malhamdale's charms, the authorities have affixed a contemporary iron handrail across the bridge. My own view is that this iron railing, although obviously required for the safe passage of pedestrians using the bridge, unfortunately spoils this beautiful and ancient clapper bridge.

HANLITH PACKHORSE BRIDGE, NEAR KIRKBY MALHAM, MALHAMDALE

The former packhorse bridge at Hanlith which was evidently widened in the nineteenth century. The joint where the extension joins the original stonework of the arch can be easily seen by accessing the underside of the bridge which can be achieved when the river is low. August 2005.

© Christine McEwen Collection.

Due south of Malham village and across the River Aire from Kirkby Malham is the tiny hamlet of Hanlith whose name derives from the personal name of an early settler in the pre-Medieval period which translates into 'the hill-slope of Hagena'. Dominating the hamlet is the impressive Hanlith Hall mostly constructed in the late nineteenth century, with parts dating back to 1668, for long the ancestral home of the Serjeantsons, one of Malhamdale's most ancient families.

Stone-built Hanlith Bridge, once a narrow packhorse bridge having one single segmental arch spans the infant River Aire in a moderate throw of ten feet. The trackway over the arch is about ten feet wide, with parapets built of coursed stones, twenty-three inches high. It is currently used as a road bridge, and by viewing the underside of the arch, it is evident that the structure has been extended in width from the narrowness of the original packhorse bridge; the

modifications probably carried out sometime in the nineteenth century.

HANLITH'S CLAPPER BRIDGES

Up river, close to where the Malham Beck and Gordale Beck converge to form the Aire, there are two small, but extremely interesting clapper bridges. The first bridge consists of a lengthy slab of what appears to be Horton Slate which rests onto large sandstone boulders at either end and about twenty-four inches above the surface of the water. There is an ancient, Blacksmith-fashioned iron handrail which is bolted through the slate that serves to safely assist those using the bridge in floods conditions or during the dark. The other bridge is lengthier and is formed from two lengths of the Horton Slate. Both bridges were a pleasure to discover being surrounded by the fabulous Malhamdale countryside.

This picture is of the first clapper bridge probably made from Horton Slate with its Blacksmith-fashioned iron handrail.

© Christine McEwen Collection.

The second clapper bridge, also of Horton Slate, yet considerably lengthier.

© Christine McEwen Collection.

CLAPHAM BECK PACKHORSE BRIDGE, RIBBLESDALE.

Clapham Beck Packhorse Bridge is one of four bridges spanning the beck in this historic, attractive Dales village. September 2003.

© Christine McEwen Collection.

Clapham village sits astride the Clapham Beck which has four old stone bridges including a packhorse bridge spanning the sparkling water course with its many delightful waterfalls. The historic village with its many eighteenth century cottages built from the local limestone together with its Manor house is dominated by the craggy 2,373 foot mountain, Ingleborough.

Set beneath the fanned-out branches of ancient, gnarled Yews and Beeches across the Clapham Beck that meanders down the centre of this charming Dales village, is the delightful stone, middle-humped packhorse bridge that spans the water course in a leap of twenty-one feet.

Around the centre of this attractive segmental-arched packhorse bridge, there is a curious joggle or kink, - perhaps a constructional mistake made by the builders, or evidence of an earlier rebuild or repair following flood damage. Nevertheless, I feel that this structural idio-syncrasy actually enhances the bridge's appear-ance. The trackway across the top - (which unfortunately has been despoiled by tarmac) –

betwixt the round-topped, thirty-eight inch random stone parapets, measures forty-one inches. The random, un-coursed gritstone from which the bridge is constructed has been extremely crudely hewn.

Clapham lying to the north-west of Settle is situated on an historic trackway extending from Kendal, Lancaster and Kirkby Lonsdale in the west to Settle via the small hamlets of Austwick and Feizor; the historic Ribblesdale town, some two hundred years back was an important crossroads for the many Jaggermen's packhorse trains that conveyed hides, woollens, coal, limestone, lead, charcoal, peat and multifarious other goods in their panniers as they passed through.

Despite me carrying out much research, unfortunately, I have drawn a blank at dating Clapham Beck Packhorse Bridge.

Clapham's claim to fame is that Michael Faraday, the experimenter of electricity was the son of the village Blacksmith.

STAINFORTH BRIDGE, STAINFORTH, RIBBLESDALE

Elegant Stainforth Bridge, a former packhorse bridge, built circa 1675 spans the River Ribble in a giant leap of fifty-seven feet. It was constructed from limestone rubble by local Quaker, Samuel Watson. September 2003.

© Christine McEwen Collection.

In the seventeenth, eighteenth and early nineteenth centuries a significant volume of Jaggermen's packhorse traffic came through the attractive north Ribblesdale village of Stainforth, which had many trackways criss-crossing the area. Stainforth is located on an ancient monastic trackway that comes over the fells from Halton Gill in Littondale, the track extending between two local mountains, Penyghent and Fountains Fell.

Stainforth Beck otherwise known as Cowside Beck, flows through the village, which is dominated by the huge overhanging limestone mass of Langcliffe Scar; below which, is a huge rock boulder comically known as Samson's Toe – perched upon a slender stone pedestal. It is here that Stainforth's hidden gem, Catrigg Force can be seen in all its awe-inspiring glory as it dramatically rushes through a narrow canyon to plunge sixty feet. Sometimes in winter, some fantastic icicles form on the lip of the rocks where the waterfall plunges over.

Langcliffe Scar is actually the face of a large disused quarry where in days gone by countless thousands of tons of limestone were extracted. The quarry closed around 1939. Around 1873, a Hoffman kiln was constructed in the quarry and thereafter produced burnt lime until it temporarily stopped operating in 1931. The kiln was shut down for six years until 1937 when it was again re-fired to produce lime until its final closure at the outbreak of war in 1939. The structure, sadly now derelict with its arched roof caved-in still remains.

Hoffman kilns were used for burning limestone, the lumps of quarried limestone being stacked within the many chambers inside the kiln, and subsequent to the burning process – the fuel being coal – the produced lime was loaded into railway waggons to be despatched all over Britain via the Settle to Carlisle railway. Ingleton Patent Limeworks was the first company in Yorkshire to operate Hoffman kilns for lime-burning.

Stainforth Bridge locally known as 'rainbow arch' – no doubt due to the attractive display of salmon 'leaping up' the series of stupendous waterfalls and cataracts known as Stainforth Force or Foss below the packhorse bridge as they head up the Ribble.

This bridge is an extremely beautiful and graceful limestone arch that spans the River Ribble in a giant leap of fifty-seven feet and was constructed circa 1675. The width of the trackway over the bridge between the thirty-six inch high parapets amounts to six feet, nine inches or thereabouts. Quaker, Samuel Watson, the builder of Knight Stainforth Hall is reputed to have constructed the bridge over the site of an ancient ford: 'staney ford' - which lends it name to Stainforth village. The bridge was evidently sited on the line of a Roman road which ran from the Roman fort at Smearsett west of the Ribble, through Stainforth then eastwardly over the heights of Malham Moor and thence into Wharfedale. The structure is now owned by the National Trust and is still used today by light vehicles going to the nearby hamlet of Little Stainforth.

Craven Lime Works – Hoffman Kiln.

© By courtesy of Yorkshire Dales National Park Authority

THORNS GILL PACKHORSE BRIDGE, GEARSTONES, NEAR RIBBLEHEAD, RIBBLESDALE

The crudely-built limestone semi-circular arch of Thorns Gill Packhorse Bridge which spans the deep chasm in the limestone that the Gayle Beck rushes down on its way to join the River Ribble. July 2004.

© Christine McEwen Collection.

Located about a mile from the remote and famous Ribblehead viaduct on the Settle to Carlisle railway, and close to the ancient farmstead and former inn, Gearstones, is Thorns Gill Bridge, - (locally known as Roman Bridge) - which spans Gayle Beck that rushes down a deep, tortuous, narrow, rocky chasm to eventually flow into the River Ribble, a short distance downstream.

Thorns Gill Bridge is undoubtedly one of the most charming examples of Dales packhorse bridges and is in the form of a crudely-built semi-circular arch which springs from the natural bedrock on either side of a deep chasm. The arch is constructed from roughly-hewn limestone slabs, which spans Gayle Beck in a leap of around fifteen feet. The structure is devoid of parapets and the overall width of the trackway across the top is six feet, six inches.

One beautifully sun-kissed afternoon in July 2004, when standing on top of the bridge amidst the overhanging Rowan trees, on me noticing the shear drop of around eighteen feet to the surface of the torrent of water roaring through the chasm, and with my imagination kicking in, I could picture the scene two hundred years ago: a pitch black winter's night, a desperately hungry and tired Jaggerman leading perhaps a string of thirty packhorses across the tight confines of the bridge en route to Gearstones after leaving Settle that morning to trod across the wild and bleak fells. Terrifying!

JAGGERMEN'S BRIDGES ON PACKHORSE TRAILS

I quickly crossed the bridge into the sunny meadows beyond which were full of colourful wild flowers. Alan then joined me and we walked two fields further on where we reached a semi-ruinous barn amid some gnarled old trees. Close by, was the derelict ancient farmhouse which, my map indicated was called Thorns, and had once been a grange belonging to Furness Abbey.

Originally Gearstones, sited about a quarter of a mile in the direction of Hawes on the Hawes-Ingleton road – (B6255), - was a prominent local corn and oatmeal market which successfully operated until the late 1860s. The historic building also once served as an inn - 'Gearstones Inn' – and is still remembered by some of the older inhabitants of this wild and remote part of upper Ribblesdale.

An interesting piece of research in old books pointed me in the direction of another ancient inn, now a farm called 'High Birkwith' which is sited about a couple of miles south-east of Thorns Gill Bridge. High Birkwith sits on an ancient Jaggermen's packhorse trail that ran up Ribblesdale from Settle via Horton-in-Ribblesdale. This track eventually ran over the wild, bleak, desolate, high moorland to Hawes and Askrigg in Wensleydale. It has been suggested by a handful of packhorse bridge scholars – notwithstanding, there not being a scrap of documentary proof, that Thorns Gill Bridge was used by packhorse trains as a short cut from Gearstones across the wild moorland hereabouts to join the Horton-in-Ribblesdale to Askrigg packhorse route.

Thorns Gill Packhorse Bridge was extensively repaired in the early 1990s.

Alan standing on the rough stones that form the trackway over Thorns Gill Packhorse Bridge. July 2004.

© Christine McEwen Collection.

LING GILL PACKHORSE BRIDGE, CAM BECK, NEAR SELSIDE, RIBBLESDALE

The pleasing lines of Ling Gill Packhorse Bridge with the cold, bleak high moorland as a backdrop.   February 2005.

© Christine McEwen Collection.

After savouring the delightful Thorns Gill Packhorse Bridge with its wild but breathtakingly beautiful surrounding fells of Ingleborough and Whernside, it was my intention for both of us to walk from the bridge across the rough moorland to High Birkwith, then to another fascinating stone bridge located at Ling Gill over Cam Beck; this ancient bridge was also used by the Jaggermen's packhorses during their journeys to and from Gearstones.

I regret to say that on that beautiful and sunny July day with the intoxicating scents of moorland grasses and wild flowers in our nostrils, and with our eyes taking in the surrounding magnificent sun-drenched views, that we indeed did not tramp across the moorland to the ancient former inn at High Birkwith once owned by Jervaulx Abbey; and in earlier days much frequented by packhorse trains. High Birkwith is now a thriving Dales farm.

Instead, due to Alan's well renowned zeal for steam engines of all types, we walked over to a peaty hill-top close to the colossal Ribblehead viaduct to await a Black Five steam locomotive that was hauling an enthusiasts' special train from Hellifield to Carlisle. After waiting what appeared to be an eternity, the locomotive suddenly appeared enveloped in clouds of billowing steam to thunder over the long, massively-built stone viaduct that spans Batty Moss, resulting in an eminently satisfied Alan.

It was therefore, some six months later, in the February of 2005, when on a freezing cold Sunday morning, the grass at the side of the road covered in hoar frost, and the water courses bedecked with icicles, that we drove up through Ribblesdale heading firstly for High Birkwith and then to Old Ing where we parked our car.

From there, on foot we enjoyed a sunny yet perishingly cold, tramp along a limestone ravine, passing an attractive icicle-clustered waterfall down which fell the freezing waters of Cam Beck. As we reached the top of the ravine we were fascinated with several colossal boulders which lay scattered about as a result of being riven from the cliff-faces by countless years of severe Pennine frosts. As we neared the top of this ravine, with the sun reflecting from the ice-covered rocks, we then arrived at our goal, Ling Gill Bridge, a former packhorse bridge that spans Cam Beck, another tributary of the River Ribble. To be sure, this is one of the most fascinating historic bridges in the whole of the Yorkshire Dales.

Packhorses heavily laden with corn, oatmeal, hides, and woollens travelling west from Hawes and other Wensleydale towns and villages destined for the important local market at Gearstones would use Ling Gill Bridge.

On our arrival at the attractive stone bridge, we both noticed a curious, prominently carved inscription on a tablet of Millstone Grit incorporated into the upstream parapet which proclaimed the importance, in earlier times of this packhorse bridge and trail. The inscribed lettering reads:

**ANNO 1765,
THIS BRIDGE
WAS REPAIR
ED AT THE
CHARGE OF
THE WHOLE W
EST RIDEING**

Note, the 'Ns' in 'ANNO' are reversed on the tablet and the date is extremely difficult to read, but appears to be between 1765 and 1768.

This remote packhorse bridge is located on the once important packhorse trackway that linked Settle to Hawes in Wensleydale via the village of Horton-in-Ribblesdale. Several stretches of the trackway are Roman and it now forms part of the Pennine Way. The single segmental arch of twenty feet spans Cam Beck, the whole structure built of neatly-laid random stone; the voussoir stones forming the exceptionally shallow arch are narrow and vertically placed. The trackway over the bridge at sixteen feet, is unusually wider than most other packhorse bridges. However, there is no visible evidence that the structure has been widened subsequent to it being originally constructed. When Cam Beck is flowing moderately, which is not often, the centre of the arch is only about four feet above the water. During the all too regular flooding of the beck, the turbulent waters rise almost to the underside of the arch. The parapets are about twenty-five inches in height and terminate in neatly-hewn round-topped cap-stones.

Downstream of the bridge Cam Beck is called Ling Gill Beck, but just prior to it joining the River Ribble, a further two miles downstream, it reverts to being called Cam Beck.

The curious carved inscription on Ling Gill Packhorse Bridge. February 2005

© Christine McEwen Collection.

WEST BURTON BLUE PACKHORSE BRIDGE, WEST BURTON, BISHOPDALE.

The charming West Burton Blue Packhorse Bridge spanning the delightful, Walden Beck. July 2004.

© Christine McEwen Collection.

Beautiful West Burton lies at the confluence of Bishopdale and Waldendale, where the breezy high ground of Wassett Fell that separates both gives way to Wensleydale, but belongs equally to the two Dales – although, the charming village actually sits astride the Walden Beck.

Just below the attractive waterfall formed in the Ice Age by melting glaciers on the Walden Beck is a truly striking stone bridge, known as West Burton Blue Bridge. Why the word 'blue' forms part of the bridge's name is somewhat of an enigma, but one of the larger houses in the village, Edgeley was once the home of a writer, Elizabeth Montagu, who chaired meetings of the 'Blue Stocking Club' in her London residence. Perhaps, this is the connection?

This splendid structure, originally built as a packhorse bridge spans Walden Beck which rises from springs on the summit of Buckden Pike, the

2,303 feet mountain at the dale head. The beck rushes down the narrow, rocky, limestone gorge which overtime has eroded the rock into bizarre-shaped formations and through tranquil, leafy West Burton with its ancient cottages, inn and verdant village green. Starting at the packhorse bridge a trackway climbs out of West Burton up to the high ground dividing Waldendale with neighbouring Coverdale: Penhill; at 1,685 feet the domed summit of the hill in the olden times was used as a warning beacon, one of a chain that extended throughout Britain. The origins of the trackway, used for centuries by packhorse trains carrying goods up from Wharfedale and from further west, Swaledale, Wensleydale and their tributary dales to Coverdale and north-east Yorkshire, is considered to be part of a Roman Road that connected Middleham to Bainbridge.

JAGGERMEN'S BRIDGES ON PACKHORSE TRAILS

Close by the waterfall, there is a ruinous, thought-inspiring ancient manorial corn mill that in days gone by was operated by the often turbulent waters of the beck. In the green lush meadows on either bank, rare ferns and ivys grow in the shade of Ash, Alder, Beech and Hawthorns, and in the areas bathed by the sun, dazzling displays of beautiful wild flowers flourish to harmonise into a most idyllic and truly bewitching panorama.

The bridge's high, single segmental arch spans the Walden Beck in a twenty-four foot leap. The trackway over the bridge is relatively narrow at just forty inches, and the stone parapets are low at thirty inches. On the downstream parapet is a stone date plaque set in which is inscribed: 1860, which probably is the date that the bridge, which to be sure was built sometime in the early eighteenth century was rebuilt following flood damage, commonplace on Dales bridges.

A close-up picture depicting the date stone inscribed 1860 which is set into the downstream parapet. July 2004.

© Christine McEwen Collection.

IVELET BRIDGE,
THE QUEEN OF SWALEDALE'S BRIDGES

Ivelet Bridge – 'The Queen of Swaledale Bridges'. July 2004.

© Christine McEwen Collection.

For over three hundred years the good folk of Swaledale and the thousands of visitors who annually throng this wild, beautiful Yorkshire Dale, know Ivelet Bridge as the 'Queen of Swaledale Bridges'. I have to agree because without a doubt, it is the finest bridge in the whole of Swaledale.

Ivelet Bridge takes the form of a gigantic humped-back, segmental arch that gracefully soars across the peat-stained fast-flowing waters of the River Swale. This fine example of a sturdily-built Dale's bridge was constructed circa 1690 of Millstone Grit with long, thinly-cleaved, vertically laid voussoir stones. This former pack-horse bridge spans the Swale in a gigantic leap of over sixty feet. The width of the trackway betwixt the three feet tall parapets is wide enough to allow the passage over of heavily ladened farm waggons and merchants' carts. A testimony to the bridge's robust construction is that modern cars and lorries regularly pass over the structure heading either up or down the Dale.

Ivelet Bridge lies approximately a mile and a half west of Gunnerside and is on an ancient trackway, that until the middle of the nineteenth century was much frequented by Jaggermen's packhorse trains carrying coal from the Tan Hill collieries, Swaledale lead, hides and leather goods, woollens and other merchandise. This trackway runs from Askrigg Common in Wensleydale to terminate hereabouts, and is part of the old Corpse Way, used in centuries past when the deceased of the many outlying, remote farms and homesteads had to be carried across the River Swale on their last journey before burial in the hallowed soil at Grinton churchyard. Set into the verge of the trackway on the north side of the bridge is a slab of stone known as 'the Coffin Stone' where pall-bearers would rest wicker baskets used to carry corpses as they walked to Grinton Church.

Some of the older Swaledale folk whisper that Ivelet Bridge is terribly haunted by the spectre of a huge headless black dog, a Bargest - a portentous creature of ill-omen. In earlier times, there were reports by Jaggermen and other travellers using the bridge that the headless, four-legged creature had suddenly appeared out of the mist to run over the bridge but then rapidly disappeared as though into thin air!

RAVEN SEAT BRIDGE, RAVEN SEAT, UPPER SWALEDALE

Bonny Raven Seat Packhorse Bridge spanning Whitsundale Beck was for centuries used by packhorse trains carrying Tan Hill coal. June 2005.

© Christine McEwen Collection.

Situated alongside a pebble-strewn ford at Raven Seat in the wilds of Upper Swaledale is a bonny, high, humped-back stone packhorse bridge that spans Whitsundale Beck in a leap of twenty four feet. The width of the segmental arch is six feet, seven inches betwixt the thirty inch parapets.

When Alan examined the bridge during one of our visits, he told me that he thought the parapets had been added much later. Fortunately, the trackway over the bridge is original – there is not a hint of tarmac - the surface being constructed from water-rounded cobbles, - (the builders probably sourced them from the bed of the beck).

The isolated hamlet of Raven Seat with its two remaining occupied farms is arguably one of the most secluded human habitats in the Yorkshire Dales.

Raven Seat, together with its equally remote neighbour, Birkdale are situated in the high, bleak, wild and beautiful heather-clad, peaty moorlands at the head of Swaledale.

This is one of the most unique of British landscapes: for encircling these out-of-the-way hamlets is a nine-mile circle or amphitheatre of hills, nay mountains; for they are all over 2,000 feet above sea-level. To the south rises the mass of Great Shunnor Fell followed by Hugh Seat Morville – (yes this is also a Pennine mountain) – and on to High Seat: – (lying on the other side of the watershed is Mallerstang where the River Eden rises, to flow down through the now defunct county of Westmorland). Then with decreasing height northwards by Fells End to Tailbrig the high ground swings to cross the pass leading from Swaledale to the modern county of Cumbria on the 1,698 contour at Hollow Mill Cross and climbs up again to the heather-clad Coldbergh Edge, to White Mossy Hill and the impressively named Nine Standard Rigg just over into Cumbria.

JAGGERMEN'S BRIDGES ON PACKHORSE TRAILS

It is within this vast, high altitude, wilderness where the River Swale springs from countless bubblings and gurglings of water that run out of the sodden, peaty bogs on Uldale Gill on Lodge Hags; one of the flanks of the mountain - High Seat. The waters meet to cascade down Birkdale Beck, where other waters, converge to drain this little dale. Two more becks, Little and Great Sleddale meet with the Birkdale Beck and this is where the Swale is born. Shortly, after the meeting of the three mountain torrents on the north side of Birkdale, a fourth stream forms from numerous trickles and cascades, to become Whitsundale Beck.

Where the Whitsundale Beck sweeps in a loop on the rocky floor of Swaledale at around 1,300 feet above sea level, is the location of the two farmsteads that is all that remains of the hamlet of Raven Seat. In centuries long past Raven Seat was used as an outpost for giving warnings, when Norsemen, and later Scots raiders entered the Dale looking for plunder.

Many of the coal-pits around Tan Hill – King's Pit, Kettlepot, Taylor Rigg and a few others were first sunk in the thirteenth century. In the seventeenth century, coal for Lady Anne Clifford's castles came from pits on Stainmore; Appleby Castle would be supplied by packhorses travelling through Brough and Warcop – (both now in Cumbria).

Packhorse traffic delivering coal to her Pendragon Castle would come through Raven Seat. The one hundred and fifty loads of coal annually required for heating and cooking in Lord Wharton's Hall in the 1670s was also transported by packhorse that must have crossed the Whitsundale Beck by the packhorse bridge in Raven Seat.

In the mid-eighteenth century a man named Moore kept an inn at Raven Seat. At this period the village was home to eleven families. A Jaggerman, called John Mason of Nateby, near Kirkby Stephen about this period regularly led a team of packhorses loaded with corn and potatoes to Raven Seat, his return loads into Westmorland – the customary two-way traffic – was Tan Hill coal. Around the first decades of the nineteenth century, the habitable houses at Raven Seat had been reduced to the two current occupied farms.

There is a macabre story relating to the former inn at Raven Seat. One dark night robbers attempted to climb in by removing the stone roof slates. But the noise roused the inn-keeper who fired shots at them. Next morning at first light, bloody tracks leading up onto the moor were discovered, and some years later human bones were found!

Jaggermen with loaded packhorses.

© Christine McEwen Collection.

ADDINGHAM'S TWO BRIDGES, NR. ILKLEY, WEST YORKSHIRE

Delightful little Moorside Bridge spanning Town Beck, Addingham. January 2010.

© *Christine McEwen Collection.*

Two and a half miles upstream from Ilkley Old Bridge close to the joining into the Wharfe of the Town Beck, the little stream that runs through the attractive, historic mill village of Addingham, there are two attractive small stone bridges spanning the beck. Despite freezing conditions with snow and ice on the ground, Alan and I had the utmost pleasure in exploring these bridges.

Addingham is a quaint little village built of Millstone Grit in a delightful hotch-potch of differing sizes and roof lines. The narrow, fast flowing Town Beck snakes its way through the village in a rocky channel. Many of the older streets are still attractively cobbled, with some of the more historic stone houses having mullioned windows, and ornately carved seventeenth and eighteenth century door lintels, often including the original owner's initials.

In the Doomsday Book, Addingham is referred to as 'Ediham', which probably meant 'home of Edi' - the Earl Edwin of Bolton Priory, three miles further up the Wharfe. The first mention of an industrial building in Addingham, was in 1315, a corn mill. The foundations of the weir slanting across the River Wharfe dates back to the Medieval period most of which were destroyed during a massive flooding of the river in 1776. It was however, re-built within the following year. During the mid-fourteenth century the main occupations of Addingham, apart from agriculture, were Iron Smelting and Blacksmithing.

JAGGERMEN'S BRIDGES ON PACKHORSE TRAILS

MOORSIDE BRIDGE

This fascinating, diminutive stone bridge spans Town Beck close to St. Peter's Church whose history harks back to 867 A.D. When Alan and I inspected the small, narrow dimensions of the structure, we felt assured that it had been built as a packhorse bridge. However, the scant available information suggests not, for the bridge was evidently built to allow parishioners who lived out of the village on the high ground known as Addingham Moorside to safely cross Town Beck enabling them to walk to the church.

Moorside Bridge received its name from this connection with Addingham Moorside. The segmental arch bridge built of locally-quarried random Millstone Grit spans Town Beck in a leap of twelve feet. From normal beck level to the underside of the arch is forty-two inches; the trackway (partially cobbled) between the fifteen inch high parapets is forty-eight inches. I consider this little bridge to be an absolute gem, and despite the wintry conditions during our visit, was well worth investigating.

The large oblong, gritstone parapets and the partially stone trackway over Moorside Bridge, Addingham. January 2010.

© Christine McEwen Collection.

BRIAN'S BRIDGE

After leaving Moorside Bridge, we walked across the ice-covered grass of the village green towards Addingham to investigate and photograph the next little bridge, known strangely as Brian's Bridge. This bridge which connects the village green into North Street, also spans Town Beck. The segmental arch has a throw across the beck of sixteen feet; the trackway is six feet, four inches wide and remains partially cobbled. When we first gingerly made our way over the extremely icy surface of the trackway with the beck in high flood condition, we both considered that the thirty-two inch high parapets were made from cut gritstone. They also appeared to have been extended sideways to increase the width of the

trackway. However, after Alan risked falling into the beck by leaning far over the parapets, he discovered they were in fact built of smoothly cement-rendered stone. Nonetheless, they most certainly enhance the overall appearance of this small, highly attractive bridge.

So why is it called Brian's Bridge? Reputedly, the bridge received its rather unusual name due to its specific location. The tiny ginnel which leads onto the trackway was originally known as Brian's Lane. On the corner of Church Street and Brian's Lane there once stood an inn called the Kings Arms whose landlord was called Brian.

JAGGERMEN'S BRIDGES ON PACKHORSE TRAILS

Again, even though this superb little bridge does indeed look like a packhorse bridge, my research suggests otherwise, for it was evidently constructed around 1755 for the purpose of providing access across Town Beck for heavy horse-drawn waggons conveying stone, mortar, timber and other building materials required by the stone masons, who at that period were building St. Peter's Church tower. This is not to say however, that packhorses did not use the bridge as a means of crossing the beck en route to Ilkley and other destinations.

Brian's Bridge across Town Beck. Note the cement-rendered parapets that jut outwith the arch. January 2010.

© Christine McEwen Collection.

The attractively cobbled, ice-covered trackway over Brian's Bridge. January 2010.

© Christine McEwen Collection.

DOB PARK BRIDGE, WASHBURNDALE, NEAR OTLEY

**The lofty arched Dob Park Bridge, Norwood, spanning the River Washburn near Otley.
1st January 2004.**

© Christine McEwen Collection.

The robustly constructed lofty segmental arch packhorse bridge, built circa 1738 from random Millstone Grit spans the River Washburn that drains beautiful Washburndale, one of the numerous tributaries of Wharfedale.

This delightful packhorse bridge is certainly one of the most graceful and architecturally pleasing amongst a number of surviving historic packhorse bridges in the Yorkshire Dales. The span across the river is of around forty-five feet and the width of the attractively cobbled trackway between the two feet high parapets is around fifty-five inches; the parapets are roughly hewn slabs of gritstone strongly fastened together with square-section staples of wrought-iron.

Dob Park Bridge lies on the old packhorse route running northwards from the historic West Riding market town of Otley in Wharfedale to the ancient, Nidderdale hamlet of Summerbridge.

Some 250 years ago, frequent Jaggermen's packhorse trains would trot over Dob Park Bridge heading south-westerly delivering lead and other minerals to the West Riding towns of Otley, Leeds and Bradford, or perhaps heading in the opposite direction, carrying manufactured leather and woollen goods north to the towns and villages in Nidderdale.

Located just a cockstride downstream of the bridge is a stony ford which pre-dates the bridge and is still regularly used by the local farmers.

Dob Park Bridge is only located about twenty miles from my home, and I thoroughly enjoyed carrying out the exploration of this historical packhorse bridge located in the beautiful, tranquil setting of the Washburndale.

Dob Park Bridge's cobbled trackway and parapets. When I made this picture with boundless enthusiasm for my subject, and perhaps due to the failing light and wintry conditions, my mind started to play tricks, for in this tranquil setting I thought I could hear the sound of a multitude of approaching Galloway packhorses. I was of course mistaken!
1st January 2004

© Christine McEwen Collection.

ILKLEY OLD BRIDGE, ILKLEY, WHARFEDALE

Ilkley Old Bridge with the tormented waters of the River Wharfe flowing through the three arches. February 2004

© Christine McEwen Collection

Ilkley is surely one of the most attractive towns in Wharfedale, and perchance in the whole of the broad acres county of Yorkshire.

The town constructed from the locally quarried honey-coloured sandstone sits beneath the dominant overhanging mass of the famous Ilkley Moor rising to the south. Up on this high, often bleak, wind-swept moorland, pre-historic man has left his legacy in the abundant rock carvings such as the many examples of the 'Cup and Ring' stones, and overlooking the town, is the unique and enigmatic Swastika stone considered to be the most ancient rock carving ever found in Yorkshire. Perched in a prominent position on the very edge of Ilkley Moor is another of the town's famous landmarks: the distinctive and natural rock formations known as the Cow and Calf Rocks.

Ilkley was a prominent Roman fort: 'Olicana' – and some intriguing remains of the fort's structure survive being incorporated into part of the foundations of the ancient All Saints Parish Church which dates back to A.D. 1074. In the churchyard there are a number of extremely interesting, rare, Saxon stone crosses.

Shortly following Victoria being crowned Queen in 1837, Ilkley, and particularly its 'hydropathic' springs became nationally re-nowned; people from all over Britain and Europe visited the Wharfedale town to 'take the waters'. These were natural mineral waters.

ILKLEY OLD BRIDGE

Ilkley Old Bridge built circa 1678, spans the fast flowing and often severely flooded River Wharfe, known for centuries as the *'terrible Wharfe'*, by three attractive stone arches: the centre arch leaps fifty feet across the middle of the river in a high jump, causing a pronounced hump in the middle. Both outer arches have a span of around thirty feet, but do not rise as high as the centre arch. To bolster the strength of the bridge against the power of the Wharfe, on either side there are two sturdily constructed, triangular-shaped sandstone cutwaters.

The trackway across the top of the bridge is about thirteen feet wide between the thirty-four inch high stone parapets and was originally used from the late eighteenth century by horse-drawn merchants' carts, oxen-hauled farm waggons and regular Jaggermen's packhorse trains. From around this period the bridge parapets were regularly damaged by these carts and wagons resulting in some of the coping stones being dislodged and falling into the Wharfe. However, the copings were expediently retrieved from the deep, fast flowing waters by local worthies who offered their services working *'in t'watter'* for ten pence per day.

Historical records mention a bridge hereabouts in 1530, which was apparently regularly damaged by flooding. Between 1638 and 1670 winter flooding of the river frequently damaged the bridge's structure causing regular and expensive repairs. Despite extensive and costly repairs being undertaken in 1673, as a result of exceptional heavy rain, the much-swollen River Wharfe ruthlessly overwhelmed the bridge which was destroyed by the phenomenal weight of the water.

Where this sixteenth century bridge spanned the Wharfe, it was superseded by the construction of Ilkley Old Bridge in circa 1678. The new bridge has proven to be significantly stronger than the earlier bridge because it has withstood the raging torrents of water that has flowed beneath its three arches for over 330 years.

The opinion of many historians regarding whether this grand old stone bridge is indeed a packhorse bridge or not, does not concern me for I have enjoyed a special relationship with Ilkley's Old Bridge for many years.

Whilst working in the town, despite the weather conditions of hail, rain or shine, I enjoyed a daily stroll across 'my Old Bridge', whilst taking my lunch. Indeed, I have walked across the trackway over the central arch's pronounced hump during some mighty, frightening rainstorms, whilst below my feet the *'terrible Wharfe'*, in highly flooded torment, thundered through the arches with a tremendous awesome roar. I used to look down into the violent, raging, white flecked, peat-coloured waters, mesmerised. But I was not fearful for 'Old Bridge' was my friend.

Ilkley Old Bridge is undoubtedly is one of the finest historic stone built bridges in the whole of Wharfedale.

Ilkley Moor Baht'at - Traditional West Riding Song

Wheer 'as ta bin sin' ah saw thee?
On Ilkley Moor Baht 'at.

Tha's been a coortin' Mary Jane,
On Ilkley Moor Baht 'at.

Tha'll go and get thi deeath o'cowd,
On Ilkley Moor Baht 'at.

Then we shall 'a 'ta bury thee,
On Ilkley Moor Baht 'at.

Then t'worms'll come an' eit thee up,
On Ilkley Moor Baht 'at.

Then t'ducks'll come and' eit up t'worms,
On Ilkley Moor Baht 'at.

Then we shall come an' eit up t'ducks,
On Ilkley Moor Baht 'at.

Then we shall all 'ave etten thee,
On Ilkley Moor Baht 'at.

TH'OWD DONKEY BRIDGE, OXENHOPE, WORTH VALLEY, WEST YORKSHIRE.

The attractively titled Th'Owd Donkey Bridge spanning Bridgehouse Beck, Oxenhope. February 2005.

© Christine McEwen Collection

After Alan and I experienced the delightful and historically interesting walk along the banks of the Bridgehouse Beck from Haworth to Oxenhope, for me, the bonus was in viewing Oxenhope's 'Th'Owd Donkey Bridge' that spans the beck near North Ives. Alan found this little bridge interesting too, but with his main passion being steam railways he was obviously in his element for running alongside the Bridgehouse Beck is the famous Keighley and Worth Valley Steam Railway, whose steam locomotive boilers he had repaired since the late 1960s.

Although a gem of a diminutive stone bridge, regrettably, little is recorded of its history. No-one appears to know who built it and when it was built. We both agreed that it was probably constructed during the early eighteenth century, but we may be wrong as it could be a seventeenth century bridge.

However, this highly attractive bridge – (considered to be a packhorse bridge) – built of random-coursed Millstone Grit and for decades known hereabouts as Th'Owd Donkey Bridge is a superb example of a South Pennine packhorse bridge.

Bridgehouse Beck flows down from the 1,400 feet wild moorland lying to the south of Oxenhope and on reaching Haworth flows into the River Worth. Th'Owd Donkey Bridge's stone arch leaps over the beck in a throw of twenty feet. The width of the trackway is extremely slender at just twenty-four inches between the huge, oblong gritstone slabs forming the sixteen inch high parapets that rise to a blunt arrow-head shape in the centre of the bridge.

JAGGERMEN'S BRIDGES ON PACKHORSE TRAILS

This trackway over the arch of the bridge appeared to us both to be relatively new, being constructed from well-laid, unworn flagstones. At each end of the bridge are three stone steps that also appear to be relatively modern. Alan thought that originally there would have been huge sloping flagstones laid at each end which would enable the horses and donkeys easy access to the top of the bridge. Perhaps these old flags have been removed in recent times, and the stone steps built for safety reasons?

Although Th'Owd Donkey Bridge was clearly built as a packhorse bridge and possibly used for almost two centuries by Jaggermen's packhorses carrying West Riding wool and other goods across the beck en route over the bleak, wild moorlands lying south-west, to destinations in Lancashire, rumour suggests that maybe a hundred and fifty years ago, some of the Worth Valley farmers and merchants employed donkeys in 'mule trains' to carry their produce. Perhaps, Th'Owd Donkey Bridge received its attractive name from the usage of these gentle, sturdy, yet often stubborn animals? Jaggermen also used donkeys in other parts of the North.

Oxenhope, the name of this Pennine village is derived from Anglo-Saxon and means – 'the head of a valley with oxen'. The village built of local gritstone lies in a cold, north-facing Pennine valley at around 600 feet above sea level. Nevertheless, the village with its attractive, early eighteenth and nineteenth century cottages, clustered around the woollen mills is an historically interesting and picturesque place to visit.

This one is for Alan – a steam locomotive heading towards Oxenhope on the Keighley and Worth Valley Railway. February 2005.

© Christine McEwen Collection.

LUMBFOOT PACKHORSE BRIDGE, WORTH VALLEY, WEST YORKSHIRE.

Lumbfoot Packhorse Bridge, the attractive little packhorse bridge spanning Ponden Beck close by the ruins of Lumbfoot Mill. July 2005.

© Christine McEwen Collection.

One beautiful, sunny and warm early evening in July 2005, following us both thoroughly enjoying our tea of Yorkshire ham and farm eggs, washed down with a pint of Timothy Taylors Landlord in the historic pub in the Worth Valley village of Stanbury, we tramped downhill out of the village and on reaching Stanbury burial ground, branched off left onto a narrow winding, stony lane down the valley side to the ruins of Lumbfoot Mill.

Lumbfoot Mill was built in the late eighteenth century as a cotton spinning mill, powered by the Ponden Beck, a tributary of the River Worth. In 1805, the mill was owned by Jonas Sugden and at that time produced worsted. While I was studying my notebooks with the attempt of tracing where the packhorse bridge was sited, Alan was excitedly clambering amongst the ruins of the mill and the huge stones that formed the mill's dam.

In earlier times, Lumbfoot Mill, together with a rake of cottages built on the bank of the Ponden Beck that drains the Sladen Valley, comprised the hamlet known as Lumbfoot. We discovered, that during the nineteenth century the nearby farmhouse was at that time the home of Lumbfoot Mill's manager. Moving twenty or so yards towards the beck I was delighted to discover Lumbfoot Bridge which had been screened from our view by close-growing, leafy

Alders, Willows and Hawthorn bushes, and what a delightful little bridge it was!

This diminutive stone bridge surrounded by the beautiful upper reaches of the Worth Valley spans the Ponden Beck in a leap of around twenty-three feet. The shallow segmental arch built of Millstone Grit springs from about five feet above normal beck level; the width betwixt the nineteen inch parapets is thirty one inches. The parapets themselves are rectangular slabs or blocks of gritstone, some being stapled together with wrought-iron. There is an iron railing surmounting both parapets. On the Lumbfoot Mill side of the bridge a large, heavy, standing stone has been sunk into the ground at the bottom of the trackway, obviously to stop vehicles crossing the bridge.

Lumbfoot Packhorse Bridge was probably used by packhorses delivering yarn to the mill and also for despatching the spun cotton, later worsteds, up the Worth Valley slopes to weaving sheds at Haworth, Oakworth, Goose-Eye, Laycock and other nearby villages and hamlets.

To escape the rich bovine smells wafting over the beck from the nearby farm which filled our nostrils, and with us having completed the exploration and photography of Lumbfoot Bridge, we decided to walk downstream to search out our next Worth Valley bridge, Long Bridge, near Haworth.

LONG BRIDGE, WORTH VALLEY
WEST YORKSHIRE.

Long Bridge across the infant River Worth. Note the unusual abutments and steps at either end and the modern concrete ford. July 2005.

© Christine McEwen Collection.

With the melodious chatter of the beck in our ears, we leisurely walked downstream through water meadows of lush, sweet grass, filled with yellow-headed buttercups, carpets of white-headed daisies and widely scattered hosts of red clover. The Ash, Alder, Bog Oaks and Hawthorns thickly growing along the banks of this Pennine stream were alive with wonderful bird song. Alan and I were delighted and enchanted to be there. "***This packhorse bridge spotting is truly delightful",*** exclaimed Alan breezily. We both pushed on, thoroughly enjoying our walk through the delicious, intoxicating countryside.

About a third of a mile downstream from Lumbfoot Bridge, on us rounding a loop, - several score yards after Ponden Beck joined forces with Sladen Beck to become the River Worth - there it was, Long Bridge, but I must admit it appeared to be a rather bizarre-looking bridge. From normal water level, the almost semi-circular stone arch leaps across the Worth in a throw of about twenty-seven feet. The width of the trackway is thirty-two inches between parapets, hewn from massive oblong gritstone blocks. In the centre of

the arch the parapets are around twenty-five inches high and increase at the ends to forty-five inches in height where they are completed by vertical jambs. Reputed to have been originally constructed as a packhorse bridge, Long Bridge - certainly is a rather strange structure, for at either end instead of there being flag stones used as access ramps to enable the packhorses to mount the trackway over the bridge, there are instead, three steps surmounting low abutments. The trackway is formed from well-worn flagstones - that are full of character. As Alan and I sat near the bottom of the bridge refreshing our hot, sweaty feet in the river, we could almost imagine the cacophony of clattering hooves as a string of Jaggermen's packhorses, their panniers bulging with merchandise, thundered over the bridge.

Long Bridge, like its upstream neighbour, Lumbfoot Bridge joins the south-facing slopes of the Worth Valley with Haworth, where from which there were other trackways leading across the moors to the larger, more important woollen manufacturing towns of Bradford and Halifax.

The stone steps and the narrow trackway of worn flag-stones. July 2005

© Christine McEwen Collection.

PACKHORSE BRIDGES OF HEBDEN BRIDGE AND THE UPPER CALDER VALLEY.

© Christine McEwen Collection.

HEBDEN BRIDGE

Straddling the lower slopes and bottom of a deep gorge created by Ice Age melt-waters, the picturesque former mill town of Hebden Bridge spans Hebden Water, the beautiful, fast-flowing stream that descends hundreds of feet from the desolate moorland wastes of Widdop, above Hardcastle Crags. In the bottom of the Calder Valley, the mountain torrent flows into the River Calder which, for centuries has had a terrible reputation for flooding. Calder is derived from Old English meaning 'violent stream'.

Because of the town's location deep in the heart of the Pennines, for almost forty years it has promoted itself as the "Pennine centre". Hebden Bridge – first mentioned in 1399, as "Heptonbryg" – takes its name from the beautiful stone packhorse bridge that spans Hebden Water. Despite its early origins the present town was mainly created in the late eighteenth century with the advent of the Rochdale Canal. This former woollen weaving town remains chock-full of character and fills the tight confines of the valley bottom with its ram-jammed packed rows of three

and four-storeyed vernacular-style dwellings, its serried lines of terraced houses – the former homes of hundreds of mill operatives who worked in the once numerous mills, the decaying remains of sprawling mills and weaving sheds – like a cork in a green glass bottle.

The township commenced its development in the late Medieval period as the only reliable and safe crossing place over Hebden Water for the frequent packhorse trains travelling the often treacherous 'Long Causeway' – the packhorse trackway over the moorland heights linking the important manufacturing towns of Halifax with neighbouring Heptonstall, sitting high upon the Buttress, and the larger towns of Burnley and Rochdale. This significantly important trackway across the wild, desolate moorlands on the border between Lancashire and the West Riding of Yorkshire was probably laid during the Neolithic period, but was subsequently much improved as the conveyance of goods by packhorses evolved.

Due to the local high rainfall conditions, the trackways over the peaty ground regularly suffered from serious erosion, the horses' hooves gouging 'hollow ways' out of the soft, waterlogged ground. Enabling these trackways to be kept open in all weathers, large, flat pieces of Millstone Grit known as 'causey stones' were laid to create the trackway.

Present-day Hebden Bridge was undoubtedly created on the back of eighteenth century industrial enterprise when the concentration of textile manufacture moved down from the small water-driven mills, often perched in remote tributaries of the Calder, such as Lumb Mill and Bob Mill in the Colden Valley – into significantly larger, purpose-built, newly-constructed mills on the valley floor. Dwelling houses, shops and inns were then rapidly built around these textile mills on the scarce left-overs of relatively flat ground, thus the community grew into the present town.

Within Hebden Bridge there are many surviving examples of vernacular 'top and bottom' dwellings. Due to the precipitous valley sides, and a paucity of level ground remaining following the construction of the mills – to house the burgeoning ranks of mill operatives tall houses were built of three and four storeys in long terraces on the steep hillsides. Each four-storey house was generally divided into two, two-storey dwellings with the upper houses being accessed from a street laid out on the higher ground at the rear.

Hebden Bridge and its satellite hill-top hamlets of the Upper Calder Valley are steeped in history. There are some splendid examples of seventeenth and eighteenth century, handloom weaving dwellings that stare down on the town and its ancient packhorse bridge from high on the shoulders of the Calder Valley; early packhorse 'paved causeways' wind their way over the high, barren moorland, and in the numerous, wooded ravines, known hereabouts as 'cloughs' – thought-inspiring, picturesque, ancient bridges of stone slabs or flags span breathtakingly beautiful cataracts that tumble downhill in their mad-cap rush to join the Calder.

Down on the bustling, busy floor of the Calder Valley, the Rochdale Canal – the first trans-Pennine canal – crosses the River Calder over the impressive four-arched, Black Pit stone aqueduct designed by John Rennie and built 1795. Let into the masonry of the town-side parapet is a large carved stone head with the date 1795. Reputedly, the gargoyle is there to protect travellers from harm due to there being **'a terrible boiling whirlpool',** here in the bed of the Calder. Also running parallel to the canal is the trans-Pennine railway, surveyed by the 'Father of Railways', George Stephenson.

HEBDEN BRIDGE - OLD PACKHORSE BRIDGE

The attractive cobbled trackway over the ancient packhorse bridge, Hebden Bridge. January 2010.

© Christine McEwen Collection.

JAGGERMEN'S BRIDGES ON PACKHORSE TRAILS

Having worked on many of Hebden Bridge's mill steam boilers ever since the 1960s, Alan has therefore, been acquainted with the remarkable and historic packhorse bridge for many years. When he first introduced me to this truly delightful structure one beautiful, sunny morning in July 2003, I then became deeply fascinated with the bridge's long history, resulting in both Alan and myself returning often to Hebden Bridge and the Calder Valley where we enjoyed exploring the surrounding leafy cloughs with their babbling streams, while searching out a number of other interesting old bridges.

The beautiful, stone packhorse bridge constructed during the first year of the reign of Henry VIII in 1510, was built to replace a structurally unsafe, rotting, timber bridge dating back to the thirteenth century. Finance for the stonemason-built bridge was raised by local subscription amongst the town's tradesmen; some hefty sums were also provided by wealthy Calder Valley landowners and prosperous merchants, all of whom clearly recognised that the construction of a new, robustly-built stone bridge was vital for the town's future prosperity. For a new bridge would allow the numerous Jaggermen's packhorse trains loaded with all manner of goods, to travel through the Calder Valley using the safe, all-weather crossing of Hebden Water, which in winter could be severely flooded – to the cloth markets of Heptonstall, Halifax, Burnley, Colne and Rochdale.

Located in the town centre, the Grade II listed bridge consists of three arches, under two of which flows Hebden Water; the third – dry arch – was originally used for returning exhaust water that had powered the Wadsworth manorial corn mill water wheel – which until the late nineteenth century was sited near to the present cast-iron St. George's Bridge. The span of the bridge is around sixty feet; the angled parapets are thirty-eight inches high and the cobbled trackway

between measures seven feet, six inches. Both piers have upstream and downstream cutwaters that strengthen the structure, the downstream ones preventing cavitation from undermining the piers. Three of the cutwaters are projected up to form pedestrian refuges on the trackway. Usually, refuges were a feature of lengthy, multi-arched bridges, which protected pedestrians walking over the bridge from packhorse trains with their heavily-laden, bulging panniers.

Set into the stone fabric of the bridge are three intriguing carved stone tablets recording repairs carried out to the structure in 1600, 1602 and 1657. On the downstream side of the bridge the stone tablet is inscribed: *"**Repaired by help of John Greenwood Sessions 1600"**.*

On the upstream side the two tablets, one of which is badly cracked, are inscribed: *"**Repaired by help of Richard Naler Sessions 1602" ------** and "**Repayred by the Ridinge: by Order of Sessions August 4 1657 by H N: R G: R G"***

During the history of the original timber bridge and following the construction of the present stone bridge in 1510, a number of local people bequeathed sums of money in wills: James Grenewode of Wadsworth bequeathed 3 shillings, 4 pence – *"**to the fabric of Hepden Bridge"**;* another local worthy left 6 shillings – *"**to a bridge called Heptenbridge"**;* another towns-man, Richard Naylor, who was possibly the landlord of the original White Lion Inn bequeathed the sum of 6 shillings, 8 pence in 1510 – *"**to the building of the bridge of Hepden"**.* Two years earlier in 1508, William Grenewode of Heptonstall, probably due to regular frustrations regarding the unsafe condition of the ancient, decaying and therefore, dangerous timber bridge, left – *"**to the fabric of Hepten bridge 13 shillings, 4 pence if those nearest it will built it of stone"**.*

Details of the three carved stone tablets displayed on the bridge's structure. January 2010.

© Christine McEwen Collection.

JAGGERMEN'S BRIDGES ON PACKHORSE TRAILS

This magnificent stone bridge which has lent its name to the town during 2010 will be five hundred years old. For almost three hundred and fifty years packhorse trains clattering down the steeply inclined, cobbled trackway known as the Buttress from Heptonstall, used the bridge to cross over treacherous Hebden Water before climbing up the Snicket to nearby Midgeley situated on the other side of the valley en route to Halifax.

One of the most prominent routes on the Lancashire-Yorkshire border used by the packhorse trains travelling from Halifax over the moors to Burnley was the 'Long Causeway'. Here is an interesting Jaggermen's rhyme dating back to the late eighteenth century:

"Burnley for ready Money,
Mearclough don't Trust,
You'll be taking a peep at Stiperden,
And call at Kebs you Must,
Blackshawhead for Travellers,
And Heptonstall for Trust,
Hepton Brig for Landladies,
Midgeley by the Moor,
Luddenden's a warm Spot,
Roil Head's very Cold,
But if you get to Halifax,
You must be very Cold."

FOSTER MILL BRIDGE, HEBDEN BRIDGE

To enable the strings of packhorses to climb up the vertiginous, rocky valley sides and to cross the often-sodden, peaty moorlands, paved stone trackways known hereabouts as 'causeways' were laid. Large proportioned, thick slabs of Millstone Grit, perhaps measuring four feet by around one foot and a half wide were laid, with the sides of the trackway made up of smaller slabs and stones, which usually extended to a width of around eight feet.

The individual villages and hamlets such as Heptonstall, Stansfield and Mankinholes usually provided their own tools used for packhorse trackway construction and repair work. Heavy hammers called mauls, mattocks and spades used for digging, crowbars and wedges for laying down the slabs of stone, and sturdy sledges were used for hauling and positioning the 'causey stones'. Money for the provision of the tools and for paying out wages to the men who laid the causeys, would be locally raised by 'rates or levies'. In 1768, Heptonstall paid out wages ranging from four pence per day for a labourer, who would do the heavy digging and the positioning of the stones, to as much as three shillings, paid to a farmer and his son for moving the stones on the sledges.

Foster Mill Bridge built in the 17th century, crossing Hebden Water. January 2010.

© Christine McEwen Collection

JAGGERMEN'S BRIDGES ON PACKHORSE TRAILS

One delightful and pleasant morning in May 2007 during one of our frequent forays around Hebden Bridge, Alan and I arrived at Foster Mill Bridge after an exhilarating downhill walk from Heptonstall using the old packhorse track, the Buttress, to finally descend by a series of extremely steep, zig-zagging tracks through lush plantings of freshly leafed Ash, Alder and Elderberry, thence to the banks of the silvery Hebden Water.

Situated about half a mile up Hebden Water from Hebden Bridge's old Packhorse Bridge, gracefully spanning the river in a throw of around thirty-three feet is the early seventeenth century packhorse bridge, known as Foster Lane Bridge, originally built for both packhorse traffic and for the Fulling Mill workers to reach their homes in Heptonstall.

Looking very similar to a number of other Yorkshire packhorse bridges, Foster Mill Bridge, built of coursed Millstone Grit in the form of a high hump-backed, segmental arch, with parapets cut from huge, rectangular slabs, is extremely attractive. To my mind, this historic bridge situated next to several atmospheric old stone buildings once part of the massive Foster Mill, a steam powered worsted mill, - (demolished 1985) - itself converted from a seventeenth century fulling mill in around 1808, and with the melodious chatter of Hebden Water – and the woodland setting – is the epitome of the special mix, of breath-takingly beautiful countryside and enigmatic industrial ruins, that is, the Upper Calder Valley.

The trackway over the bridge is around seventy-five inches in width, down the centre the cobbled surface has been severely worn into a hollow, the result of centuries of heavily burdened packhorses crossing the bridge heading away from Foster's Fulling Mill, or crossing from the other direction after trotting down from Heptonstall delivering loads of coarse woollens requiring fulling.

The well-worn cobbled trackway over Foster Mill Bridge, Hebden Bridge. January 2010.

© Christine McEwen Collection

Stone 'finger' posts located near Heptonstall. January 2010.

© Christine McEwen Collection.

HEPTONSTALL – A Woollen Weaving Hamlet

Precariously perched on a high spine of Millstone Grit between the valleys of Hebden Water and Colden Clough several hundred feet above the huge gouge of the Calder Valley far below, is the charming, historic, woollen-weaving township of Heptonstall with its steeply cobbled lane that climbs up from the main valley floor and its many mullion-windowed gritstone weavers' cottages.

Heptonstall is an ancient settlement, its name comes from Old English and means: 'hep-den' – a valley where Rose hips grow. Until the end of the eighteenth century it was an archetypal Yorkshire woollen weaving village, but when the new steam-powered mills built down in and around Hebden Bridge brought a rapid decline in trade, consequently, many of Heptonstall's folk were then forced to daily tramp down the steep hill, the Buttress, to find work in the mills of Hebden Bridge.

Heptonstall built its own Cloth Hall in 1545, which generated a considerable volume of packhorse traffic delivering and taking away, raw wool, yarns and finished woven woollen 'pieces'. Clothiers based in the Cloth Hall regularly employed strings of packhorses which created tremendous economic benefits for the township and the surrounding area.

These packhorse trains would leave Heptonstall and trot down the cobbled Buttress and to cross Hebden Water on the old packhorse bridge in Hebden Bridge.

JAGGERMEN'S BRIDGES ON PACKHORSE TRAILS

LUMB BRIDGE, OR HORSE BRIDGE, CRIMSWORTH DENE, NEAR HEBDEN BRIDGE

Lumb Bridge, otherwise known as Horse Bridge, Crimsworth Dene. April 2005.

© Christine McEwen Collection.

It was one of those rare winter days when the sun shines to warm up and to beautify the freezing Pennine scenery which for the researcher, explorer and photographer of packhorse bridges makes life very much more rewarding.

On the last day of December 2004, after Alan and I had parked his Picasso in the car park at Hardcastle Craggs, and following the usual frenzied donning of warm, waterproof jackets and changing into stout walking boots, we both set off along the well worn stony track to sample the delights of Crimsworth Dene, a little Pennine clough, and to hopefully view a gem of a packhorse bridge known hereabouts as Lumb Bridge or Horse Bridge.

As we cheerfully tramped up this stunning Pennine clough, we met a goodly number of fellow walkers, some with children and excited dogs. We kept stopping to consult our map and the hastily scribbled directions for locating Lumb Bridge, which I had jotted down on a small note pad. After walking another quarter of a mile, we then rested beneath the denuded branches of an ancient, gnarled Oak, where again I consulted my notes. Both Alan and I were concentrating heavily, when suddenly a deep male locally accented voice rang out, "**Mornin' folks, are you lost?**". Looking up, we saw a tall sixty-ish aged man dressed in heavy tweeds with an attractive green deerstalker on his head.

"**Yes, er, morning, we are actually looking for Lumb Bridge, the old packhorse bridge**", I replied. "**Well you're in the wrong shop up 'ere on't valley side**", said Deerstalker, whilst pointing down into the bottom of the clough. "**See them theer Hawthorn bushes? Well, make for them and walk down until you reach the beck. You will see the old bridge quite a bit higher upstream. You can't miss it, and by the way, round here it's called Horse Bridge**". After me explaining that I was researching packhorse bridges for a book I was one day hoping to write, we both thanked our new friend Deerstalker for his kindly assistance, and commenced working our way down to the bottom of the clough.

JAGGERMEN'S BRIDGES ON PACKHORSE TRAILS

It was Alan who first spotted the bridge among some stunted bushes of Alder and Bog Oak just upstream of a lovely watery cascade called Lumb Hole Waterfall that thundered into a hole in the bed of the beck. **"What a bonny wee bridge"**, shouted Alan in his Lancastrian Doric in his attempt to make me hear over the sound of the waterfall.

Located in an idyllic spot and surrounded with a magnificent backdrop of dark brown hills and drystone walled fields, the packhorse bridge, built of red lichen-covered Millstone Grit spans the Crimsworth Dene Beck with its segmental, almost semi-circular arch in a leap of around fifteen feet; the width of the trackway, which regrettably, is partially tarmaced, is five feet. There are no parapets, but I feel that the bridge's attractiveness has been slightly lessened by the fitting of iron railings.

Standing on the bridge and looking up both the western and eastern flanks of the clough, we could make out the drystone walled packhorse trackways leading down the steep hillsides to the striking little bridge. From the maps and notes that I had copied from a tatty old volume of early roads and packhorse tracks, purchased from a Mancunian second-hand bookshop, I guessed that the packhorse trackways converging at Lumb Bridge most probably included trackways between Hebden Bridge and Keighley, Hebden Bridge and Burnley – reached over Gorple Gate; – and the 'Limer's Gate' running down from Clitheroe.

HEBBLE HOLE, COLDEN WATER, COLDEN CLOUGH

Numerous Jaggermen's packhorse trains crossed the often swollen Colden Water over this wonderful Clam Bridge. Hebble Hole, Colden Clough. January 2005.

© Christine McEwen Collection.

JAGGERMEN'S BRIDGES ON PACKHORSE TRAILS

Immediately lying westwards of the ancient woollen weaving hamlet of Heptonstall is another deep and wooded canyon, Colden Clough. Just below the hamlet of Jack Bridge which sits upon the ancient monastic and packhorse trackway over the moorlands to Burnley, – the 'Long Causeway' – is a clam bridge called Hebble Hole Bridge that spans Colden Water.

Prior to Jack Bridge being built at the top of the clough, this interesting bridge carried the 'Long Causeway' over Colden Water, another often swollen beck that drains the high moorland fells at the head of Colden Clough, to eventually discharge the waters into the River Calder. The modern Heptonstall to Burnley - 'on the tops' - road passes over Jack Bridge to follow the ancient route of the 'Long Causeway'.

Following our adventure prospecting for Lumb Bridge in Crimsworth Dene, around a fortnight later in January 2005, Alan and I returned to the Upper Calder Valley, where in the wilds of Colden Clough, he promised to show me another interesting bridge he knew of, a clam bridge.

With beautiful sunshine illuminating the contours of the high, barren moorland, during our car journey over the 'Long Causeway' from where it starts at Mereclough, near Burnley, arriving at Heptonstall, and after photographing two interesting old stone mileage finger posts, we enjoyed a lovely lunch in the historic, White Lion Inn on Towngate.

At around two o'clock, with the sun sinking quite rapidly behind the hills to the west, we drove out of Heptonstall down the cobbled Buttress until we reached the Todmorden Road down on the floor of the Calder Valley. From here, after negotiating the 'turning circle' – and heading back towards Hebden Bridge, we then drove up a very narrow un-metalled road heading up Colden Clough, with the river in full spate on our right hand side.

Alan knew the way quite well, for many years earlier, he had, over several trips, photographed the many remains of long demolished mills located by the river. On arriving at the thought-inspiring ruin of Bob Mill, now just a time-blackened heap of large lumps of Millstone Grit and a tall cylindrical chimney that long ago belched black smoke coming from the coal-burning steam engine boilers, because the track had but disappeared, we were forced to park the car.

Leaving the enigmatic ruin of Bob Mill behind, we then commenced pushing up the clough, forcing our way through a jungle of high-arching branches of Blackberry and attempting to avoid being pricked to death by the dense thickets of Blackthorn and Hawthorn that grew in profusion on either side of the fast-flowing, swirling waters of the river.

Soon, the sad remains of another long-abandoned cotton mill came into view, Lumb Mill. We walked on, both of us taking pictures with our 35mm film cameras, heading in the direction of Jack Bridge. Suddenly, with the winter afternoon's pale light becoming noticeably less, on rounding a bend in the river where the trees and thorn bushes were starting to give way to the high moorland, we then saw a most thrilling example of a clam bridge: Hebble Hole Bridge.

With the light now perceptibly dying, we nevertheless, fired off a goodly number of photographs. Alan clambered on top of the bridge to carry out a detailed examination of the structure, which from where I stood, looked like it was built from one huge stone block.

This bridge spanning Colden Water comprises four, roughly dressed, rectangular-shaped slabs of Millstone Grit. The whole structure rests upon three, huge natural slabs of rock, stacked one on top of another; this pillar of rock, itself rises up from a massive water-worn stone monolith that rises above the surface of the water.

At the west side of the bridge there are two vertical standing stones that leave just a small gap for foot traffic only. Connected to the larger of the two upright stones is an iron handrail. Surely, most welcome for travellers attempting to cross the narrow bridge in the dark, in fog or when the river is in spate.

The larger of the two stone pillars was evidently placed at the Blackshaw Head end of the bridge sometime in the nineteenth century to force packhorse traffic to use nearby Jack Bridge.

With evening approaching fast, Alan and I hurriedly retraced our steps to head down river to where our car was parked near Bob Mill. I really enjoyed our winter afternoon's adventure up Colden Clough, and with my appetite whetted further our next foray was to see another unusual bridge, a clam bridge, located up the equally wild, Jumble Hole Clough.

UPPER CALDER VALLEY CLAM BRIDGES

The clam bridges of the Upper Calder Valley and many other Pennine locations are constructed from slabs of locally quarried stone, usually sandstone or Millstone Grit.

These huge, roughly hewn slabs of stone would be manoeuvred into place to form a clam bridge spanning a beck running in a narrow defile or ravine. The rock surfaces on either side of the beck where the ends of the stone slabs were to be placed were probably carefully prepared beforehand. The slabs were then placed into position on a bed of lime mortar, or clamped into position by iron bars driven around each end into prepared holes drilled into the rock. Another method was to mortar other large pieces of stone around the end of the clam-slabs, making the whole structure secure for packhorses and foot traffic. 'Clam' when associated with these types of bridges means the clamping e.g. the securing of the slabs. This is where the generic name, clam bridges is derived.

The majority of clam bridges are in the form of a single slab, such as the fine example at Jumble Hole Clough, or are constructed from two or more huge slabs. My favourite clam bridge is Hebble Hole Bridge which consists of four, huge slabs of Millstone Grit. I am particularly fascinated with these clam bridges and have often wondered just how the men who built them actually handled these huge, weighty slabs of stone, lifting them into position across the water courses without any of the modern cranes we take for granted. Alan informed me that the slabs would be loaded onto wooden sledges where they were quarried and then hauled to where they would form the clam bridge, either by oxen or heavy horses. Once the slabs had been delivered to the beck side, the men using wooden rollers and long iron crow-bars would then manoeuvre the slabs as close to the final position as possible. The final lifting into place of the slabs would probably be carried out by ropes suspended over pulley wheels fastened at the top of shear-legs fashioned from three suitable tree trunks, using a horse or an ox to take the load.

JUMBLE HOLE CLOUGH, CHARLESTOWN, NEAR HEBDEN BRIDGE

Jumble Hole Clough Clam Bridge. September 2005.

© Christine McEwen Collection.

JAGGERMEN'S BRIDGES ON PACKHORSE TRAILS

It was an early Sunday morning in September 2005, the weather was behaving itself with not a cloud to be seen in a deep azure sky.

Alan and I were both extremely hot and sweaty as we battled our way up the steep, rocky sides of Jumble Hole Clough, near Hebden Bridge.

For quite some time, Alan, who knew this wild Pennine clough quite well, had promised me a treat. He was going to show me a superb, little clam bridge spanning the mountain torrent that raced down the clough. There was however, method in his madness, for he wanted to photograph a romantic eighteenth century cotton mill ruin, Staups Mill, that is remotely sited by the beck, in the wilderness near the head of Jumble Hole Clough.

'Jumble Hole' – what a fantastic name for a Pennine clough, and the chance of seeing another clam bridge. I couldn't wait to set off. Alan being keen to see the cotton mill ruin, was around thirty yards in front and I had just nettled my bare right arm in the attempt to fight off a swarm of flies that were dive-bombing my sweaty body from every direction.

"Christine, your clam bridge is here", Alan shouted above the roar of the beck whilst pointing into a green jungle of Hazel, Ash, Silver Birch and Hawthorn growing thickly right down to the water's edge. Puffing and panting, feeling really hot and the large white nettle rash on my arm dreadfully hurting, I raced to join Alan, who by now was proudly standing on the slab of rock forming the clam bridge that was peeping out from a dense mass of giant fern-like plants.

"What a lovely example of a clam bridge in a truly tranquil, beautiful setting", I exclaimed cheerfully. Using Alan's trusty, but rather battered elderly, Olympus 35mm camera, I fired off a number of photographs of the clam bridge, whilst he was on his hands and knees investigating the structure.

We could both see that one huge, oblong piece of gritstone, its ends resting upon a number of stone blocks, formed the bridge. This stone slab measured around eight feet in length, the width being around eighteen inches and the thickness about nine inches. A light, iron handrail completed the structure. There are old records that mention this clam bridge was used by packhorses loaded with cloth destined for Heptonstall Cloth Hall.

Despite my hot, tired and nettled condition, I was extremely satisfied with our morning's adventure in wild and beautiful Jumble Hole Clough.

LOWER STRINES, COLDEN WATER, NEAR HEBDEN BRIDGE

This fascinating example of an old packhorse bridge known as Lower Strines Bridge, spans Colden Water, Near Hebden Bridge. September 2005.

© Christine McEwen Collection.

JAGGERMEN'S BRIDGES ON PACKHORSE TRAILS

As my interest in packhorse bridges appeared to know no bounds, and in particular my fascination with the splendid gems of packhorse bridges around Hebden Bridge and the Upper Calder Valley, Alan and I made frequent visits, which would take less than one hour, from our home in Cowling, near Keighley.

Lower Strines Bridge is a striking example of a stone packhorse bridge and spans upper Colden Water around a few hundred yards from the hamlet of Jack Bridge on the 'Long Causeway'. The high-humped segmental arch spans the beck in a leap of around twenty-two feet. The width of the trackway betwixt the eighteen inch high parapets is very narrow at thirty-two inches. The parapets are built from rough slabs of Millstone Grit and were once stapled together with wrought-iron bars, now virtually rusted away. The trackway consists of several small flagstones, except for the centre which has a thin concrete render over the arch stones, which I consider ruins the attractiveness of this historical structure. At each end of the bridge there is a narrow stone stile. This arrangement was probably built to deter Jaggermen's packhorses from crossing, following the building of the wider bridge at Jack Bridge. A narrow, grass-covered, cobbled causeway leads from the east to Lower Strines Bridge which probably, originally, connected it with the hamlet of Blackshaw Head and the 'Long Causeway'.

Alan and I visited this packhorse bridge one rather cool morning in September 2005 and immensely enjoyed our walk up beautiful, tranquil Colden Water.

HIPPINS CLOUGH, STAUPS MOOR, NEAR BLACKSHAW HEAD

Just peeping from beneath its covering of heather and moorland grasses is the tiny, enigmatic Hippins Clough Packhorse Bridge located on Staups Moor, Near Blackshaw Head. September 2005

© Christine McEwen Collection.

To illustrate the wide variety of packhorse bridges that abound in the wild moorland cloughs between Hebden Bridge and Todmorden in the Upper Calder Valley, is the dwarf-size, beautifully-built packhorse bridge that spans a tiny beck at the top of Hippins Clough, on Staups Moor, near Blackshaw Head.

This diminutive well-constructed stone bridge leaps across the tiny watercourse in a span of just fifty-five inches between the abutments of the segmental arch, and is just twenty-six inches above the water. The bridge is five feet wide and the worn surface of the top of the arch suggests the structure has experienced considerable passage of hoofed feet.

This bonny little bridge is situated on an early packhorse trackway known as Harley Wood Gate, essentially forming a section of the route from the historic hill-top hamlet of Shore-in-Stansfield to Heptonstall Cloth Hall.

Our endeavours to find this midget of a packhorse bridge in September 2005, encouraged the sun to shine, and so blessed with lovely warm early autumn sunshine, Alan and I set off across the swampy, undulating terrain of Staups Moor with just a few lines of instructions of where the bridge could be located.

Hippins Clough Bridge certainly sounded unique, but with it being so small, the question in my head was, would we be able to find it among the tall swamp rushes and lank moorland grasses that flourished over the extensive wilderness of Staups Moor.

As we tramped over the soaking peat, we had to be mindful of the numerous, dangerous, water-filled holes that were naturally camouflaged by the tall reeds that thickly grew around them. More than once, after I placed my heavy walking boot down on to what appeared to be terra firma, my booted leg sunk deeply into black, smelly liquid peat, which required Alan's assistance to pull me out.

After around three quarters of an hour of searching for the elusive bridge over the desolate moorland, I suddenly noticed about thirty yards to my left what appeared to be a low stack of stones. Urging Alan to join me, I made my way over to the stones, and on getting closer it dawned on me that this was the tiny Hippins Clough packhorse bridge. Surrounded by dense clumps of purple-flowering heather and swamp grasses was a stone arch-like structure, which at first glance appeared to be a natural stone outcrop. With Alan joining me, we both knelt down to clear away with our hands some of the grasses that were hanging over the entrance of the arch. Once completed, we could clearly see that it was a neatly-built bridge, perhaps several centuries old, spanning a shallow, sluggish watercourse.

I was truly amazed and delighted with our discovery of Hippins Clough packhorse bridge, and after us both becoming acquainted with three inquisitive ponies that had been grazing nearby, fully satisfied with our achievements, we set off back across the moor to where we had parked our car.

Alan sat on top of the bridge taking a well-earned breather. September 2005.

© Christine McEwen Collection.

CLOSE GATE BRIDGE, MARSDEN, COLNE VALLEY

Spanning Close Gate Brook, near Marsden, this delightful example of a packhorse bridge known as Close Gate, Eastergate or Th'Owd Gate Bridge is situated in isolation amidst stark, barren, moorland. January 2004.

© Christine McEwen Collection.

It was a clear, brilliant January day but frosty and cold, and we were both ensconced upon a long-ago fallen stone gate post looking down from our high moorland eyrie onto the small, attractive stone-built Pennine town of Marsden. The town is dominated by the wild heights of Standedge which at 1,300 feet above sea level carries the modern A62 trunk road over the Pennines to Oldham. Early Engineers pierced the bulk of this massive hill with tunnels that carry the Huddersfield Narrow Canal – (the highest canal in Britain) – and the Huddersfield to Manchester railway line.

Marsden has an infamous reputation for severe flooding, no doubt due to numerous streams that drain the wastes of Wessenden Moor converging in close proximity to the town which during frequent rain storms become severely swollen on their downhill journey to the River Colne.

Despite the cold, my thoughts were focused on an interesting snippet I had read in an old book on Marsden's history which had

dramatically proclaimed: " *.... before Man ruined for ever this tranquil, unspoilt Yorkshire valley with the building of many massive mills, weaving sheds, colossal engine houses and ever-belching, tall smoke stacks, which He calls progress, ... a squirrel could leap from branch to branch the whole seven miles from Marsden down to Huddersfield at the bottom of the Colne Valley without placing a foot on the ground; and in the forests around Marsden and high upon the wastes of the moors, for centuries, stags were regularly hunted.* "

Marsden, or 'Marches Dene' meaning a 'boundary valley' is first mentioned in a document dated 1067. A number of local place names are of Norse origin. In the Doomsday Book, Marsden is described as 'waste'. Right up until the Victorian period, the descriptive word – 'waste', was applied to much of the extensive high altitude moorlands throughout the Pennines.

JAGGERMEN'S BRIDGES ON PACKHORSE TRAILS

The former mill-town of Marsden once famous for manufacturing silk shawls, woollens, and during the nineteenth century for iron-founding, textile machinery and steam boiler manufacture, straddles the River Colne which gains its life from countless minor water courses and small becks that drain the high Pennine watershed hereabouts: the bleak moorland barrier that separates West Yorkshire from Lancashire. The infant river inexorably gathers strength and purpose as it rapidly flows down the steeply inclined vee-shaped bottom of the Colne Valley until it reaches Huddersfield.

For over six centuries, the handloom weaving of wool was carried out in the hamlets of the Colne Valley; for there were at hand abundant supplies of soft Pennine water. Whole families won their bread by spinning and weaving wool, the raw material generally being sourced by the children who gathered the wool deposited by sheep on the branches of Blackthorn, Hawthorn, Gorse and Bilberry bushes.

Another important early industry in Marsden was the fulling of woollen cloth which was carried out in a number of water-powered Fulling Mills, the water required for powering the waterwheels being provided by numerous small streams and watercourses. By the late eighteenth century, many of Marsden's mills specialised in the manufacture of silk shawls, and in Crimble Clough in 1832, a stone-built mill was specifically constructed for the manufacture of silk shawls. Between the mid-nineteenth and the first decades of the twentieth centuries, many new, massive mills constructed from locally-quarried Millstone Grit were built in Marsden and down the Colne Valley by many of the long-established, locally prominent handloom weaving families: famous local family names such as: Hirst, Hoyle, Beaumont, Mallinson and Crowther.

This surge of mill-building activity resulted in the Colne Valley from Marsden down to Huddersfield becoming jam-packed with huge, stone, woollen-spinning and weaving manufactories, gigantic saw-edge roofed weaving sheds, opulent-designed engine houses, large boiler houses, clusters of soaring mill chimneys and serried ranks of mill workers dwellings. By this period, these colossal mills were powered by gigantic steam engines, whose many boilers, consumed weekly, many hundreds of tons of locally mined coal.

It was supplying the customers with products from Marsden's mills, particularly from earliest times until around the mid-nineteenth century that packhorses were used. Coal was also carried on the backs of packhorses which was delivered to Marsden's mills for steam production.

These early Jaggermen's packhorse trains loaded with silk shawls, woollens or miscellaneous other goods and destined for customers in Rochdale, Oldham or Manchester when travelling out of Marsden would normally avoid the summits of the surrounding high hills, often enveloped in low cloud, by skirting around the contours above the sodden peat and dense woodlands of the valley bottoms. One of the most important packhorse trackways leading out of Marsden over the splendid stone packhorse bridge, known either as Close Gate Bridge or the more popular local names of Eastergate and Th'Owd – is the 'Rapes Highway'.

CLOSE GATE, EASTERGATE OR TH'OWD GATE BRIDGE

Located around two miles west of Marsden where a number of small moorland streams merge to become the head waters of the River Colne, there is a superb specimen of a packhorse bridge, intriguingly known by three separate names: Close Gate, Eastergate or Th'Owd Gate Bridge. This little packhorse bridge is surrounded by some of the most desolate, barren, moorland and small rocky, narrow cloughs that can be found almost anywhere in the South Pennines.

The segmental arch of Millstone Grit spans Close Moss Brook in a leap of about eighteen feet, and the width of the trackway between the twenty-four inch parapets is fifty inches. The parapets are formed from rectangular shaped blocks and finished by lengthy sections of round-topped coping stones that display evidence of originally being fastened together with leaded-in iron staples. The cobbled trackway is well worn and pleasingly enhances the overall appearance of what I consider is a fantastic gem of a South Pennine packhorse bridge.

We had walked to the bridge from the nearby hamlet of Hey Green, where in a frost-covered field, a man we had stopped to ask directions to the packhorse bridge, enthusiastically spent a good half hour giving us a most interesting potted history of Marsden together with its surrounding hills and cloughs. Our new-found friend, a sprightly octogenarian named Billy, lustily informed us that the bridge-with-three-names was called Close Gate because it was on the track to the cloughs: the bridge spans the brook draining Moss Brook Clough; in the locality of the bridge there was once a pub, the Packhorse Inn, which was kept by a woman called Esther Schofield and was much frequented by Jaggermen.

Billy told us that overtime the inn-keeper's first name, Esther, became corrupted to Easter, thus 'Eastergate'. The last name, 'Th'Owd Gate', just means the old way leading onto the moors.

Our octogenarian friend also told us about the ancient trackway, 'Rapes Highway' – probably of medieval origin – which heads away from the packhorse bridge and across the desolate reaches of high-altitude Clowes Moor that spans the Lancashire and Yorkshire border to finally reach Newhey, a former hand-loom weaving village near Rochdale.

Consequently, with old Billy's description of Rapes Highway giving us much food for thought, we did some research regarding this interesting old packhorse route over the Pennines, and discovered that from leaving Eastergate Bridge, the trackway goes by way of Pace Gate where there is a splendid, although much-weathered, stone guide stoop with the faintly inscribed words: Pace Gate. From here the trackway, after crossing the modern A640 trans-Pennine road then skirts around the shoulder of bulky, Great Hill, then continues across rough moorland until another old moorland inn is reached, the Rams Head; it then passes Piethorn Reservoir – across yet again more desolate wild moorland – until the scant remains of what was once a packhorse hostelry – now just a few stones – are reached. Close by is a paddock evidently once used for resting and the grazing of packhorses. Further on the remains are soon reached of old pony corrals, which may have been used for stabling packhorses. Eventually, the trackway enters the ancient village of Newhey. This former packhorse route of approximately eleven miles was in regular use by strings of Jaggermen's packhorses until around 1820.

Jaggerman 'Lame Luke O'Marsden'

My further research regarding Marsden's packhorse trains flagged up some fascinating information from a book written by the famous Lancashire dialect poet Edwin Waugh – **'Roads out of Manchester'**.

Waugh writes that in the early nineteenth century a Jaggerman known as Lame Luke O'Marsden supplied oatmeal and flour which he delivered to small grocers by a string of packhorses. Luke was regularly seen riding his lead packhorse, the five or six brass bells hanging from the horse's neck melodiously ringing out, as

he led his team of heavily-laden packhorses out of Marsden and onto the long, often treacherous route over Standedge and down through the Saddleworth villages to Oldham and finally to Failsworth on the edge of Manchester.

After arriving in Failsworth, then a quiet country hamlet, and distributing the flour, oatmeal and other goods, he would then spend the night at an ancient wayside inn, the Packhorse. After turning out his horses in the paddock behind the pub, where there was much grass, hay and water, he would partake of the offered refreshments. Early the next day Luke would set off on the long, weary trek back over the Pennines to Marsden, his packhorse's panniers loaded with coal, candles, cotton goods and miscellaneous types of other goods, which he would sell to the country grocers on his way home.

After I read Waugh's fascinating account, I asked Alan, who originates from Middleton in Lancashire, and therefore well acquainted with Failsworth, if he would take me there for I had a strange feeling that the Packhorse Inn mentioned by Edwin Waugh might still be there. Alan, as ever, full of enthusiasm for a spot of historical detective work cheerily agreed, and the next morning, which I remember being bright yet very cold, we set off. After driving over the Pennines, Alan drove through a maze of busy roads between Rochdale and Oldham, until we entered the A62, the Oldham to Manchester trunk road, where we headed in the direction of Manchester. With eyes peeled staring out of the car's windscreen, we both searched for the old loop road mentioned by Waugh, which Alan thought could be on the right-hand side of the trunk road. There were numerous pubs; the locals hereabouts, to be sure, liked their ale! Just as we were heading out of Failsworth, Alan suddenly shouted, ***"There it is, and what a wonderful old building."*** He pulled into the street on the right and then parked the car. I couldn't believe that this historic old inn, which Alan considered dated back to the early eighteenth century, was still standing. I thought that I was dreaming, and I had to painfully pinch my arm, for this was the inn where Lame Luke, the Marsden Jaggerman often stayed. We both agreed, you could almost taste the history!

After us both taking many photographs, fully satisfied with the pleasing outcome of our quest, we headed back over the Pennines to our home in Cowling.

JAGGERMEN'S BRIDGES ON PACKHORSE TRAILS

The stone fabric of the bridge, particularly the huge round-topped coping stones are an attractive green colour, this is due to the mosses and lichens that flourish in the damp Pennine climate. I find the higgledy-piggledy time-worn cobble stones on the trackway incredibly thought-inspiring. How many packhorses have clattered over these historic cobbles? January 2004.

© Christine McEwen Collection.

The Packhorse Inn, Failsworth, near Manchester. Once the haunt of Jaggermen. What a pity this eighteenth century wayside inn has been defaced with modern brewery signs and the offending street furniture. January 2004.

© Christine McEwen Collection.

These lovely old stone steps once used for mounting horses are located at the front of the Packhorse Inn. Did Lame Luke O'Marsden ever use these steps? January 2004.

© Christine McEwen Collection.

MELLOR BRIDGE, MARSDEN

Marsden can also boast of another striking packhorse bridge, Mellor Bridge, which was probably used by countless packhorses, their panniers bulging with corn and oats from the manorial corn mill whilst heading out of the town towards Close Gate Bridge and beyond to Rapes Highway – destination Rochdale.

This quaint, lovely little bridge certainly fired my imagination during our visit, and just like neighbouring Close Gate Bridge it is attractively blanketed with the greenest of lichens and mosses. In a leap of thirty-three feet the bridge spans the Wessenden Brook just before it merges with the River Colne. The three feet high parapets are pleasingly arched and topped with huge, round-headed coping stones of Millstone Grit. The cobbled trackway over the bridge betwixt the parapets measures thirty-four inches; a very narrow bridge indeed.

Even though the day was bitterly cold, the sun kept peeping from behind voluminous dark snow clouds. Alan and I stood close to the bottom of the bridge up against an iron railing below which was the icy waters of the Wessenden Brook. We were thoroughly enjoying a well-earned lunch of delicious fish and chips to which liberal shakings of salt and vinegar had been sprinkled before wrapping up in newspaper. As we enjoyed this delicious repast, we were entertained by the antics of hoards of Mallard ducks who were swimming below us in the brook. At the same time we were being serenaded by the sonorous tones of St. Bartholomew's Church bells. Despite the cold, we were both at peace with our surroundings and were amused by the ducks who were fighting each other for the odd potato chip we threw into the water.

Alan stands on the bank of the Wessenden Brook with Mellor Bridge to the rear. January 2004.

© Christine McEwen Collection.

Mellor Bridge. I found the splayed stone approached of the arched parapets and the worn cobbled stones of the trackway most pleasing. January 2004.

© Christine McEwen Collection.

HOLME END'S BRIDGE, ALCOMDEN WATER, WALSHAW DENE.

Substantially built of gritstone, the isolated Holme End's two-arched packhorse bridge spanning Alcomden Water. On the hill above is the ruined, last remaining building in the hamlet of Holme End. January 2010

© Christine McEwen Collection.

One brilliant, sunny, but extremely cold Saturday in early January 2010, leaving home just after first light we drove over sheets of black ice on the high Pennine road across Widdop Moor between Colne and Heptonstall, our mission was to search for an old packhorse bridge, known as Holme End's Bridge, in remote Walshaw Dene above Hebden Dale. The beautiful sunshine was indeed most welcome and had followed an extremely cold, but moonlit night. For more than two months the South Pennines had endured unusually deep snow and day after day of Arctic conditions. Our following bridge spotting adventure bathed in beautiful sunshine was therefore, very gratifying.

Alan and I left our car on the United Utilities car park about half a mile along the Widdop Gate road, above the historic, pictur-esque Packhorse Inn – once the haunt of Jagger-men and Drovers – and close to Blake Dene. With maps, note books, and cameras to hand, we commenced walking along the tarmac-surfaced Water Board road that leads to Walshaw Lower Reservoir. Notwithstanding, the biting chill, we heartily tramped along, passing on our left a large Sitka conifer plantation. The big sky above was a deep azure blue and the brilliant sunshine illuminated the frost-covered surrounding moorland sheep pastures. We walked passed a frozen spring, now solid with a mass of icicles hanging down from where normally a trickle of water dropped to fill an old, semi-buried gritstone trough at the side of the road. The sun's dazzling rays dancing and shimmering lit up the mass of monster icicles like a cache of glittering diamonds.

JAGGERMEN'S BRIDGES ON PACKHORSE TRAILS

Descending a steep hill through a sparse-copse of massive, ancient Elms and Beeches, we passed several mounds of moss-covered dressed stones: the melancholy remains of a seventeenth century laithe house, originally comprising a small farm cottage with attached barn. Walking further downhill, we noticed to our left at the bottom of the shallow, almost treeless clough, a small beck, – Alcomden Water – the overflow of the Lower Walshaw Reservoir – flowing downhill, its waters sparkling in the brilliant sunshine, the over-hanging reeds and grasses bedecked with long, glistening icicles.

Leaning against the massive trunk of an ancient Elm, we consulted our much-battered copy of a local history guide book dating back to the 1950s which informed us that Alcom in the title 'Alcomden' comes from the Old British Celtic tongue meaning – 'a stream', – and 'kumb' – meaning a dingle or a small secluded valley. Maybe in pre-Roman times there could have been a Celtic village hereabouts? Alan, who had loved most aspects of history from being a small boy, I noticed, was deep in thought. Looking at my white-haired, white-bearded husband, I guessed that his imagination was running riot: he was probably imagining an early British settlement with huts down by the stream and men and women hard at work in the fields, and children laughing and splashing in the stream.

A couple of hundred yards further down at the bottom of the clough, we were delighted to see the attractive stone bridge spanning the stream. Nearby, standing on higher ground was the only remaining building in this tiny hamlet known as Holme End. This was another laithe house consisting of a cottage built of fine dressed stone and an adjoining barn with a huge attractive arched doorway. Unfortunately, the whole structure looked to be in a terrible ruinous and dangerous state of repair, and totally roofless.

Before reaching the bridge we both climbed up the steep hill side to closely look at the remains, of what many years ago, would have been a fine looking building with commanding views over the Alcomden Valley. Peering through the empty spaces of doors and windows, we saw huge, worm-eaten timber roof beams laying drunkenly about after falling from above, and the small rooms filled with broken masonry and heaps of dried sheep's droppings.

The ruins of Holme End laithe house overlooking Holme End's Bridge. January 2010.

© Christine McEwen Collection.

JAGGERMEN'S BRIDGES ON PACKHORSE TRAILS

Leaving the old farmhouse, we quickly arrived at the very pleasant-looking two-arched gritstone-built bridge, and out came our cameras, notebooks and pens. Alan, delved deep into one of the cavernous pockets of his jacket and pulled out his weighty, metal 50 metre tape measure. Apart from a friendly, lone mountain-biker, who momentarily stopped to ask directions to Lower Walshaw Reservoir, we saw no-one else. Above the reassuring sound of the stream's laughter as it raced down the bottom of the clough, there was that increasingly rare phenomenon in modern Britain: peace and tranquillity, with only the mournful bleating of sheep to rent the silence.

This attractive looking bridge, built of the local Millstone Grit in the early nineteenth century has two, robustly-built arches. The main arch is semi-circular and spans Alcomden Water in a leap of thirteen feet, four inches; the secondary arch, which, in normal conditions is dry, is segmental with a span of thirteen feet. The trackway over the bridge consists of rolled limestone quarry waste which unfortunately covers the original cobbles; the width between the two feet high by sixteen inch wide parapets is ten feet. The parapets are finished with large, flat-topped gritstone copings around forty eight inches in length by six inches thick. The mid-stream piers are neatly constructed, incorporating triangular cutwaters both on the upstream and downstream sides.

The metalled road that we had walked down, in earlier days was one of the many packhorse trackways that criss-crossed the 'Limer's Gate', the ancient packhorse route linking the limestone 'hushes' at Thursden, near Colne and at Shedden Clough, near Cliviger, with Hebden Bridge, Halifax and other parts of West Yorkshire. Across the bridge the trackway runs up and over the steep escarpment, thence along the left-hand side of Hebden Dale and down to Hebden Bridge.

Alan and I were extremely pleased with our interesting foray to Alcomden Water and we delighted in the sun-lit amble back to the car park. Subsequent to finishing a most enjoyable lunch which we ate sat upon a large slab of gritstone in a disused stone delve-hole near Shore-in-Stansfield, we then made ready for the afternoon's pilgrimage to find our next packhorse bridge, which was evidently close by, – Hudson Bridge over Redmires Water.

The attractive PACK HORSE INN sign which displays a Jaggerman leading his heavily laden packhorse on the old packhorse trackway past the inn on Widdop Moor. January 2010.

© Christine McEwen Collection.

HUDSON BRIDGE, NEAR SHORE-IN-STANSFIELD, TODMORDEN

Hudson Bridge that crosses Redmire's Water. This simple, yet pleasing structure typically belies great robustness. January 2010.

© Christine McEwen Collection.

Hudson Bridge is located near Shore-in-Stansfield, which is one of the wettest, wildest parts of the Upper Calder Valley which encourages significant amounts of heather, cotton grass and Bilberry to flourish on these high moorlands. It is documented that within the parish between the start of the eighteenth century and the 1750s there were around thirty farms whose occupants carried out both farming and woollen handloom weaving. There was also an inn, a busy Blacksmith's forge, a shoe maker and quite a number of Jaggermen who lived in the area. Around this period, the Long Causeway would have been extremely busy with numerous packhorse trains travelling daily in each direction between Halifax and Burnley.

Around mid-day on arriving at the bottom of Pudsey Clough, Cornholme in brilliant sunshine, we drove up the steep, meandering, narrow hill road that leads to the hill top hamlet of

Shore, where, shortly after turning into the curiously named, Pudding Lane at a Tee junction, we then drove again around a number of tight switchbacks until we reached Blue Bell Lane.

Though not warm, it felt like a spring morning, the beautiful sunshine illuminating the moors and fells all around, and in the clear air, we could see for miles. As we drove uphill along Blue Bell Lane, we passed several attractive late seventeenth or early eighteenth century farm-houses and cottages: the whole surrounding tiny hill top hamlets appeared to be full of historic character. As we reached the top of Blue Bell Lane, we saw a rough looking man walking a scruffy mongrel dog. Alan brought the car to a halt and poking his head through the window breezily asked the man if he knew the whereabouts of Hudson Bridge.

"Awreet, mornin'", the man replied displaying a mouthful of bad teeth. *"Just drive round t'corner mate, and enter Hartley Royd Farm, where they might let you park your car"*, he said, whilst pointing beyond a thin plantation of conifers.

"Thanks a million", replied Alan. *"You sound as if you are a local. Do you know anything about the old packhorse tracks, and also Hudson Bridge?"*

With a slight puffing out of his chest, Brown Teeth said, whilst pointing to a small triangular-shaped field in the direction of Hartley Royd Farm, *"Yon field over theer behind t'farmhouse was in th'olden days a sort of coral which the packhorse men used for resting their packhorses"*.

"Aye, thanks, that's fantastic inform-ation", said Alan whilst waving to our Brown-toothed friend.

We then drove around the conifer plantation and entered a short drive between an enormous, ancient, mullioned-windowed stone farmhouse and a couple of cottages. Alan stopped the car in front of a large barn. We both got out and whilst Alan was enthusiastically studying the architectural details of the old farmhouse, I walked across the yard to knock on the door of a small cottage.

The cottage door was quickly opened by a tall, friendly looking, brown-haired man. I introduced myself, explaining that my husband and I wanted to see Hudson Bridge and would it be acceptable for us to park our car for around half an hour in the farmyard.

"No problem love, you're very welcome. It's a grand day", the man pleasantly said.

So after thanking him and bidding him good morning, we set off with me clutching my old, worn leather bag bulging with the usual bridge-spotting gear. Alan and I walked across the stone flagged yard and whilst passing the ancient farmhouse, Alan reckoned it had been built around 1725 as a yeoman farmer's house. After a short walk we came to a small wooden gate set at the top of a 'hollow lane' paved with causey stones. We walked for around forty yards, taking our time over the treacherous ice that covered the causeys, until we reached Hudson Bridge.

This curious little stone packhorse bridge spans Redmire's Water about a quarter of a mile downstream from the long disused Redmire's Dam situated to the north on the shoulder of high moorland above the Long Causeway. Perched higher still, is an enigmatic grouping of ancient rocks, known as Hawks Stones. Hereabouts, there are a number of similar groupings of gritstone boulders that can be found on the high moorland between Hebden Bridge, Todmorden and Burnley; and these natural clusters of huge rocks have been endowed with some extremely strange names: Whirlaw Stones, Bridestones, Stannally Stones and Orchan Stones.

This lovely little gritstone structure known as Hudson Bridge – (nobody appears to know why it is so named) – was, on the morning of our visit bathed in beautiful rays of sunshine which were reflected beautifully from the surface of the laughing, chattering and gurgling waters of the stream. We were also fascinated with the display of long tentacles of ice, suspended from the overhanging reeds and grasses which were slowly melting in the pleasantly warm sunshine. Alan and I agreed that the stunning packhorse bridge, the causey stone-paved trackways, and of course, the beautiful chattering stream was a most wonderfully, becalming, tranquil place.

The span of the segmental stone arch across the stream is six feet; the trackway width between the parapets measures six feet, six inches; the parapets are built from heavy slabs of Millstone Grit, fourteen to fifteen inches wide by twenty seven inches in height.

At the western end of the bridge is a gritstone gatepost which has three or four, square cut- holes which was probably used for restricting access across the bridge by the insertion of stout wooden poles.

The western approach to the bridge is by a causey stone-paved hollow way; the eastern trackway is also paved with causey stones, and after leaving the bridge ascends a small hill to run across Hudson Moor. Another trackway follows the course of the stream down to Lydgate on the valley floor.

The western approach down to Hudson Bridge via a causey stone-paved 'hollow way'.
January 2010.

© Christine McEwen Collection.

FROM MOUNT CROSS TO PUDSEY CLOUGH.

Mount Cross, an ancient guide post. Was it created by the monks from Whalley Abbey, or by the Vikings? January 2010.

© Christine McEwen Collection.

Alan and I were reluctant to leave the peaceful, sunbathed, idyllic setting of Hudson Bridge, but as we were both keen to photograph Mount Cross, an ancient guide stoop, which was sited closeby, we set off to walk back over the bridge and on the ice-covered causey stones of the hollow way packhorse track until we reached our car. I felt quite elated with our morning's adventures, and now I looked forward to seeing a rather enigmatic, ancient stone guide post.

Tilting at a drunken angle, Mount Cross stands on the edge of a sheep pasture behind an old dry stone wall on Cross Hill. We got there by driving down the evocatively named local lanes, Blue Bell Lane which crossed Sugar Lane, then down Pudding Lane, then turning sharp right into Gall Lane – (so named for the connection with 'Lime Gals', lime-carrying packhorses) – and finally up the severely inclined Mount Lane. Alan parked the car outside a lonely farmhouse at the Tee Junction of Mount Lane and a rough, old stony track, Delf Lane around fifty yards from Mount Cross, which we both could now clearly

see. I was so thrilled at seeing this ancient stone guide post, and in spite of the icy conditions under foot, clutching my camera I hurriedly walked up the track towards the cross. Quickly glancing back to see if Alan was following me, I was amused to see that he was busily engaged feeding a handful of broken biscuits to a flock of inquisitive Guinea fowl that had popped out of a hole in a dry stone wall in front of the farmhouse.

Mount Cross, otherwise known as Idol Cross is situated at a cross roads of old packhorse tracks; it is of hewn gritstone, around five feet in height, and is considered by some to have been carved by the monks of Whalley Abbey as a guide post; others, reckon that the cross was carved by the Vikings, but no-one knows for certain. The cross has evidently been relocated from an earlier position, and it is one of six similar stone crosses to be found between Burnley and Kebs on the Long Causeway. The packhorse drivers, the Jaggermen no doubt used these stone crosses as route marking stoops.

HUDSTONE BRIDGE, PAUL CLOUGH, NEAR CORNHOLME, TODMORDEN.

In the dramatic setting of the Ice Age carved gorge known as Paul Clough, the unusual circular Hudstone Bridge spans the stream. The picture was taken in the early autumn of 1998 by geologist Paul Kabrna who kindly donated the photograph.

Photo © Paul Kabrna, Craven & Pendle Geological Society (1998)

After photographing the enigmatic Mount Cross, we drove on to the Long Causeway and parked in a rough lay-by at Stiperden. The next bridge on my 'bridges to get' list – was the rare, unusually shaped, circular Hudstone Bridge located in the depths of Paul Clough, a tributary of the larger Pudsey Clough.

After partaking of a pleasant lunch and leaving the car, we set off in search of the elusive bridge by going through a stout, old gate and tramping down an ancient-looking trackway which our map informed us was originally a section of the Long Causeway. Walking down this track for about a quarter of a mile, we reached Lower Stiperden Farm, where we could see a young man in a heavily padded check shirt, his head under the raised bonnet of an elderly Landover.

Alan walked across the farm yard to ask the young farmer if he knew where Hudstone Bridge was to be found in Paul Clough.

"**Aye, no problem, I think the bridge you're seeking is about three quarters of a mile from here, reet deep in t'clough bottom**", said the young, friendly farmer.

He then gave us a few directions of how to actually get down into the clough, and also warned us about the extremely dangerous conditions of the clough sides owing to them being covered with frost and ice.

After thanking him, we both turned right at the gable end of his farmhouse and squelching through an unpleasant porridgy mixture of broken ice, mud and sheep droppings, we headed off downhill, passing an interesting, but forlorn-looking empty eighteenth century farmhand's cottage.

In spite of us being bathed in brilliant sunshine, it was extremely cold and there was much compacted ice underfoot, which made our progress down the top edge of the steep clough extremely hazardous.

JAGGERMEN'S BRIDGES ON PACKHORSE TRAILS

We came to a much-battered, old wooden gate, which we opened to proceed along a straight causey stone trackway between crumbling dry stone walls. Alan and I agreed, despite a lack of information in the two books I had in my leather bag, this was most definitely a packhorse trackway that had once joined the Long Causeway to run downhill passing through Lower Stiperden Farm, then by the side of another ancient farm that we could clearly see ahead of us. Our guess was that the trackway would eventually run down into Paul Clough which would be crossed by Hudstone Bridge, the trackway eventually dropping down to Cornholme via Pudsey Clough.

However, after about a hundred and fifty yards the causey stone surface trackway disappeared under a muddy morass. Alan went on ahead towards the farm to see if the trackway re-appeared. But it did not. From where I sat upon a large piece of gritstone at the end of the causey stone trackway, there was no discernable evidence whatsoever.

After quite a bit of head scratching and surveying our surroundings through Alan's binoculars, reluctantly we decided to walk back up the clough to our car and then to drive down through Shore to the village of Cornholme on the valley floor, then up Pudsey Clough, from where we should be able to enter Paul Clough. And this is what we did; arriving at around three o'clock in Pudsey Clough, where we parked our car in a small lay-by past the end of a row of old stone cottages near a concrete reinforced bridge.

Near the top of Paul Clough between crumbling dry stone walls and beneath ice and frost covered grass this old packhorse trackway has some good stretches of causey stones. The trackway descends into the clough where it crosses Hudstone Bridge and then enters the larger Pudsey Clough where it traverses down until Cornholme is reached at the bottom of the valley. January 2010.

© Christine McEwen Collection.

Alan went off to scout the area leaving me warm and comfortable in the car. After about ten minutes he came back looking tired and somewhat puzzled, at the same time looking down at the map in his hands.

"**This map can't be correct as it's showing Paul Clough to be an extension of Pudsey Clough. But it can't be, for a farmer I have just spoken with further up the clough, has told me that another half a mile and this clough, Pudsey Clough, actually runs into Coal Clough, where the wind turbines are located. He also informed me that the entrance into Paul Clough is located between where we are parked and the row of cottages behind us**".

"Wow, let's go and explore", I exclaimed, a feeling of excitement coursing through me.

We both walked the short distance from our car back towards the stone cottages and noticed that we had actually driven over a narrow, unpretentious farm-type bridge which spanned a deep narrow gorge heading north-eastwards. Alan opened a small wooden gate set into a fence on the bridge, and I could see that my husband was just about as excited as me. "**We've found it, this has to be Paul Clough and the bloody map is incorrect**", shouted Alan.

Despite the rapidly failing sunlight of the January afternoon, through the rickerty wooden gate we both went to enter the tightly confined gorge by walking along a narrow pathway, undoubtedly used as a bridleway, for there was an abundance of well-trampled horse manure underfoot. Down on our right, we could just about make out in the failing light, about eighty feet below the trackway, a stream racing down the clough. To the front of us all along the clough, there were huge rocky outcrops softened by thick blankets of frost, and down at the water's edge on either side of the stream we could make out, albeit in the poor prevailing light, many solidly frozen ice cataracts.

As usual, Alan's excitement to see anything to do with Britain's industrial history induced him to race on ahead along the frozen trackway until I could see he had suddenly stopped around two hundred yards ahead.

The packhorse trackway across the top of the bridge that leads up the clough side, eventually to the vicinity of the Long Causeway near Stiperden. January 2010.

© *Christine McEwen Collection.*

JAGGERMEN'S BRIDGES ON PACKHORSE TRAILS

"I've found the bridge love, come on, hurry up", he excitedly shouted, A few seconds later, I found myself scampering along the trackway. And what a curiosity Hudstone Bridge turned out to be: a conspicuous rarity of a packhorse bridge. In spite of the heavy covering of frost on the grass, Alan, tape measure in hand carefully worked his way down on the downstream side of the bridge to take dimensional measurements at stream level.

"Internal diameter of the bridge, six feet, two inches", he shouted up to where I stood on the trackway over the bridge. Looking down to where my husband stood balancing on an icy lump of rock mid-stream, I could see a strange shaped pool of deep water just beyond him. Later, we learnt that in the 19th century the local children employed in the cotton mills down in Cornholme at the bottom of Pudsey Clough, would come up to Hudstone Bridge, where they jumped off the top into this deep pool. These cotton mill kids called the pool, 'the Frying Pan'.

Alan clambered to safety up the ice and frost-covered almost vertical bank of the stream and joined me on the top of the bridge. We then measured the width of the trackway over the bridge, which at twelve feet, we considered to be very wide for a packhorse bridge; also there was no parapets. Nonetheless, we both considered the unusually configured Hudstone Bridge – to have been used by packhorses, for a tell-tale sign was the trackway that we could see working its way up the opposite steep side of the clough to head in the direction of Stiperden, near the Long Causeway, which we had explored earlier that afternoon.

By this time, the winter's late afternoon light had all but died, leaving a rather eerie glow in the bottom of the clough, which I will now admit felt rather forbidding, so quickly we packed up our few scattered belongings and treading carefully we picked our way back along the ice and mud-covered trackway and worked our way out of the clough. On entering the much wider Pudsey Clough we found the light was much better, and so within a few minutes we arrived at our car.

With Alan driving us home, and my frost-bitten fingers slowly thawing out, I reflected on our long, packhorse bridge-spotting day involving the searching out of Hudson Bridge at Shore, photographing ancient Mount Cross, our early afternoon's foray where we discovered the dry stone walled, causey stone paved, packhorse trackway below Lower Stiperden Farm, and our late afternoon's adventure to locate Hudstone Bridge in the deep, eerie gorge known as Paul Clough – a most wonderful and exhilarating adventure.

The unusually shaped Hudstone Bridge. The bridge has evidently been rebuilt in recent times for there are a number of plastic drain pipes that can be seen in the photograph. January 2010.

© Christine McEwen Collection.

BECKFOOT PACKHORSE BRIDGE, BINGLEY, WEST YORKSHIRE.

Beckfoot Packhorse Bridge spanning Harden Beck was built for the cost of £10 in 1723. The ancient ford lies in the centre of the picture with the early 17th century built Beckfoot Farm behind.

© Christine McEwen Collection.

In 1722, on a bitterly cold February morning in the Old White Horse Inn in the township of Bingley, a number of local dignitaries sat around a rough deal table in front of a warm fireside, drinking strong ale and smoking clay pipes. Sat amongst them were two young Stonemasons, both natives of Bingley, Benjamin Craven and Joshua Scott.

With grave expressions, the township's elders have just accepted a tender document presented by Craven and Scott for the construction of a new stone bridge as a replacement for the ancient, flood-damaged wooden bridge spanning the often rain-swollen Harden Beck.

Staring back at the circle of grim faces both young stonemasons pledge they will within a year, build a strong bridge of stone across the stream known as the Harden Beck for the sum of ten pounds. With the covenant in place, the whole gathering raised their ale tankards and let out a loud hurrah.

Bingley is mentioned in the Doomsday Book of A.D. 1086 as 'Bingheleia' – a manor comprising four carucates of taxable land useful for two ploughs. During the medieval period Bingley was an important township extending for several miles up and down the valley of the River Aire.

In 1212, King John granted Bingley a market charter, and by this period the township was part of the West Riding of Yorkshire. By the late fourteenth century, Bingley was the most prominent town in Airedale, with a population of around five hundred people. The other closely sited townships of Leeds, Halifax and Bradford were less important.

JAGGERMEN'S BRIDGES ON PACKHORSE TRAILS

The first houses were built at Beckfoot, where there was a natural ford across Harden Beck. Ever since the Middle Ages, bridges built of timber were used for packhorse trains and foot traffic, particularly when the river was in full spate. The wooden bridges were regularly damaged by flood and were therefore, regularly under repair, or being rebuilt at great expense to the town.

The location of the bridge at the foot of Harden Beck was on the important packhorse trackway, probably established by the monks of Rievaulx Abbey who operated an iron bloomery at Harden. This route was the main north-south packhorse trackway from Scotland down to the south of England, the bridge spanning Harden Beck being the only mid-Aire Valley crossing point prior to the later constructed Ireland Bridge and Cottingley Bridge. The trackway was the only route linking Bingley with Haworth in the Worth Valley, and was much frequented with regular packhorse trains carrying woollens, coal, salt, metaliferous ores, Cobbydale iron nails, Cumberland woollen stockings and tanned leather.

The trackway coming down from Haworth came by the hilltop hamlet of Crossroads, where a number of packhorse tracks converged; then over the wild moorland on appropriately named Bell Horse Lane, eventually arriving near Goff Well.

The crossing of the Harden Beck was therefore, significantly important for the future wealth of Bingley. The urgent need for a new stone built bridge was the reason why the important meeting of the townsmen with Ben Craven and his partner Joshua Scott took place on that freezing February morning in 1722.

The Stonemasons kept their word and built the superb, single segmental arch bridge of local stone which leaps across Harden Beck in a span of about thirty three feet. Parapets were excluded, and the trackway over the top measures sixty two inches. The men clearly, were masters at producing good stonework for the voussoir stones forming the arch are cleverly slotted into place using alternate long and short stones that are all well dressed.

Alan making an effort to decipher the inscribed wording cut into this splendid old millstone. February 2010.

© Christine McEwen Collection.

Twelve months subsequent to that first meeting, on the 7th of February 1723, there was another gathering of Bingley's finest and the two young Stonemasons, now masters at building fine and robust stone bridges. Again, in the Old White Horse Inn on another frosty February morning the town's Constable, William Ellison, handed over the sum of ten pounds to Benjamin Craven and Joshua Scott as payment for their bridge. Part of the original covenant between the town's elders and the two Stonemasons included that the bridge was to be maintained, and if needed, repaired by Craven and Scott.

Hereunder, are the interesting, historic details of that meeting:

'7th, 2nd, 1723 – Whereas the Constabulary or Township of Bingley have this day paid by Willm. Ellison, the p'sent Constable, to Benja. Craven and Josa. Scott, Masons ye sum of Ten Pounds, consideration whereof ye said Benja. Craven and Joshua Scott doe hereby promise joyfully and severally to uphold and keep the sd Bridge in good and sufficient repair during the terme of seaven years from the day hereof, as witness our hands this day and year above sd.

TEST: WILLM. ELLISON   BENJ. CRAVEN

JOSHUA SMITH

The mark of – JOSHUA X SCOTT.

Our Visit To Beckfoot Bridge.

Whilst passing through Bingley one afternoon, because Alan had never actually seen Beckfoot Bridge and I previously had, I therefore offered to give him a conducted tour. He enthuseiastically agreed, and shortly we parked our car near the mill cottages at the bottom of Beckfoot Lane. Leaving the car we walked down the old packhorse trackway framed by young ivy-covered Beeches and Alders, to the bridge.

Despite a chill in the air, the wintry sun peeping around dark clouds reflected from the rippled surface of the stream flowing sluggishly under the striking stone packhorse bridge whose segmental arch gracefully leapt across Harden Beck. Regrettably, topping the structure to form a parapet was a wooden fence which definitely did not enhance the bridge. Probably 'elf n' safety' – I muttered to myself.

To my right, due to the low water level, I could make out the ford running alongside the bridge. Across the beck to the rear of the historic packhorse trackway was the delightful, stone mullion-windowed Beckfoot Farm which dates back to the early seventeenth century. Later, I noticed over the front door a date stone inscribed 1617 ER. IR. AR.

After taking many photographs, Alan and I spent some minutes studying the old moss-covered mill stone that was propped up against the upstream abutment, which had some unusual inscribed lettering cut into the surface. Alan thought they could be mason's marks, and that the stone had originally been used in Beckfoot Farm, which may have once operated a water-powered corn mill. The trackway over the top of the bridge was an interesting mix of large cobble stones and worn flag stones, which we thought was most attractive. The nearby field dry stone walling was also of interest to us, and at the north end of the bridge the wall's coping stones included two old 'boskin stones' – used in laithe house floors for supporting wooden uprights.

Finally, we were extremely satisfied with our afternoon's exploration of historic Beckfoot Bridge, and whilst driving home I could imagine back in the eighteenth century a string of packhorses clattering over the cobble stones of the bridge.

An interesting mixture of time-worn flagstones and cobbles form the trackway over Beckfoot Packhorse bridge. Unfortunately, there are no parapets of stone but rather unsightly timber fencing panels that despoil the graceful aesthetical lines of the stone structure. February 2010.

© Christine McEwen Collection.

OXYGRAINS OLD BRIDGE, RISHWORTH, CALDERDALE.

Oxygrains Packhorse Bridge; this unpretentious but attractive little packhorse bridge, probably built in the early 17th century spans Oxygrains Beck near to Rishworth in the Ryburn Valley. To the rear is the huge stone bridge that carries the A672 Oldham to Ripponden road.   February 2010.

© Christine McEwen Collection.

Beneath a scouring, steel-eyed early February sky threatening a fall of sleet, Alan and I found ourselves stood on the icy wastes of Blackstone Edge, where he was enthusing over the Aiggin Stone, an enigma of a medieval wayfarers guide stone set at the side of an important trans-Pennine packhorse trackway that follows the causey stoned route of an arrow-straight road known hereabouts as the 'Roman Road'. Nearby, there was a cairn, a mountain in miniature of piled-up Millstone Grit rocks and stones that during frequent rain and misty weather act as a guide for weary hill walkers.

Alan pointed over to a mass of craggy boulders strewn about the foot of some forbidding-looking high cliffs, Robin Hood's Bed. **"That's where we're heading up onto the top of Robin Hood's Bed"**, he said. **"Come on lass,**

let's roll. From the top of the 'Bed', it's only a couple of miles to Oxygrains Old Bridge". The old packhorse bridge spanning Oxygrains Brook was our destination, for we wanted to carry out one of our bridge-spotting sessions and to take some photographs for my book.

As we set off to clump over the frozen tundra of the barren moorland, looking all around me, I noticed that the boulders and rocks of Millstone Grit were all of a sombre black colour. I thought, no wonder this desolate Pennine moorland on the high watershed between Oldham and Rochdale on the Red Rose county side – and on the White Rose side, Ripponden and Rishworth in Calderdale – was known as Blackstone Edge.

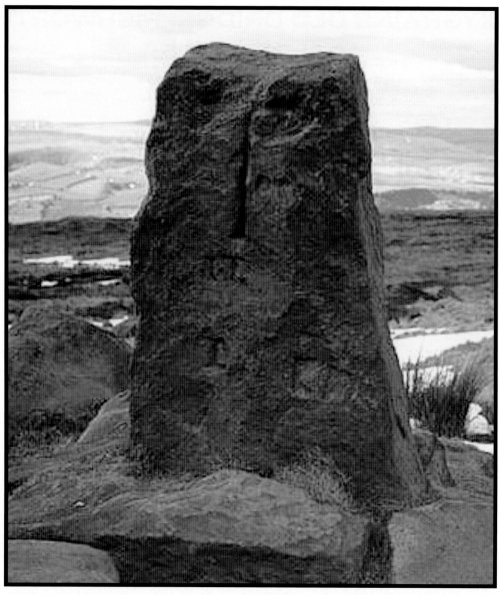

Sighted on the breast of the steep incline at the top of the 'Roman Road' stands the Aiggin Stone, a Medieval Period wayfarers guide stone fashioned from a rough slab of local Millstone Grit; crudely carved onto one face of this is a cross; beneath are the letters 'IT' . February 2010.

© Christine McEwen Collection.

After us both picking our way like mountain goats around massive, weather-rounded gritstone boulders and tramping knee deep in crisp snowdrifts, we finally made the stiff climb onto the top of the brooding, dark cliffs of Robin Hood's Bed. **"By golly, Christine, I haven't been up here for well over forty years"**, exclaimed Alan breathlessly. Then suddenly, the smiling face of the sun burst through the clouds to brightly bathe the surrounding moorland in fabulous, welcoming sunshine.

From our high eerie looking west we could see the sparkling, sun-lit waters of Hollingworth Lake and behind, the dark-grey urban sprawl of Rochdale, Oldham and further still the panoramic spread of Greater Manchester.

Celia Fiennes, an intrepid traveller who having trekked over the heights of Blackstone Edge was certainly in awe of the wilderness, for in 1698, she wrote:

"Then I came to Blackstone Edge, Noted all over England for a Dismal high Precipice and Steep in the Ascent and Descent on Either End; its Very Moorish ground all About and Even just at the Top, tho' so High ...... (she mentions the causey stoned trackway) **...... that you travel on a Causey wch is Very Troublesome as its a Moist ground soe as is Usual on these High Hills; they Stagnate the Air and hold Mist and Rains almost Perpetually".**

JAGGERMEN'S BRIDGES ON PACKHORSE TRAILS

In August 1724, Daniel Defoe also journeyed from Rochdale over Blackstone Edge into Yorkshire and conveyed in this extraction below, his highly atmospheric description of his experience:

"**Here**, (in Rochdale) **for our Greater Encouragement, though we were but at the Middle of August and in some places the Harvest hardly Gathered in, we saw the Mountains covered in Snow, and Felt the cold Very Acute and Piercing; but even Here we Found, so in all these Northern counties is the case, the People had an Extraordinary way of Mixing the Warm with the Cold very happily Together; for the store of good Ale which flows Plentifully in the most Mountainous parts of this country seems Abundantly to make up for All the inclemencies of the Season or Difficulties of Travelling, adding also the Plenty of Coals for firing, which these Hills are Full of.**

We mounted the Hills, Fortified with the same Precaution, early in the Morning, and thought the Snow which had fallen in the Night lay a little on the Ground, yet we Thought it was not Much; and the Morning being Calm and Clear, we had no Apprehension of an uneasy Passage, neither did the People at Rochdale, who Kindly directed us the Way, and even Offered to Guide us over the first Mountains, Apprehend any Difficulty for us; so we Complimented ourselves out of their Assistance, Which we Afterwards very much Wanted.

It is not easy to Express the Consternation we were in when we came near the Top of the Mountain; the Wind Blew Exceedingly Hard, and Blew the Snow so Directly in our Faces, and so Thick, that it was Impossible to Keep our Eyes open to see our Way. The Ground also was so Covered in Snow, that we could see no Track, or when we were in the Way or When out; Except we were Showed it by a Fearful Precipice on one Hand and Uneven Ground on the Other.

In the Middle of this Difficulty, and as we Began to Call on one Another to turn Back Again, not knowing what Dangers might still be Before us, came a surprising Clap of Thunder, the First that ever I Heard in a Storm of Snow, or, I Believe, Ever shall; Nor did we Perceive any Lightning to Precede the Thunder as must Naturally be the Case; but we Supposed the Thick Falling of Snow must Prevent our Sight........

Upon this We Made a Full Stop, and Coming all Together, for we were three in Company, with two Servants, we began to Talk Seriously of Going back again to Rochdale, but just Then one of our Men Called out to us and Said He was Upon the Top of the Hill and could see Over into Yorkshire, and that there was a Plain way Down on the Other side ...."

In fantastic, bright sunlight, we set off from Robin Hood's Bed and headed across a wilderness of semi-frozen peat and dead heather to the watercourse called Rishworth Drain. As we walked through a drift of slowly melting, deep snow, suddenly, quick as a bullet leaving a gun barrel, we were fortunate to witness the extremely rare sighting of a white hare as it raced across the moorland. With the wintry sunshine rapidly thawing out the frozen tundra, we decided to contour around the north east side of Green Withens Reservoir and to head off down into shallow Green Withens Clough. Passing a natural grouping of gritstones, Castle Dean Rocks, we eventually reached Oxygrains Clough, whose little beck acts as an overflow drain for the expansive Green Withens Reservoir.

Looking south westward from our high moorland plateau, we could see the bright sunlight glancing off the windscreens of the countless cars, vans and huge juggernauts frantically hurtling along the carriageways of the incongruous trans-Pennine M62 motorway. On us reaching the A672 road, not only could we clearly see the massive volume of traffic using the motorway, but the cacophony of ear-splitting noise, we both agreed, utterly destroyed the peace and tranquillity, that but for the last few minutes of our trek over the moorland heights, had been serenely pleasant.

Choosing each step carefully, we gingerly picked our way through a porridgy mess of sun-melted snow, ice and mud on the banks of Oxygrains Beck until we reached the huge stone bridge that carries the A672, the Oldham to Ripponden road. Beneath the bridge, the fast flowing water appeared to be about eighteen inches deep, but undaunted, both of us by now sporting cold, wet feet, by stepping onto semi-submerged rocks, we made our way under the bridge to emerge into bright sunlight that bathed the snowy sides of the clough. As ever, Alan was around fifty yards in front of me, and as I squelched through deep, soaking wet peat up the side of the bank of the beck, I suddenly heard him excitedly shout, **"There's your Oxygrains Packhorse Bridge, and what a bonny little bridge it is!"**

JAGGERMEN'S BRIDGES ON PACKHORSE TRAILS

Notwithstanding, the awesome clamour of twenty first century traffic resonating in our eardrums, we were both indeed delighted to reach ancient Oxygrains Packhorse Bridge which we found to be consisting of a simple segmental arch of Millstone Grit that spanned the gurgling beck in a leap of around sixteen feet. The arch itself comprised twelve roughly hewn, gritstone voussoir stones set on either side of the massive key stone. There were no parapets, and the eight feet, six inches wide trackway over the top of the arch consisted of no other than the surface of the outwards protruding voussoir stones; the whole structure being crudely constructed, but nevertheless extremely attractive. On the side nearest the A672 road, a crudely-built staircase of huge, roughly squared gritstone slabs affords access onto the bridge for foot traffic and in times gone by for packhorses.

Following us measuring and photographing Oxygrains Packhorse Bridge, we searched across the rough moorland grass to the south west with the hope of establishing the whereabouts of the old packhorse trackway. Unfortunately however, there was virtually no evidence to be seen.

From what I have read, evidently, the original packhorse trackway climbed up the western flanks of the Pennines from Oldham to cross Oxygrains Beck on the little parapet-less bridge, thence down into Ryburndale to eventually reach Halifax.

Crude, stone slabs form access onto the top of Oxygrains Packhorse Bridge. February 2010.

Oxygrains Packhorse Bridge across Oxygrains Beck. February 2010.

© Christine McEwen Collection.

NEWSHOLME DEAN CANTILEVER BRIDGE.

The Cantilever Bridge spanning Dean Beck in Newsholme Dean is either of Neolithic origin or, Medieval. July 2004.

© Christine McEwen Collection.

Not far from my home, a small laughing, chattering, gurgling beck flows down from high upon Keighley Moor to meander and weave its course along a thin, rocky gorge until it flows behind the ancient farmstead at Higher Slippery Ford before cascading down into beautiful Newsholme Dean – a charming, peaceful wooded clough – before plunging through the historic cotton-weaving and paper-making hamlet of Goose Eye on the stream's final descent down to Keighley in the Aire Valley.

It was a beautiful sun kissed evening in July with the clean moorland air heavily scented with delicious fragrances of moorland grasses and wild flowers, and as Alan and I leisurely walked on a heavy flagstone paved track leading us steeply downhill into the verdant depths of Newsholme Dean, we found ourselves becoming intoxicated with the natural beauty of our surroundings. Accompanied by my husband, I was on a mission to bag me an extremely unique bridge: an incredibly ancient cantilever bridge, which had fired my imagination for quite some considerable time.

Spanning Dean Beck in the grassy bottom of this delightful dean or clough is a profound rarity amongst early bridges: a cantilever bridge cleverly constructed from massive, naturally shaped gritstone slabs. This bizarre, yet stunningly attractive little bridge was almost certainly used by packhorses to-ing and fro-ing with their loads of cotton, woollens, iron tools and implements, lead, limestone and miscellaneous merchandise from Lancashire; the trackway coming over the wild moorland from Wycoller near Colne. Once across Dean Beck, the trackway went up the steep, rocky east flank of the dean, thence to head over rough, boggy moorland to Laycock, from where the track would head down the side of the Aire Valley to the hamlet of Utley, where there was a ford crossing the River Aire. Packhorses heading over to Lancashire, after crossing Dean Beck's cantilever bridge, – which owing to its unusual construction – would at most times be hazardous, would then climb up the western flank of the dean on a zig-zag trackway to emerge close to the ancient hamlet of Newsholme. From here, the route would go via Oakworth and Hare Hill, thence over a ten mile stretch of bleak, high, water-logged moorland and down to Wycoller.

JAGGERMEN'S BRIDGES ON PACKHORSE TRAILS

The massive flagstone trackway leading down into Newsholme Dean was probably built for the transporting of stone out of a number of quarries on the sides of the dean. There is no suggestion that it was used specifically by packhorses. July 2004.

© Christine McEwen Collection.

Cantilever bridges were often built by the early British Neolithic peoples long before the Roman invasion of Britain. Others were also built during the Middle Ages. The design allows heavy loads to be carried across the streams without the requirement of a centre supporting pillar rising from the river bed. The construction involved massive slabs of stone – (in the Pennines, usually Millstone Grit) – to be located on either side of the banks of the water course usually about five or six feet above the flood level; projecting out over the water and being well-packed underneath with more huge slabs set at right-angles to achieve upward sloping. These slabs were counter-weighted by another slab being placed at such an angle to partially rest on the back end of the projecting slab, with the other end resting on the ground. This design achieved a profoundly robust structure. The bridge was finally completed by the placing of the centre stone slab, which was usually considerably longer, wider and thicker than the others.

Walking along the flagstone trackway bordered on both sides with tumbled down dry-stone walls, were many ancient wind-contorted Oaks, Birches, Alders, and Hollies growing high above the sheep-filled pastures on the floor of the dean. On reaching an enormous gritstone boulder, we abruptly turned to head downhill, passing some brightly flowering yellow brooms competing with great swathes of buttercups

We reached a stone-roofed, gritstone cottage, where just over a low stone wall, a portly, fiftyish-aged, salt and pepper-bearded man was lustily and noisily engaged with a smoking chain saw cutting down a much-gnarled, ancient Apple tree. We stopped walking to watch the man for a minute or so. Alan shouted a greeting and the man killed the chain saw's noisy engine. Placing the chain saw carefully on the grass among a pile of Apple logs, he walked through a narrow gateway in the wall to greet us. **"Lost your map, are you lost?"** the man jokingly asked. We explained that we wanted to find the old stone bridges crossing Dean Beck. Our bearded friend walked about three or four yards to the edge of the dean and pointed down towards a gigantic, dense thicket of white blossom-covered Hawthorn. **"Just about a couple o' hundred yards passed them theer thorn bushes and you'll come t'bridges",** he said in broad Yorkshire, smiling. Thanking him, Alan enquired if the man was going to burn the Apple logs on the cottage hearth during the coming winter. Surprisingly, the man said he was going to try and sell them by advertising in the local free ads newspaper. Quick as a flash, Alan made him a cash offer, which was readily accepted. Later, Alan collected around three quarters of a ton of Apple logs in our van.

Walking around the heavily perfumed greenery of the Hawthorns, we were delighted to see below, spanning the Dean Beck, the strong summer evening light falling onto two lovely, small stone bridges. On us reaching the first bridge which is incorrectly called a packhorse bridge, the sun's heat was so strong that we were both freely perspiring. Alan then came up with a jolly good idea: **"Christine, why not take off your boots and thick woollen socks and sit down with your feet in the beck"** he said, gesturing me to join him where he was sat ensconced upon a stone slab, his bare feet immersed in the clear, cold waters of this mountain stream. So I did, and what a delightful ease it induced to my hot, sweaty feet. We sat drinking in the beauty of our tranquil surroundings. Nearby, were a mass of strongly growing purple foxgloves, and in the pasture to our front I could see over a dozen rabbits happily gorging on the sweet grass. Looking downstream, I saw the proud, upright, statuesque figure of a heron standing mid-stream. It was obviously patiently waiting to catch one of the brown trout common hereabouts, for its supper. We were then entertained with the comical antics of two, courting blue dragonflies, madly chasing and tormenting each other. After re-socking and booting up, the cameras came out and we thoroughly enjoyed photographing both bridges.

The attractive farm bridge built by James Lund sits alongside the ancient cantilever bridge. July 2004.

© Christine McEwen Collection.

JAGGERMEN'S BRIDGES ON PACKHORSE TRAILS

THE 'PACKHORSE BRIDGE'

Crudely built of local gritstone, its shallow segmental arch spans the beck in a leap of around thirteen feet; the width of the trackway across the top being around ten feet. The parapets are constructed from random pieces of stone, and the whole bridge appeared to have been recently re-pointed with lime mortar. Although an attractive structure, this bridge is definitely not a packhorse bridge. It was built by local farmer James Lund for the princely sum of £10, and has well served the farmers of Newsholme Dean ever since its construction in the late nineteenth century.

THE CANTILEVER BRIDGE

The age of this thought-inspiring, ingeniously built little bridge could well be several thousand years. On the other hand, it may not be incredibly old, for it may have been built in the Medieval Period. The truth is, no-one really knows. But Alan and I agreed that its building involving the manoeuvring, lifting and placing of the massively heavy gritstone slabs, would have been a truly daunting endeavour without any form of mechanical lifting equipment. The centre slab, measuring around eight feet long by two feet in width and about ten inches thick, must weigh over a ton. The other slabs, also massive, probably weigh between a quarter and half a ton apiece.

With his Engineer's eye for detail, Alan reckoned that the slabs originally would have been riven out of local gritstone beds and transported on wooden rollers or sleds hauled by teams of men. This would be during the summer period when the beck would be at its lowest level. The slabs forming the bridge's abutments would be manoevoured into position on the sides of the beck, by long wooden levers, possibly fashioned from stout branches. The counter-weighting slabs would be prised and levered into position, and then tightly packed with small stones and clay.

The massive centre slab would be manoevoured to a position alongside the abutments, and then jacked up by levering and building up a firm base of flat stones beneath, until, the slab had reached a height of a few inches higher than the abutments. The centre slab would then be carefully manoevoured sideways by levering it into the position we see it in today, after which it would then have been lowered. More small stones and clay would have been tightly packed in around the whole structure making the bridge extremely strong. Countless centuries ago, it would have been a stirring sight to behold a tribe of dirty-looking, straggly-haired, heavily-bearded, muscular men engaged in the construction of this unique, cantilever bridge.

I am certain that the Jaggermen of old would have treated with the utmost respect the crossing of this cantilever bridge by their strings of packhorses.

We concluded our enjoyable foray into Newsholme Dean by strolling alongside the beck as it meandered down the dean; negotiating our path with difficulty over rough, swampy ground whilst being eaten alive with swarms of moorland midges and large, evil-looking bluebottles.

Soon, we came to an old iron footbridge, that in former times, would both morning and evening, have echoed to the sounds of countless millworkers' feet as they either hurried from where they lived in the small hill village of Newsholme to the Rag Mill at Goose Eye further downstream, or dog tired, were returning home.

With the beck gathering momentum as it raced down the dean, we next came to more signs of Man's ingenuity, for hereabouts among carpets of late flowering bluebells and the all-pervading aroma of wild garlic, were the crumbling remains of stone-built goits and launders used for conveying water from the beck. There was a large rusty, threaded, iron bar, rising from a weed-choked door-plate. Alan told me it was a Clow valve for controlling the flow of water from the beck.

Rounding a bend in the path thronged with stinging nettles, a large dam came into sight, the sun's rays dancing off the surface of the vast sheet of still water. Sat around were one or two lonesome anglers trying their luck at catching a brown trout supper.

I had read somewhere that the dam because of its distinctive shape, was known as Teapot Dam and was built in 1791 to power Brow End Mill, a cotton-spinning 'manufactory'. Later, the mill was used for rag-grinding for paper manufacture, which was subsequently carried out at the extensive Goose Eye Mill, specifically built for paper-making.

After walking across another interesting little stone footbridge spanning Dean Beck at the front of 'the Rag Mill', dog-tired, we entered the historic Turkey Inn, in Goose Eye Village where with locally brewed ale, we slaked our thirst.

Six months later during the long, dark, cold winter nights in the comfort of our living room sitting around our wood-burner with its doors open, Alan and I greatly relished the sight and sounds of the brightly burning, crackling logs providing warmth, with the bonus of the enchanting, delicious apple-wood perfume scenting the air.

ENCHANTING WYCOLLER, NEAR COLNE, LANCASHIRE.

On a cold February morning Wycoller's curious looking, crooked, double-arched packhorse bridge spanning Wycoller Beck with the ruinous Wycoller Hall to the rear. February 2010.

© Christine McEwen Collection.

The charming East Lancashire village of Wycoller with its architecturally renowned eighteenth century stone houses and its ruinous, reputedly haunted, Wycoller Hall, straddles Wycoller Beck that meanders down the beautiful Pennine valley, Wycoller Dene to drain the high moorland to the east that extends over to Haworth in West Yorkshire.

Anyone approaching Wycoller could not help but notice the wild silhouettes of gnarled, wind-bent ancient Oaks, Alders, Ash and Birches against the sky. Wycoller received it name from the Anglo-Saxon: - 'wic-air' – which translates into, 'the dairy farm amongst the Alders'. Middle Stone Age man lived and hunted on the encircling high moorland that dominates Wycoller.

Early records mention – (circa 1196) – there were two cattle rearing farms, known as 'vaccaries' in Wycoller. It is probable that vac-aries were established for the breeding of oxen. These powerful, sturdy animals were the main beasts of burden for centuries. Each village required eight oxen to pull the plough, and it was the Wycoller vaccaries that provided the oxen.

The unusual looking, enigmatic vaccary walls, built of massive, weirdly-shaped gritstone slabs are a striking feature of the fields around Wycoller. Their existence alongside the ancient trackways where they stand up like giant jagged teeth against the sky, are a testament to the men who erected them centuries ago. These walls of gritstone slabs were built to act as enclosures for the safeguarding of the farm's oxen, cattle and sheep, and were probably erected during the mid-thirteenth century when many new vaccaries were established in nearby Pendle Forest, Rossendale Forest and elsewhere in Pennine Lancashire.

'A row of giant jagged teeth against the sky'. A section of vaccary walling on the fell side above Wycoller Dene. February 2010.

© *Christine McEwen Collection.*

By 1527, the two Wycoller vaccaries had developed into a hamlet. Between the Tudors and the stirrings of the Industrial Revolution, Wycoller developed into a locally important, handloom weaving village, which by this period lay astride the packhorse trackway from nearby Colne to Keighley on the other side of the Pennines in the West Riding of Yorkshire.

Wycoller village, together with the verdant, leafy Wycoller Dene with its beautiful stream, has for over forty years been a favourite place to visit for my husband Alan, and also for myself ever since I became lovingly acquainted with its charms in 2002. The area abounds with wildlife; and we have frequently observed kestrels hovering above the village in search of mice, rats, stoats, weasels and young rabbits. In Wycoller Beck, we have been regularly delighted in seeing heron gracefully standing in the beck fishing for the abundant brown trout. On a number of other occasions I have been thrilled on seeing the typical flash of bright plumage as a kingfisher races above the surface of the busy, chattering Wycoller Beck searching for a meal. Alan also enjoys a passion for wild flowers, so in spring we often take a most delightful stroll along Wycoller Beck where we are rewarded with seeing hosts of bluebells, wood sorrel, celandines, and those unusually looking plants, butterburs. In summer, the edges of the steeply sloping meadows are awash with the colour of tall foxgloves, dog violets and germander speedwell. A truly delightful, enchanting and serene haven for wildlife and for Man.

WYCOLLER'S FAMOUS UNIQUE BRIDGES

Wycoller straddles one of the earliest important packhorse trackways across the Pennines between Colne, once an important cloth-making town, and over into the West Riding of Yorkshire, Keighley and Bradford in the Aire Valley.

Wycoller is renowned for its seven stone bridges that span Wycoller Beck, three being unique specimens of the bridge builders art. On entering Wycoller the first of these three bridges, the packhorse bridge can be seen spanning the beck a cockstride downstream of a cobble stone-bottomed ford.

THE PACKHORSE BRIDGE

The famous packhorse bridge is a fascinating specimen of a double-arched bridge. Some say it dates back to the thirteenth century, whilst other say the fifteenth century. However, I am sure its true age will never be revealed but the ancient structure has withstood the constant passage of Jaggermen and his strings of packhorses for centuries.

The whole bridge is built from the local Millstone Grit. The voussoirs: the stones that comprise the double arches actually extend the full width of the bridge and display evidence that in the distant past the arch stones themselves were the actual paving. Also due to the bridge's foundation stones being laid in an uneven fashion, the whole structure, and in particular the 'village side' arch looks to be in a precarious state of health. How long the bridge has been in this predicament nobody seems to know, but in 1948 the Ministry of Works issued a fascinating condition report on the bridge which, I feel is worth adding in full:

"At first glance this appears to be in a precarious state but it is considered mainly an optical effect due to the extra ordinary method employed in springing the arch – (entirely built of long stones) – direct from the rock without any attempt to level it first; the distortion of the arch does not appear to be a recent fault and in fact may never have been true. The bridge is not falling over as appearance suggests. Mortar in the joints is mainly lacking and they should be thoroughly consolidated. Original path surface and low parapets are missing and the backs of the arch stones now form the surface. When this is washed out and consolidated, it would perhaps. Be as well to lay a layer of concrete over the whole bridge, within the parapets of course, to form a saddle and provide a proper surface, care, however, would be necessary to provide a pleasing surface ......"

When I read this document, I was truly horrified at the prospect of the Ministry of Work's builders covering this striking, ancient packhorse bridge with so hideous a material as concrete! Gladly they did not do so.

The packhorse bridge is affectionately known hereabouts as Sally's Bridge. So who was Sally? Local tradition has it way back in the mists of time, a local lass named Sally influenced the construction of this amazing bridge. A one time resident of Wycoller Hall, Squire Henry Cunliffe had a favourite niece, Sally Scargill, who evidently delighted in spending time at the hall, which she had enjoyed ever since being a wee lass. This Sally, probably was a young well-born woman, Sarah Scargill, who was locally known as Sally. She eventually married into the prominent Cunliffe family, thereafter being known as Sally Owen Cunliffe. Later, she gave birth to a boy, Henry Owen Cunliffe, who in time became the last Squire of Wycoller Hall.

When I have viewed this fascinating, double-arched, old stone bridge from its upstream side, the crooked left-hand arch referred to above, appears to be most strange. Nevertheless, the quirky, malformed configuration, whether intentionally built in, or the result of an early partial collapse of the structure, actually accentuates the overall attractiveness and appeal of this stunning pre-industrial packhorse bridge which countless visitors to Wycoller take pleasure in photographing.

The 'crooked' arch has a span of around fourteen feet. The 'main' arch leaps from the centre stone pillar, a distance of around twelve feet to the bank. The overall span of the bridge across Wycoller Beck amounts to around twenty six feet. The centre stone pillar rising from the middle of the beck acts as cutwaters on both upstream and downstream sides.

The twenty six inch wide trackway over the bridge consists of severely worn cobbles and flagstones. The random stone parapets are approximately ten inches high. These were probably rebuilt by the Ministry of Works around 1948.

Two or three yards upstream is an attractive stony-bottomed ford, and several stepping stones. Both ford and stepping stones originally would have been used by herdsmen whilst leading cattle and sheep across the beck. When in full spate, the beck would no doubt be difficult to cross, and particularly so for packhorses with their heavily loaded panniers, perhaps containing oats, corn, wheat, woollens, cotton – which had to be kept dry, this is probably the reason the packhorse bridge was constructed.

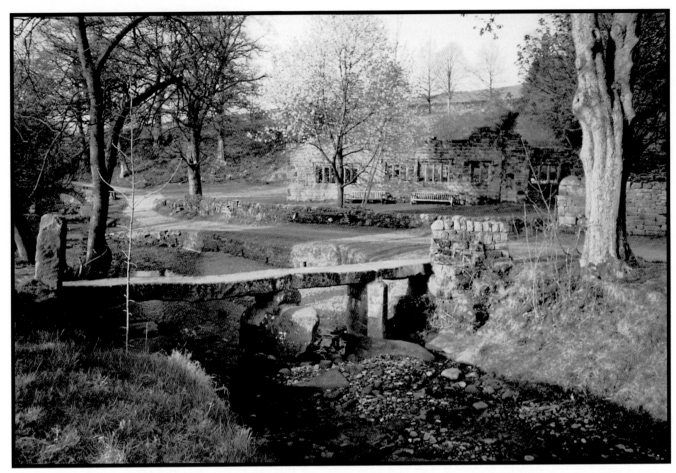

On a beautiful April morning I took this picture of Wycoller's ancient Clapper Bridge crossing the beck near the front of Wycoller Hall. April 2005.

© Christine McEwen Collection.

THE CLAPPER BRIDGE

This superb specimen of a clapper bridge spans the beck in the shadow of the broken down walls of enigmatic Wycoller Hall. Hereabouts, the beck was too wide to be spanned by a single-slab bridge, such as the clam bridge located about a half a mile upstream. Although somewhat primitive looking, clapper bridges of these proportions in Northern England are a profound rarity, and the age of this bridge is the subject of much head-scratching amongst historians. It is safe to say, however, that Wycoller's clapper bridge is among the rarest of its type to be found anywhere in Britain. In Devon, in the village of Postbridge there is a similarly striking clapper bridge, but the date of its construction is unknown.

The clapper bridge is also quite unusual, as it is known hereabouts by three different names: Th'Hall Bridge; Weavers' Bridge and Druids' Bridge. Its colourful, varying names derive from the centuries old traditions that surround the ancient structure. It is known as Th'Hall Bridge because it crosses the beck right in front of Wycoller Hall; Weavers' Bridge, no doubt, recalls several centuries of village handloom weavers who crossed the bridge with their 'pieces' – sheets of coarse woollens to hang out to dry in the Tenter field then located at the rear of the Hall. Local legend spins that in the Dark Ages, local Druid priests carried out human sacrifices in an amphitheatre located on the side of the beck where the Hall was later constructed. Evidently, these ancient Druid rites are now recalled in the clapper bridge's thought-inspiring name.

Currently, the clapper bridge consists of three massive gritstone slabs resting on two supporting pillars. However, local legend says that early in the nineteenth century there were only two slabs, until the slab on the Wycoller Hall side of the beck was broken in half due to a falling, heavy tree. This resulted in the two broken sections of the slab being subsequently repaired, and being supported from the bed of the beck by a stout, Oak log. Later, the log was replaced by the current concrete pillar.

So this is the reason why the bridge now comprises of three huge slabs of local Millstone Grit to span this wide section of Wycoller Beck. The slabs have an average width of thirty eight inches by eleven inches in thickness.

In the middle of the beck there is a massive arrowhead-shaped gritstone boulder, seven feet, six inches long by three feet high which tapers at the downstream side from thirty eight inches down to six inches. This boulder, an Ice Age erratic, together with two squarish lumps of stone stacked on top acts as the main support pillar; on the upstream side the arrowhead acts as a cutwater.

The main slab which even for a large section of Millstone Grit is, at fourteen feet, eight inches a considerable length. One end of this huge slab on the 'village' side of the beck rests on crudely built abutments constructed from huge, roughly-squared, natural pieces of stone. The other end sits mid-way on the supporting stone pillar. Between this natural stone pillar and the 'hall' side of the beck, acting as an additional support pillar, is the most unappealing, incongruous, concrete support. The middle slab, some seven feet in length is supported by the huge stone column and the concrete pillar. The third slab measures around seven feet, four inches and is also supported at one end by the concrete pillar and the other end by large pieces of stone let into the bank of the beck.

The present top surface of the clapper bridge is relatively smooth. Most modern footwear is not iron-tipped like the handloom weavers' clogs of old, or the heavy leather boots once worn by farmers, and therefore, do not cause grooves to be worn into the stone. However, past generations of foot traffic did indeed, over time, wear extremely deep troughs along the centre of the upper surface of the stone slabs.

These ever-deepening grooves, obviously made walking across the bridge increasingly difficult, particularly at night when it would be pitch-black, or during bad weather when the conditions could be hazardous. Local legend spins that the grooves were in fact chiselled flat by a Wycoller farmer following the tragic death of his daughter who evidently drowned in the flooded beck resulting from her missing her footing in the deep grooves and falling into the raging torrent.

Although not specifically mentioned as a packhorse bridge, I believe this broad-topped clapper bridge pre-dates the packhorse bridge and therefore, would be regularly used by the Jaggermen's heavily ladened packhorses, as well as farmers driving their cattle and sheep across the beck.

CLAM BRIDGE

Located about a third of a mile upstream from the clapper bridge is an excellent specimen of a stone beam or clam bridge, which comprises a massive, single slab of Millstone Grit which is laid resembling a huge tree trunk across the beck. This clam bridge is the most primitive-looking of Wycoller's bridges, its design harking back to earlier times when man would use large tree trunks for crossing streams.

In the mountainous regions of Northern England, where there was an abundance of stone, for example, the Millstone Grit areas of the South Pennines, large slabs hewn from gritstone and other suitable sandstones were considerably commonplace.

The massive, natural-looking slab used in the Wycoller clam bridge originally may have been discovered among the numerous piles of erratic boulders left scattered about Wycoller Dene during the last Ice Age; for there is no distinct evidence in the form of mason's tool marks to be seen anywhere on the stone.

The quarrying of such a large slab, and particularly so in the pre-Medieval Period would have been a significant undertaking. The transportation of the slab, due to the rocky terrain of the dene, unless sourced from nearby would also have been virtually impossible; and the final lifting into place of the slab, would be a most hazardous and practically challenging task.

Regarding the age of the clam bridge, some historians suggest it was built in ancient times, - (between 1000 and 3000 years) - while others say it is relatively modern, probably late eighteenth or early nineteenth century.

Just like dating many of these enigmatic bridges – who knows? I have only added the Wycoller clam bridge into the book – because it is one of the well-known 'Wycoller three bridges', and because I just find the old clam bridge absolutely fascinating.

The author and granddaughter Emily precariously standing upon Wycoller's Clam Bridge. In the foreground is an ancient ford with some large vaccary stones embedded in the beck. April 2005.

© Christine McEwen Collection.

The overall length of this huge slab of Millstone Grit, the main component of the bridge, is a massive fifteen feet and the width varies between thirty two and twenty eight inches. The thickness of the slab ranges from fifteen inches down to around twelve inches. There are two square holes measuring approximately two inches square which have been cut into the top, presumably, for securing an iron handrail, now long gone.

Rather precariously, the slab spans Wycoller Beck with just around three or four inches of purchase on top of a large, irregular-shaped rock embedded in the bank by the road side. The other end of the slab sits on a crudely constructed abutment of large, rough blocks of gritstone built into the side of the beck.

Almost unbelievably, on the 19th of May 1989, a tremendous, powerful wall of flood water thundering down the beck, ripped the giant slab from its position and washed it several yards downstream, resulting in it being cracked across in two different places. The bridge owners, Lancashire County Council, successfully recovered the slab, and subsequent to carrying out specialised repairs involving pinning and bonding the cracks together with special mortar, it was re-sited, where it had withstood many a ferocious Pennine storm for countless years.

Immediately downstream of the clam bridge is the remains of a ford and embedded in the bed of the beck are a number of large 'vaccary' stones which must have been removed from one of the local field walls.

Having many times visited these three fascinating old bridges, and marvelled at their construction, I have found myself becoming more and more appreciative of how they enhance the enchanting atmosphere of beautiful Wycoller Dene, and I just wonder when and by whom these historic stone bridges were built.

WYCOLLER'S GHOSTS

Legends of ghostly visitations embrace ancient Wycoller as they cling to perhaps just a few other secluded Pennine villages. But it isn't surprising, for the tiny hamlet of Wycoller lies in seclusion in its bowl-like valley encircled with high altitude, misty moorland; surely the perfect spot for ghostly hauntings, boggarts and worst, terrible Guytrash Padfoot.

During the summer days, Wycoller with its beautiful stream flowing peacefully between banks of colourful, perfumed wild flowers is a charming and peaceful location. But during those pitch black, moonless, late autumn nights, with swirling blankets of mist rising above the beck, it would be easy to let your imagination dwell on the local legends of ghostly happenings that for centuries have haunted the village, and in particular the broken down ruins of Wycoller Hall.

Just imagine, in the dead of night, walking across either the Packhorse Bridge or the Clapper Bridge, the mist swirling around you, to then enter the roofless old Hall and to stand close to the huge stone fireplace. Even for the stoutest heart naturally, this would be a fearsome place because a number of ghostly happenings have occurred hereabouts. Wycoller's ghost stories are well documented and more than one involve two of the historic bridges.

'THE SPECTRE HORSEMAN'

The legendary Spectre Horseman is undoubtedly the most well documented, famous Wycoller ghost. From back in the mists of time, local tradition says that the ghost appears on just one night each year, and only then when the night is as black as a grave, the wind howling down from the high, bleak moorland and rain barrelling down in torrents. On nights such as this when there is no moon to light up the secluded, dark and foggy lanes, the village folk of Wycoller would not stir from their hearths.

The haunting of the Packhorse Bridge by the Spectre Horseman is dramatically recorded in Harland and Wilkinson's, 'Lancashire Legends' dated 1882:

"He is attired in the costume of the early Stuart Period and the trappings of his horse are one of the most uncouth description. When the wind howls, the loudest horseman can be heard dashing up the road at full speed, and after crossing the narrow bridge, he suddenly stops at the door of the Hall. The rider then dismounts and makes his way up the broad open stairs into one of the rooms of the Hall. Dreadful screams, as from a woman, are then heard, which soon subsides into groans. The horseman then makes his appearance at the door ---- at once mounts his steed ---- and gallops off the road he came. His body can be seen through by those who may be chance to be present; his horse appears to be wild with rage and its nostrils steam with fire."

This tale, records one of the Cunliffe family members murdering his wife in one of the Hall's upstairs bedrooms. The ghostly apparition, - the Spectre Horseman - is the ghost of Cunliffe, the wife-killer who is doomed forever to re-enact the terrible, bloody scene of the heinous crime.

There is an even more dramatic telling of the same story in Halliwell Sutcliffe's *'Mistress Barbara Cunliffe',* who dates the murder during the reign of Charles II.

"Well, he went a-hunting once on a day ---- it was in Charles the Second's time, we're told ---- and the fox led them a five-mile chase across the moors until he came to Wycoller Dene. He crossed the stream between the straight bridge and the double-arched, and would have turned down the village; but the hounds headed him, and he ran straight as a die through the open main door of the Hall, and up the stair here: the hounds followed, and after them the old Squire spurred his horse right up the stair, and into his wife's room, where she had been busy with her tiring maid until the entry of the fox disturbed them. The wife screamed aloud in terror for the hounds' teeth were already in the fox, and the music of the hunt was deafening --- and Simon Cunliffe swore a great oath, and cursed her chicken-heartedness, and raised his hunting-crop as if to strike her. That and the fright together killed her, so they say, and all in haste the Squire drove out the hounds, lest they should turn upon his fallen lady."

The ghost in this tale is supposedly Squire Simon Cunliffe – who in fact was a fictitious character invented by the author Halliwell Sutcliffe. Nevertheless, it is a most disturbing ghostly tale.

Alan and I have visited the ruins of Wycoller Hall in the wee small hours of a dark winter night, and notwithstanding the creepiness of the ruins, alas, we went back home to bed without seeing or hearing any ghostly happenings. Alan was really disappointed!

The ruins of Wycoller Hall, the haunt of the ghostly 'Spectre Horseman'. February 2010.

© Christine McEwen Collection.

OLD LOWER HODDER OR CROMWELL'S BRIDGE, NEAR GREAT MITTON, CLITHEROE.

The graceful lines of Cromwell's Bridge whose three stone arches span the beautiful River Hodder. March 2010.

© Christine McEwen Collection.

A day early in the year, the 4th of March 2010, and with it the urge for Alan and I to visit one of the most charming and thought-inspiring packhorse bridges to be found in Lancashire, Cromwell's Bridge or Old Lower Hodder Bridge, that spans the Hodder at Great Mitton, three miles from Clitheroe. With brilliant sunshine glinting from the silvery surface of the wide, River Hodder and welcoming blankets of white snowdrops lighting up the banks, Alan and I made our way through a jungle of high-arching, razor-barbed Dog Rose thickly growing on both sides of a stony narrow path. Our lovely walk marched downstream through a stand of truncated ancient

Beeches, their trunks luxuriously clothed in ivy, until we reached the triple-arched bridge of stone, that General Cromwell is said to have rode over with his battalions of marching Ironsides.

THE RIVER HODDER – LANCASHIRE'S TOTALLY RURAL AND MOST BEAUTEOUS OF RIVERS.

Historically, the ancient county of Lancashire stretched from the River Mersey to the River Duddon, now in Cumbria. Between these, the Rivers Irwell, Ribble and Lune with their many tributaries drain the Pennine uplands to eventually flow westwards into the Irish Sea.

After flowing down from the enchanting limestone country of Upper Ribblesdale, the River Ribble already swollen with the waters of the Calder, Darwen and lastly the Hodder, meets the sea at Preston. The Hodder, a totally rural river commences its journey as a number of small streams that drain the southern slopes of the Bowland Fells above the charming village of Slaidburn. From this beautiful location, it meanders through the lower flanks of the Bowland Fells, whilst collecting the waters from the River Dunsop and the Langden Brook; it then flows circuitously around the mass of Longridge Fell, before flowing beneath the 'modern' well-engineered stone, Lower Hodder Bridge and the beautiful, thought-inspiring sixteenth century Cromwell's Bridge, to finally merge with the River Ribble near Mitton, a few miles away from historic Clitheroe.

CROMWELL'S BRIDGE

This graceful, triple-arched bridge of stone spanning the River Hodder, was built in 1562 by Master Stonemason Roger Crossley for the sum of £70. Sir Richard Shireburne of Stoneyhurst Hall provided the stone and paid the mason in instalments of £10 until the bridge was completed.

An 'indenture' or contract dated 30th December 1561 between Sir Richard, other local 'gentlemen' and Master Stonemason Roger Crossley set out the requirements for the building of a bridge to span the Hodder. The contract documents named Stonemason Crossley together with Sir Richard Shireburne; Richard Shireburne of Bailey, Edmund Shireburne, John Holden and James Shuttleworth.

Within the contract, Crossley agreed to build *'one sufficient and abyll bryge of Stone'* .... the *'breidth and wideness of the sayd bryge'* ...... one to be similar to another local bridge, Edisford Bridge; ...... *'after the Samepyll of Edysforth bryge.'*

The contract stipulated that apart from actually constructing the bridge, Crossley will also be responsible for the quarrying of the stone at nearby Malmerdene Quarry, (probably a 'delve hole' in the deep chasm of Dean Brook), *'he is to breke the stones in Mawm(er)den.'*

Roger Crossley agreed that he would complete the building of the bridge before Michaelmas 1563. The £10 payments to Crossley were to be made on the following dates: Feast of the Purification of Our Lady, 2nd February 1562; the Feast of St. John the Baptist, 24th June 1562; and at Martinmas, 11th November 1562; and with four more £10 payments until the contract was completed.

Close-up of the pebbled construction of the trackway over the eastern arch. Note the robust construction of the triangular cutwaters and combined piers. March 2010.

© Christine McEwen Collection.

JAGGERMEN'S BRIDGES ON PACKHORSE TRAILS

Sir Richard Shireburne's part of the contract was to cart the stone from the quarry at Malmerdene to the bridge construction site and they were to set up suitable coffer dams on the river bed to enable the masons to build the bridge piers: *'they were to make Casis or other Conveyance to sett the grownde Work dry.'*

There is also mention of Shireburne's men having to dismantle the remains of an earlier bridge that stood on the site of the bridge Crossley was to construct: *'..... to helpe to Remove the old lwelles* (piers) *from the ground where they Stand.'*

Shireburne and his partners had also to provide lime and sand for mortar, and the timber for scaffolding and for the arch formers.

Finally, Sir Richard Shireburne and his cohorts were obviously shrewd businessmen for within the bridge building contract there was a penalty clause amounting to £100; this figure being £30 greater than Crossley's agreed price of £70.

Owing to local roads being virtually non-existent, it is probable that some of the bridge building materials: lime, sand, wood ashes for mortar-making, would be brought to the site by packhorses. The huge stones would have to be conveyed by oxen-hauled carts or waggons.

On the 16th of August 1648 whilst marching from Gisburn to Preston, General Cromwell's army – a body of around eight thousand men crossed the Hodder, the officers riding their mounts over Sir Richard Shireburne's bridge, while the weary foot soldiers struggling with their heavy ordnance pieces probably used the nearby ford.

That evening Cromwell quartered his troops in the fields adjoining Stonyhurst Hall. Together with his senior officers, Cromwell stayed the night in the Hall as the guests of the incumbent Royalist and Catholic, Sir Richard Shireburne. It is said that due to being amongst the Royalist occupiers of the Hall, Cromwell, was greatly in fear of being assassinated and therefore, ordered a large oak table to be positioned in the dining hall upon which he bedded down, his gunpowder charged and loaded pistols and sword by his side!

Whilst resting at Stonyhurst, Cromwell and his officers deliberated whether it would be a wise move to directly intercept the Royalist army at Preston, or alternatively, to cut them off by contouring around Blackburn and Chorley to attack the enemy from the south. However, the consensus was to head straight across to Preston which Cromwell did, mercilessly routing the Royalist army on Ribbleton Moor.

Cromwell wrote: ***"Last night we lay at Mr. Shireburne of Stone-hurst ...... we advanced betimes in next morning towards Preston with a desire to engage the enemy."***

Another intriguing tale about Cromwell's Bridge involves paranormal phenomena for the bridge is apparently haunted with *'a bridge devil',* a poltergeist. In 1690, Richard Atkinson, a drunken scoundrel, who lived in Clitheroe and locally known as *'a profane, drunken baliff,'* who pleasured himself by terrorising his fellow townsfolk with much swearing, drunkenness and uncouth behaviour,

'reproached and cursed the town's faithful followers of Christ when he could not otherwise persecute them ......'.

One day, following a severe bout of nasty behaviour, Atkinson was riding over the bridge when suddenly,

'the Bridge Devil appeared from thin air. The beast effortlessly lifted the terrified man from his snorting horse and with great violence threw him, causing his body to somersault thrice before plunging a drop of thirty feet into the raging, swollen waters of the Hodder.'

It was said that the fright of seeing the *'bridge devil'* caused his death before he hit the water.

From earliest times around Bowland, because strings of packhorses could easily ascend the high fells and rough moorland, the carrying of diverse merchandise by packhorses was significantly more common than the use of oxen-hauled carts and waggons that were forced to use pot-holed trackways in the valley bottoms; in winter mostly un-passable. By the advent of the sixteenth century, due to the ever-burgeoning trade in woollens, large amounts of packhorse traffic were daily travelling all over Northern England, their pack-saddles loaded with bolts of cloth.

A good example of the magnitude of the packhorse trade is displayed by the fact that churchman, Dean Nowell was able to purchase during one week in 1569, nearly two thousand, five hundred yards of woollen cloth from several dozen cloth merchants operating from Blackburn, Whalley and Burnley. Much of this cloth would be carried by packhorses over Cromwell's Bridge, day or night, summer or winter.

The triple segmental-arched bridge built of local stone ashlar comprises one large arch and two smaller side arches. The large centre arch stands around thirty feet above the normal river water level. This arch appears to have lost its covering of mortared rubble which now consists only of protruding, neatly-cut voussoir stones. There are no parapets. The two side arches still contain a partial covering of mortared rubble, and also what appears to be the remnants of low parapets.

The bed of the trackway over both side arches comprise of large cobbles or water-worn pebbles set into mortar. All piers have triangular cut-waters extending the full height. The total span of the bridge amounts to around one hundred and thirty feet; the total width around ten feet. When originally built the bridge probably had low parapets, and by taking measurement of the trackway between the remains of these, the width would have been around seven feet. There are no approach roads at either end of the bridge and also no discernable evidence of a ford, despite being earlier mentioned.

After we had both completed the enjoyable work of photographing Cromwell's Bridge, we fed some broken ginger biscuits to a forlorn-looking pony that had inquisitively joined us.

The late afternoon sky was beautifully tinted with rose and gold, with the distant Bowland Fells a dazzle, until the early spring sun dipped turning the hills to shades of purple and indigo. It was time for home, so after tackling once more the spiny Dog Roses, we headed back to the comfort of our car.

The author standing on top of the key stone of the centre arch. To the rear is the 'new' Lower Hodder Bridge built 1819. This fantastic structure displays fine levels of the Stonemason's craft. March 2010.

© Christine McEwen Collection

HIGHERFORD OLD BRIDGE, BARROWFORD, PENDLE.

**Higherford Old Bridge or 'Th'Owd Brig' spanning Pendle Water.
March 2010.**

© Christine McEwen Collection.

Situated around eight miles from my house at Cowling, is the well known 'Roman Bridge' or 'Th'Owd Brig'. This highly attractive stone packhorse bridge spans Pendle Water in a graceful leap of thirty six feet. The structure was not however, built by the Romans, but was constructed circa 1620.

This impressive single segmental arched bridge comprises two attractive, double layered rings of chamfered voussoir stones. Both of the massive stone abutments spring from solid sandstone bedrock forming the sides of the river bank.

The bridge was originally built without parapets; the current parapets were added to the structure circa 1815 and consist of six courses of gritstone topped with iron-stapled rectangular slabs which rise to a steep apex on the centreline of the bridge. The width of the trackway over the top is approximately nine feet.

Surprisingly, the cobbled surface of the trackway was laid in 1984 when the bridge was repaired by the local authority. Perhaps this work has unfortunately taken something away, however slightly, from what is a splendid display of early seventeenth century stone masonry. This superb bridge is undoubtedly one of the finest packhorse bridges in Lancashire.

The recently built steps and the addition of an iron handrail, although obviously of benefit to pedestrians using the bridge, regrettably, also spoils the historic character of the structure.

JAGGERMEN'S BRIDGES ON PACKHORSE TRAILS

The bridge, sited just a stone's throw upstream from Higherford Mill on the old Nelson to Gisburn turnpike, forms a link in the chain of old packhorse trackways linking 'Bonny Colne on the Hill', and its important Cloth Hall, with the many woollen weaving communities scattered throughout Pendle Forest; it was also used by regular packhorse trains bringing coal won from the many drift mines and bell pits from around Gisburn, as well as lime carried from the massive limestone workings at Lothersdale. Packhorses delivering goods into East Lancashire from Kendal, the Lake District, and the Yorkshire Dales, would also cross Higherford Old Bridge.

In 1774, the famous Methodist John Wesley is said to have preached from the top of the bridge to a large crowd which apparently did not appreciate his vitriolic rantings and became hostile, threatening the preacher which forced him to seek refuge in a local inn: nowadays called The White Bear.

An interesting snippet in the bridge's long history mentions that in earlier times a large brass bell was suspended from the underside of the arch to dangle above the normal stream level. In times of severe flooding - which could be frequent - the rising waters would cause the bell to ring out a warning of an impending flood.

Those of us who live in the Craven and Pendle Districts on the border between Lancashire and Yorkshire are in my view, extremely blessed to have the wealth of beautiful surrounding countryside, in which are sited almost a dozen superb specimens of historic stone packhorse bridges.

(Left) The massive stone abutments spring from the solid sandstone bedrock. (Right) A close-up of the attractively chamfered, double rings of voussoir stones forming the arch. March 2010.

© Christine McEwen Collection.

The cobbled trackway laid by the local authority in 1984 and the steps and iron handrail installed more recently. October 2004.

© Christine McEwen Collection.

CATLOW BOTTOMS PACKHORSE BRIDGE, NEAR NELSON.

An early undated photograph depicting Catlow Bottoms Packhorse Bridge as it may have looked before its unsympathetic restoration.

Several years back due to an unfortunate incident, I became somewhat acquainted with Catlow Bottoms, but at that time I did not know that the attractive little, humped, stone packhorse bridge had originally been built for Jaggermen's packhorses.

One late November night, Alan and I were taking a regular short-cut from Briercliffe by driving over the 'tops' to Cowling via Colne, which required us to drive down the old 'holloways' leading downhill into Catlow Bottoms which with its two fords over Catlow Brook is a good short cut home. It was foggy with a steady drizzle falling, making visibility difficult. However, Alan was well acquainted with the route, having used the lonely, pitch-dark country lane, originally a packhorse trackway, for many years.

After driving down Robin House Lane, Alan had just driven the car across the first ford, which though unusually deep, the small beck being flooded – did not pose any problems.

Just as the front wheels of the car entered the deep water streaming across the second ford there was an almighty bang from beneath the vehicle. We both jumped because the noise was that of a bursting tyre.

"Hell's Teeth! We've got us a blow-out, a puncture," shouted Alan. *"And we're not in a good spot to change a wheel."*

Within a few minutes, he had reversed the car to the side of the narrow track and commenced breaking out his jack and tools required for changing the wheel. Fortunately, we were well wrapped up, having our walking boots and winter coats in the car boot. We also had two large torches, one of which I switched on, illuminating Alan, who was crouching at the front off-side wheel. Suddenly, we both heard the alarming sound of movement in the nearby thorn bushes making us both feel rather uneasy.

**Catlow Bottom's Packhorse Bridge displaying the rather incongruous battlemented parapets.
January 2005.**

© *Christine McEwen Collection.*

"Christine, I don't wish to frighten you but it's been said that Catlow Bottoms is haunted by Boggarts," whispered Alan, whilst kneeling in about two inches of water. However, to re-assure me he said he considered the sound coming from the bushes was probably nothing more lethal than a barn cat. Between struggling with wheel nuts, car-jack and the wheels, he clearly delighted in regaling me with tales of ghostly happenings in this dark and forbidding place.

"Owd Rennie, my late dear friend who came from these parts told me that Catlow Bottoms was haunted by a Boggart as big as a woolsack with eyes like flaming coals."

Looking about me at the bottom of this wet, foggy clough with just the sound of the beck in full spate to break the silence, I must say, it was quite unnerving.

"That's it, the spare wheel's on. Home-ward bound. Let's roll", said Alan breezily.

Whilst driving the few miles over the deserted, misty, hill roads back to our home in Cowling, I asked Alan if he believed in the Catlow Bottoms Boggart tale.

"I am a Lancastrian, we were brought up with stories about Boggarts. My mother used to take me as a child to Boggart Hole Clough, where we enjoyed picnics there."

Later, when researching material for this book, I learnt that the old Jaggermen, when passing through certain areas, particularly in the bottoms of gloomy cloughs near fords such as at Catlow Bottoms, were often troubled by sightings of 'Boggarts' that frightened the horses. Known areas of the packhorse trackways troubled by Boggart hauntings were suppressed by the setting up of wayside stone posts which had a hole cut through close to the top. The idea was to dilute the potent sorcery of the Boggarts, in the hope they would no longer *'jump out in the path of the packhorses and frighten the Jaggermen and their horses.'*

JAGGERMEN'S BRIDGES ON PACKHORSE TRAILS

This concept of a holed wayside stone post was a consequence of popular belief that Boggarts usually concealed themselves in dark places or behind a stone post where they would suddenly rise up, *'shrieking and roaring'*. A wayside post having a large hole hewn through its top permitted the approaching Jaggermen to see in advance whether a dreadful looking creature resembling *'a wool sack with flaming eyes'* was waiting to pounce. Superstition being rife, it was a wide belief that Boggarts could not cross becks flowing across packhorse trackways.

At Catlow Bottoms, my question is, was the Boggart trapped between the two fords giving rise to the tale? Alan believes it to be true!! I do not!!

The attractive little, semi-circular pack-horse bridge, built of local stone spans Catlow Bottoms in a leap of around ten feet, and is situated a stones throw downstream of the main ford. A few yards away on Robin House Lane is the smaller ford. We changed our punctured tyre in between both fords. Undoubtedly, it is a most curious looking structure due to the three feet high battlemented parapets, which were probably added in modern times. The early undated photograph shows the bridge in a semi-ruinous state, and without parapets. My opinion is they spoil an otherwise beautiful, charming little bridge. The trackway over the top has been finished in 'crazy paving' and is around two feet wide. Again, I feel together with the battlemented parapets this re-building work applied to what is probably a typical early eighteenth century packhorse bridge, is rather incongruous.

Despite its name Catlow 'Bottoms', this tiny hamlet is perched high on the hillside above the former cotton towns of Colne, Nelson and Burnley, and the packhorse trackway that the bridge is sited on was once part of the important route linking Skipton-in-Craven with Burnley, and also Clitheroe with Halifax via the Long Causeway. Packhorses using Catlow Bottom's Bridge carried lime, lead, woollens, and a multitude of other goods.

The end aspect of the bridge showing the crazy paving of the trackway. January 2005.

© Christine McEwen Collection.

CADSHAW BRIDGE, CADSHAW, DARWEN.

The substantially constructed Cadshaw Bridge spanning Cadshaw Brook high above the Darwen Valley. September 2006

© Christine McEwen Collection.

Situated at above the 1000 feet contour, on the original packhorse trackway spanning the Cadshaw Brook on the breezy heights of the West Pennine Moors between Darwen and Bolton, is the crumbling remains of an eighteenth century stone bridge. Cadshaw Bridge is on the ancient road that linked the two Lancashire towns before the Bolton to Blackburn Turnpike – (the modern A666) – was built in 1797. The bridge was the only crossing point of the brook, which when flooded, would have been difficult to cross.

What few passable roads there were in the seventeenth and eighteenth centuries, were generally poorly laid with maintenance being virtually non-existent. In 1781, the preacher, John Wesley in his journal moaned about the **"miserable roads between Blackburn and Bolton."** During the long winter months, the road that trailed over the high Pennine hills linking south Lancashire with the north Lancashire towns of Blackburn, Preston and Lancaster was often impassable to carts and waggons. In summer, the

route over the bleak, often misty hills, was not much better, therefore, **'hail, rain or snow'** – all manner of goods, for example: domestic pottery from the Stoke-on-Trent potteries; salt, used for salting meat and fish and for the preparation of animal hides etc; nails from the Black Country forges; wooden bobbins for the cotton mills; and virtually every other type of industrial, commercial and domestic manufac-tures and commodities were carried on the backs of the Jaggermen's strings of packhorses.

On several occasions, I had noticed this interesting looking, little stone bridge near the isolated hamlet of Cadshaw, situated high above the Darwen Valley, when driving on the A666 from Darwen to Bolton.

One fine September afternoon, together with Alan, I decided to have a recce. From the mid-eighteenth century Cadshaw was most industrious with many handloom weavers operating from the farmhouses and cottages.

JAGGERMEN'S BRIDGES ON PACKHORSE TRAILS

Coal was mined from numerous bell-pits scattered around the hamlet, and the local thick seams of quality clay were extracted for brick manufacture and pipe-making down in Darwen. By the turn of the nineteenth century at Old Lyons at the head of the valley, there were a number of extensive coal mines. Large quantities of coal and clay, together with the produce of the handloom weavers were transported by packhorses to Darwen and Blackburn.

With high clouds scudding across big skies and fine light affording us magnificent long distant views westwards over the high, barren moorland, Alan and I hurried past a rake of ancient, wind-tortured Hawthorns that stood beside a stony track whilst heading directly towards the yellow, smiling face of the sun.

After, perhaps a couple of hundred yards of brisk walking, Alan's keen eyes noticed the poorly defined outline of a grass-covered trackway veering off to our right which ran parallel to the side of a dry stone wall bordering old Bolton Water Work's buildings, and a conifer plantation. Walking further on, we both could make out the interesting bridge, which from our new perspective did not at all resemble the structure we had previously seen from the trunk road.

Five minutes or so later, after we had circum-navigated a patch of boggy ground covering a long, narrow depression, it dawned on us both, that this was the grass and swamp reed-covered remains of the ancient packhorse track-way that up ahead crossed the bridge spanning Cadshaw Brook. Reaching the bridge, we realised it was considerably larger than was previously thought. The structure spanned a stone-built trough ducting the brook towards the southeast where, once across the trunk road it would flow into the Entwistle Reservoir. The arch was formed from well-dressed voussoir stones on to which was laid a ring of six inch thick stone slabs; the span across the brook was twenty eight feet. We walked around a large mature Hawthorn bedecked with clusters of bright red haws. We then clambered up on to the top of the ruinous trackway, which I suppose was a little foolhardy, due to the dangerous condition of its crumbling, loose masonry. The trackway width was, we discovered, eight feet, six inches.

We were both thrilled with our afternoon's exploration of Cadshaw Bridge, and after partaking of a picnic of delicious Lancashire cheese and Southport tomatoes, we headed back home.

The author standing in the middle of the stony, semi-ruinous trackway. It was difficult to appreciate that before 1797 this was the main road between Bolton and Darwen. September 2006.

© Christine McEwen Collection.

BLEASDALE BRIDGE, BROOKS FARM, BLEASDALE, FOREST OF BOWLAND.

Beautiful little Bleasdale Bridge that spans the River Brock. April 2004.

© Christine McEwen Collection.

This bonny little stone bridge is situated in an enchanting, almost fairy-like hollow. During our visit Alan and I were blessed with lovely spring sunshine which glinted like a chest of diamonds from the surface of a chattering, bubbling, and busy little brook. Our approach was by walking down a leafy lane of old Oaks, Alders and Hawthorn, followed by picking our way across lush, sweet grass carpeted with a host of bluebells on the cusp of flowering. Poking up here and there were clusters of delightful bright yellow daffodils, their heads nodding in the light breeze to welcome anybody entering this secret little dell.

This single-arch stone bridge probably built for packhorses, spans the River Brock in a leap of thirteen feet. The trackway over the humped top is formed from flagstones and measures thirty-three inches in width betwixt parapets fourteen inches high comprised of round-nosed stone slabs.

The north end of the bridge extends into several intriguing stone walled enclosures. After closely studying these unusual structures, we wondered if they were originally used for corralling packhorses whilst changing over tired horses for fresher ones. Our feelings were that these enclosures were most probably associated with the packhorse bridge, and we do not recall seeing any other examples. My research in old books suggests the bridge was probably used by packhorse trains travelling down from Lancaster, then by skirting around the southern flanks of the high ground of Grizedale Fell, Bleasdale Moors and Blindhurst Fell whilst heading for Chipping, they would eventually reach the bustling ancient market town of Clitheroe.

It has been suggested by others that the steep hillside on the southern bank of the brook would have been far too severe an incline for laden packhorse trains to ascend. However, this slope certainly appears no steeper than many others I have seen around Todmorden in the Calder Valley. Therefore, I do consider this bridge was used by packhorses, until that is, it can be proven otherwise.

The interesting trackway over the bridge leading into the unusual stone walled 'corrals'
April 2004.

© Christine McEwen Collection.

MONK'S BRIDGE, NEAR RIMINGTON, CLITHEROE.

The graceful span of Monk's Bridge is clearly reflected in the waters of the Swanside Beck. March 2010.

© Christine McEwen Collection.

Our regular research pointed the way to a fine example of a packhorse bridge located in a beautiful, secluded glen between the historic, picturesque villages of Downham and Rimington in the Ribble Valley near Clitheroe. Both villages are dominated by the whaleback mass of Pendle Hill, infamous for witch lore, whilst Rimington straddles the ancient border between Lancashire and the West Riding of Yorkshire.

One fine March day, we decided to seek out this appealing bridge. Alan and I found ourselves tramping through a marshy meadow heading towards the massive, stone-built, twelve-arched Lancashire and Yorkshire Railway viaduct that carries the Blackburn to Hellifield railway line. With wind-bent Hawthorns on our right close to a huge pile of broken stone we reached the viaduct. To our front was a post and wire fence and a broken, rickety, old wooden five-bar gate. To our

left, after snaking this way and that way around many hilly contours, a stream, Ings Beck flowed under one of the tall viaduct arches. Alan, clearly fascinated with the towering viaduct's construction, was busy taking digital pictures. Suddenly, he excitedly shouted, **"By golly, I have discovered an L&YR tombstone,"** pointing down to a round-topped, time-blackened, upright stone, incised with the letters L&YR. He explained to me that his find was a boundary stone that marked the edges of the land once owned by the Lancashire & Yorkshire Railway Company which had gone out of existence in 1923. After poking around underneath the arches we discovered two more of these old railway curiosities. Leaving the viaduct to head downhill we were suddenly arrested by the fascinating sight of a red breasted robin, its beak spearing tasty creepy-crawlies with military precision out of a rotten lower limb of a gigantic Oak.

JAGGERMEN'S BRIDGES ON PACKHORSE TRAILS

Just beyond the monster Oak we could clearly see the spot where the Ings Beck meets a larger stream, the Swanside Beck, which hurried down a beautiful glen bordered on both sides with peaty banks on which flourished many large Oaks, Ash, Alders and clumps of thorny Hawthorn. Looking down stream, I could see we had now reached our goal, for partially hidden by the trees was a stone bridge on its high humped arch gracefully leaping across the beck. Pointing ahead, I shouted over to Alan, **"There's Monk's Bridge."** Yes, this little venerable packhorse bridge is known by not one, but by two names. Hereabouts it is known as Swanside Bridge, for it crosses the Swanside Beck; its alternative ecclesiastical name, Monk's Bridge, because it was evidently used by the Monks of nearby Whalley and Sawley Abbeys. My personal favourite name for the bridge is Monk's Bridge.

After hurrying along the extensive pebbly beaches and crawling beneath a barbed wire fence, we reached the east foot of the bridge where we were greeted by the fantastic display of a large clump of beautiful yellow daffodils sprouting at the side of the abutments. We both agreed the bridge was a truly amazing example of a picturesque packhorse bridge. The high humped arch comprised of roughly hewn slabs of local stone spans the beck in a leap of around twenty-two feet. The voussoir stones were cut from crudely worked sandstone blocks. The underside of the arch was covered in attractive, brownish lichens; green ferns emerged from cracks and crannies, and a large specimen plant of maiden hair spleenwort sprouted luxuriantly from a mini crevasse behind the downstream keystone. Hanging down also were a number of ghostly-looking stalactites. There were no parapets, and the six foot wide trackway over the top of the bridge was formed from pebbles set in mortar. From the bottom of the bridge on either side of the beck, we could easily make out the grass covered trackways, once trodden by the Jaggermen and their strings of laden packhorses.

We both heartily agreed, that Monk's Bridge was indeed a gem of an ancient packhorse bridge located in the truly, breathtakingly beautiful Ribble Valley.

The left image is the Lancashire and Yorkshire Railway Boundary Stone. On the right shows the Rimington & Middop signpost, our starting point. March 2010.

© Christine McEwen Collection.

THE FAIRY BRIDGE, CLOUGH BOTTOMS, NEAR BASHALL EAVES, CLITHEROE.

The Fairy Bridge spanning Bashall Brook at Clough Bottoms. June 2005.

© Christine McEwen Collection.

A few years earlier of our Monk's Bridge adventure, also in the Ribble Valley near to the small hamlet of Bashall Eaves, that stands on the banks of the River Hodder, Alan and I delighted in searching for another fascinating packhorse bridge – 'a saddle bridge' – called the Fairy Bridge, and hereabouts said to have been built in just one night by a host of kindly fairies in the act of assisting an old local woodcutter to cross the stream, who was being chased by witches from nearby Pendle Hill.

Small, high, humped-back packhorse bridges are uncommon, and are known as 'saddle bridges' due to the configuration of the structures usually jumping up high over small, narrow streams, and also due to having stone parapets. The structures therefore, lend themselves to the appearance of the wooden and leather pack-saddles used for the equal distribution of loads across the backs of packhorses.

This delightful gem of a bridge spans the Bashall Brook at Clough Bottoms near Bashall Eaves. This enchanting location with its dense overhanging foliage, and in spring and early summer carpets of dazzling, colourful wild flowers, many being rare species, is very much like the picture that one can imagine of a secret fairy dell.

When we visited the spot one pleasantly warm June afternoon in 2005, after walking to the bridge, Alan and I quickly divested ourselves of our walking boots and thick tweed stockings. We then sat down in the shade of overhanging trees among wild flowers on the bank of the stream, into which we immersed our hot, weary feet in the soothing, cool, refreshing water.

The Fairy Bridge consists of one segmental arch built of local gritstone which spans Bashall Brook in a high leap of around twenty-five feet; the width of the trackway is around four feet betwixt parapets of random stone, approximately three feet high at the ends, reducing down to around twenty four inches on the centreline of the hump. This fairy dell where the bridge is located can be reached by walking through a farm yard, then by following the brook downhill. This was a most memorable visit to a very lovely 'far from the madding crowd' sort of place.

LONGHOLME PACKHORSE BRIDGE, RAWTENSTALL, ROSSENDALE.

The double-arched Longholme Packhorse Bridge crossing the flooded River Irwell. September 2008.

© Christine McEwen Collection.

Rawtenstall is situated at an elevation of 825 feet, at the confluence of the River Irwell and the Limy Water, in the Rossendale Fells. Rawtenstall is derived from Anglo-Saxon meaning **'roaring pool or stream'**. During the Medieval Period, Rawtenstall was a vaccary – such as at Wycoller near Colne. The nearby village of Crawshawbooth that straddles Limy Water was a summertime shieling, later developing into a small village. The 'booths' and 'folds' that predominate all over Rossendale are indicators of this medieval pastoralism. During the late eighteenth and the early nineteenth centuries Rawtenstall developed to become an important Lancashire cotton town.

The Rossendale Valley is a deep cleft cut by glacial melt-waters into the Millstone Grit that over-burdens limestone, once the bed of an ancient sea, and is located in the Rossendale Fells at the western extremity of the Pennine range.

Due to the prevailing rain-laden westerlies that rip across the Manchester plain to become abruptly halted by the steeply rising uplands, the whole district of Rossendale has a significantly higher rainfall than either the Peak District to the south, or the Yorkshire Dales to the north. The highest hills rise to just 1,550 feet, the persistent wet climate however, leads to the creation of countless small cataracts and streams that cascade down the steep fell sides to join the River Irwell which, together with its tributaries, drain the valley during its long downhill journey to Manchester.

JAGGERMEN'S BRIDGES ON PACKHORSE TRAILS

Until around the early sixteenth century, the whole Rossendale Valley was densely covered in forests of Oak, Rowan, Alder, Ash and other native deciduous trees: it was known as the Forest of Rossendale. The often wet, boggy valley floor was virtually impassable being intersected by numerous fast-flowing streams. These boggy conditions were the haunt of robbers and other outlaws who preyed on anyone attempting to pass by.

From the early Medieval Period pack-horses would have been used for carrying all manner of goods throughout Rossendale. However, it was around the dawning of the sixteenth century that the first packhorse trackways were established, clinging high on the wind-swept shoulders of the valley above the thickly growing woodlands and the streams.

Packhorses carrying lime from Burnley and Clitheroe traversed the shoulders of the hills above Limy Water, a tributary stream of the Irwell, whilst making their way down through Craw-shawbooth, where an ancient stone packhorse bridge spanned the stream; from here the Jaggermen would lead their packhorses down into Rawtenstall where they would use the double-arched, Longholme Bridge over the Irwell, close to where the Limy Water merged into the larger river. Once safely across the deep waters of the Irwell, the packhorse trains would head south through Balladen, thence down the Irwell Valley to Bury and beyond.

Longholme double-arched packhorse bridge, probably built sometime in the sixteenth century was sited in the most convenient location on the Irwell near to the township of Rawtenstall. The bridge straddles the Irwell a few yards upstream of the confluence of the river and Limy Water, the structure's total span amounting to around forty-two feet. The whole bridge is built from random gritstone; the voussoir stones forming both arches are crudely hewn.

The arch on the Rawtenstall side of the Irwell has a span of twenty feet, whilst the other arch is twenty two feet. The trackway which is comprised of old flagstones and setts, having been rebuilt in recent years by the local authority, is ten feet wide betwixt the random stone walls, of the thirty seven inch high parapets. There is one substantially-built triangular-shaped cutwater formed from the centre pier on the upstream side.

Longholme Bridge, is without doubt, the oldest surviving packhorse bridge in Rossendale. It is a most appealing, ancient structure and during our regular visits to the district, we generally visit the bridge, where we stand on the trackway in awe of the *'roaring stream'* beneath our feet, as the turbulent Irwell thunders down the Rossendale Valley.

The triangular cutwater of the centre pier.

The neatly-laid old flagstones and sandstone setts laid by the local authority to form the trackway.

September 2008.

© Christine McEwen Collection.

Longholme Packhorse Bridge taken from a painting by Robin Sharples of Cowpe, Rossendale.

© With courtesy of artist Robin Sharples.

TOWN BRIDGE,
CROSTON, NEAR CHORLEY.

**The seventeenth century Town Bridge spanning the River Yarrow at Croston.
September 2007.**

© Christine McEwen Collection.

For quite a number of years whilst motoring over to friends who live near Southport, Alan and I have frequently driven past the charming, late seventeenth century, high-humped, stone packhorse bridge: Town Bridge, that spans the River Yarrow in Croston, a small, pleasantly located village of ancient mellow brick and gritstone houses.

This lovely old Grade II listed bridge, constructed of blocks of sandstone ashlar stands on the north side of St. Michael's Church. On the downstream parapet there is a date stone inscribed 1682. However, an old document records that the bridge was actually built in 1671 – and for just a few pence less than £30!

The single, segmental arch spans the River Yarrow in a graceful leap of thirty nine feet. Strengthening bands of iron are afixed by large bolts to both faces of the arch. The trackway over measures around eight feet, six inches between the parapets, which commence at either end from sixteen inches in height, extending to slightly over three feet high on the centreline. The attractive, cobbled trackway named 'The Hillocks' is still used by light motor vehicles. The slabby copings are connected together with leaded-in iron staples, both across the top and some connecting vertically down into the parapet walls.

My research into Croston Bridge informed me that the famous seventeenth century traveller and diarist, Celia Fiennes, chronicled the journey she made on horseback in 1698, whilst travelling between Wigan and Preston. In her diary she mentions: **"Passing bye many Vary Large Arches that were only Single ones .... they are but Narrow Bridges for Foote or Horse .... I passed bye at least a Dozen of these High Single Arches .... over their Greatest Rivers."**

JAGGERMEN'S BRIDGES ON PACKHORSE TRAILS

During the period of her journey, she would have encountered several streams and brooks, but the two largest rivers flowing between Wigan and Preston would have been the River Douglas and the River Yarrow. During the time of Celia Fiennes' travels, the majority of the land hereabouts would have been almost trackless, dangerous mossland and marsh. Therefore, you do not need a great deal of imagination to conclude that Celia Fiennes probably crossed over the Yarrow on Croston's Town Bridge. Undoubtedly, this woman was an immensely brave and inveterate traveller and explorer.

During one of our regular journeys through Croston, Alan and I purposely parked our car near the Grapes Inn. It was early September and we were blessed with beautiful sunny weather. We enjoyed a leisurely stroll around the village which included exploring the old bridge. The iron railings separating the busy road from the river were a riot of colour coming from the many suspended flower-filled planters. The bridge's parapet coping stones were also garlanded with fabulous displays of beautiful, multi-coloured flowers which were a delight to behold.

Croston's name is derived from Anglo Saxon and translates as 'The Town of the Preaching Cross'. A stone preaching cross was set up prior to A.D. 651. This ancient cross still survives and is set up in Church Street which has been rightly described as having one of the finest surviving rows of seventeenth century brick cottages in Lancashire. In earlier times, much of the flat, low lying area of west Lancashire was a huge lake which extended westwards from the Pennine foothills east of Chorley and Preston to cross the Lancashire plain to Southport on the coast. This vast lake was drained during the eighteenth century leaving behind excellent growing land.

Until the turnpike roads came through Croston in the late eighteenth and early nineteenth centuries, regular packhorse trains, carrying all manner of goods would cross Town Bridge as they travelled through the village which was an important cross-roads linking the principal towns and villages of central and west Lancashire.

Framed by beautiful flowers, the 1682 date stone at the apex of the bridge's parapets.
September 2007

© Christine McEwen Collection.

The attractive cobbled trackway, 'The Hillocks' over the bridge. September 2007

© Christine McEwen Collection.

Documents dated 1671 detailing the costs and labour involved during the construction of Town Bridge.

© By kind permission of Lancashire County Library and Information Service.

PRESTOLEE PACKHORSE BRIDGE, KEARSLEY, BOLTON.

The remarkable Prestolee Packhorse Bridge. To the rear is the all-dominating concrete utilities bridge and behind furthermore, the splendid Manchester, Bury and Bolton Canal Aqueduct. July 2006.

© Christine McEwen Collection.

Prestolee is a small, historic hamlet located on the north bank of the River Irwell amidst the nineteenth century industrial suburbs between Salford, Bolton, Radcliffe and Bury. The Manchester, Bolton and Bury Canal with its impressive Nob End locks and the magnificent aqueduct that carries the canal over the River Irwell are also within Prestolee.

Both the location and the configuration of Prestolee packhorse bridge, built between 1781 and 1803, are noteworthy. It spans the River Irwell, a cockstride upstream of the confluence with the smaller River Croal that flows down from Bolton. Within striking distance of each other, three bridges span the river.

Downstream, is the superb specimen of a packhorse bridge, built of well dressed local stone that spans the Irwell with five semi-circular arches springing from tall piers with triangular cutwaters on both the upstream and downstream sides. The total span is around one hundred and fifty feet, and the trackway between the forty-four inch high stone parapets, is five feet wide. Intriguingly carved on the inward facing stones of the upstream parapet, at around the centreline, is: PRESTOLEE BRIDGE C.C. together with other indecipherable wording.

I consider this packhorse bridge to be a most beautiful bridge, despite there being just a few feet away further upstream, a hideous concrete bowstring bridge that carries a large sewage pipe. This utility monstrosity was incongruously built between the ancient packhorse bridge and the equally attractive, stone aqueduct that carries the now defunct Manchester, Bury and Bolton Canal across the Irwell.

**The carved inscription on the stonework of the upstream parapet.
March 2010.**

© Christine McEwen Collection.

The River Irwell rises high in the Rossendale Fells above Bacup and during the Industrial Revolution was one of the most over-worked rivers in Britain. It has a notorious reputation for flooding, the water rising rapidly to great depths that thunder down the western flanks of the Pennines on its journey to Manchester. During its course, the Irwell is joined by a number of tributary rivers and streams: the Roch coming down from Rochdale merges with the Irwell near Bury and the River Croal flowing south-westerly from Bolton merges with the Irwell around a quarter of a mile downstream from the packhorse bridge.

The location of the packhorse bridge is within a curious muddle of semi-rural and industrial land, once heavily polluted by alkaline wastes dumped during the nineteenth century. Between the River Croal and the south approach trackway of the packhorse bridge, this whole area was occupied by the Prestolee Chemical Works, established in 1805 by Benjamin Rawson for the manufacturing of specialised textile bleaching and printing chemicals. In 1844, another chemical manufacturer, Edward Wilson took over the works, where he manufactured washing soda. This vast chemical works closed down in 1875, the buildings demolished and the site levelled.

During the seventy years of the chemical work's existence, significant quantities of alkaline wastes and effluents were disposed of by burying on the site. Overtime, despite this serious level of pollution, nature has played its restorative hand resulting in several types of uncommon wild flowers, including orchids, now flourishing hereabouts.

During the nineteenth century all along the banks of the Croal and the Irwell, the many collieries, cotton mills, papermaking factories, chemical works, gas-plants etc., dumped toxic chemicals and wastes into both rivers: gas-tar, gas-lime, paper sludge, colliery drainings. In 1860, the Irwell was described as, *'almost proverbial for the foulness of its waters; receiving the refuse of cotton factories, coal mines, print works, bleach works, dye works, chemical works, paper works, almost every kind of industry.'*

In 1862, the Scots geologist Hugh Miller described the River Irwell in his book: FIRST IMPRESSIONS: THE ENGLISH PEOPLE - as:

'The hapless river — a pretty enough stream a few miles higher up, with trees overhanging its banks, and fringes of green sedge set thick along its edges — loses caste as it gets among the mills and the print works.

JAGGERMEN'S BRIDGES ON PACKHORSE TRAILS

There are myriads of dirty things given it to wash, and whole waggon-loads of poisons from dye-houses and bleach yards thrown into it to carry away; steam-boilers discharge into it their seething contents, and drains and sewers their fetid impurities; till at length it rolls on — here between tall dingy walls, there under precipices of red sandstone — considerably less a river than a flood of liquid manure, in which all life dies, whether animal or vegetable, and which resembles nothing in nature, except, perhaps, the stream thrown out in eruption by some mud-volcano.'

Thankfully, today most of the pollution has disappeared leaving the waters of the Irwell and Croal considerably cleaner and, significantly clearer than they have been for over two hundred and fifty years. Now, there is fish aplenty, herons, mute swans, kingfishers together with many species of ducks and geese regularly frequent both rivers.

One sunkissed Sunday morning in July 2006 with the sky a brilliant azure and with the promise of viewing Prestolee packhorse bridge and glimpsing perchance a rare flowering orchid, it did not take much to entice Alan to accompany me on a trip to Prestolee.

After an uneventful trip down to Bolton we parked in Moses Gate Country Park to enjoy a wonderful stroll through the Beech tree lined banks of the River Croal, which is truly a wildlife haven. Near to where the Croal unites with the River Irwell, we walked across a mini-wilderness of scrub Willow and Hawthorn towards the packhorse bridge and its incongruous, neighbouring sewage pipe bridge, that we automatically recognised from the photographs we carried. Beneath our feet was the site of the former Prestolee Chemical Works, and there were masses of colourful wild flowers: brown knapweed, moon daisies, horseshoe vetch, star-of-bethlehem ..... and many beautiful, cowslips of the deepest yellow.

The splayed approach of Prestolee Packhorse Bridge from the village side. March 2010.

© Christine McEwen Collection.

JAGGERMEN'S BRIDGES ON PACKHORSE TRAILS

We arrived at the southern end of the packhorse bridge, where upon I sat down in the shade of a massive, venerable Willow.

Clutching camera and note book, Alan gingerly clambered down a dangerous, derelict broken-down stone wall to reach the river bank, about twenty feet below. I could just make out his mop of silver-white hair as he cut his way with a stick through the shoulder-height, densely growing Himalayan balsam with their beautiful pinkish flowers that smothered both banks of the Irwell.

We spent a couple of very pleasant hours in glorious sunshine surveying and photographing, not only the packhorse bridge, but the Manchester, Bury and Bolton aqueduct, which in itself is a remarkable feat of bridge engineering.

On the Prestolee village side of the bridge, the former packhorse trackway had become a well-used bridleway; the route originally, would have headed down to Salford and Manchester. In the opposite direction the Jaggermen's packhorse trains would have taken locally mined coal to the mills of Radcliffe, Bury and Bolton.

Clearly, Prestolee Packhorse Bridge was a significant crossing point on the Irwell for the Jaggermen's packhorse trains prior to the opening of the Manchester, Bury and Bolton Canal in the 1790s. It is probable, that for several following decades the packhorses delivered to and also collected goods from the canal barges.

Photograph taken November 1928 of Prestolee Packhorse Bridge, and at the rear the MB&B Canal Aqueduct. Note the bowstring bridge carrying the sewer pipe has not yet been constructed.

© By courtesy of Manchester, Bury and Bolton Canal Society.

LAD HILL PACKHORSE BRIDGE, GREENFIELD, SADDLEWORTH, OLDHAM.

The picture post card of Lad Hill Packhorse Bridge spanning the River Chew in Greenfield, and displaying the unusual, massive, rough-hewn, gritstone parapets.

© By kind permission of David Ford, Oldham.

One bright, chilly January morning there was a loud knock on the kitchen door. On opening it, stood there huddled in a heavy woollen winter coat was my close friend Sue, **"Good morning Christine, I've brought you a little present,"** she said, whilst hurrying past me into the warmth of my kitchen. Dipping inside her coat, she pulled out a plastic envelope, one of those protective transparent types, used for storing photographs, stamps or old coins. Sue, deftly opened up the envelope to extricate an old post card depicting a picture of a stone packhorse bridge. **"Last week Christine, I was rummaging in the post card box of a second-hand bookshop down in Manchester, and out popped this post card of an old looking stone bridge. With knowing that you collect pictures of old bridges, I purchased the card for the princely sum of £2.50,"** she said smilingly. I warmly informed her how delighted I was in receiving such an interesting post card, and particularly because it featured a packhorse bridge. So after us both enjoying a warming cup of tea and a slice of hot oat cake, I thanked her again and because she was in a hurry to sort out other matters, off she went home.

Unfortunately, Sue's post card actually turned out to be relatively modern, but nonetheless, was extremely interesting and featured an artist's impression in the form a painting of a stone packhorse bridge in the Saddleworth village of Greenfield. Also in the picture was a row of old stone cottages forming a background to the bridge with stark winter denuded trees, the whole scene overshadowed by high snow-covered hills. I couldn't wait for Alan to come home, so that I could show him Sue's interesting post card.

JAGGERMEN'S BRIDGES ON PACKHORSE TRAILS

Later that afternoon, after Alan had closely studied the post card for several minutes, looking up, he said, **"Greenfield is a small Pennine village in Saddleworth located on the old West Riding side of Oldham. This packhorse bridge looks most interesting; I suggest we have a run down there tomorrow morning to take a look."**

At around ten o'clock next morning, following us experiencing some hair-raising and rather tricky driving conditions over the snow-covered and icy Pennine village roads for a distance of around forty five miles, we eventually arrived in the small hill village of Greenfield, which was dominated by high, encircling snowy hills. After stopping to study our map, we then drove down Oak View Road and headed steeply down into the bottom of the Chew Valley.

With the bright wintry sunshine dazzling our eyes, looking ahead through the windscreen I suddenly saw just ahead the unmistakable outline of an old packhorse bridge spanning the river. Parking the car nearby, and clutching our cameras, a long tape measure and notebooks, we headed over to the curious-looking old stone bridge. Alan pulled from the inside pocket of his jacket, a photocopy of the packhorse bridge post card that Sue had kindly presented to me.

"By Golly, where we are now standing is the exact position as shown in the picture," enthused Alan, his eyes studying the scene before us of the bridge, the cottages and the dominating snowy hills behind, just like on the post card. Since making the decision to visit the bridge, the studying of several historic tomes had revealed the packhorse bridge was actually called Lad Hill Bridge.

In fantastic, bright sunlight, we both spent an unforgettable and most enjoyable hour taking pictures from all angles of Lad Hill Bridge, and then using the long metal tape measure we set to recording the dimensions of this ancient, interesting stone structure. Alan was so intent on photographing the underside of the bridge's double arches, that when he stepped on what he considered to be a mud-covered stone, his polished brown brogue and trouser leg up to his knee suddenly disappeared in deep, smelly mud causing him to fall forwards towards the fast-flowing deep water. He was, however, fortunate

because there was a rusty iron bracket bolted to the bridge abutment, which he quickly grabbed, otherwise he would have fallen into the river.

Subsequently, we discovered Lad Hill Bridge, had been constructed in the early eighteenth century as a packhorse bridge to enable the frequent, heavily ladened packhorse trains coming over the high watershed from the Huddersfield area of Yorkshire to cross the River Chew that roared down the Chew Valley. In 1781, the inhabitants of the hamlets of Lordsmere and Shawmere were prosecuted by the West Riding authorities for not maintaining,

'This bridge over a certain rivulet called Greenfield Water in the pack and primeway from Marsden to Mottram'.

Fortunately, the poor, hapless people were found not guilty.

My survey of the bridge revealed that it is built from Millstone Grit in the form of a double-arch spanning the River Chew in a leap of forty-five feet. The width of the trackway across the top between the massive, rough-hewn gritstone parapets is eleven feet. I feel these bizarre-looking, nine inch thick by thirty eight inches high parapets, despite them being chunky, con-siderably enhance the appearance of this striking old packhorse bridge.

Due to them being stood on top of a row of horizontally laid slabs, we both consider these parapets had been added subsequent to the date of the bridge's construction, perhaps in the early nineteenth century when it would be used regularly, not only by the packhorse trains, but also daily by crowds of workers crossing to the nearby busy cotton mills. To safeguard these pedestrians from falling into the Chew, particularly on dark, winter nights, it is probable this is the reason the massive stone parapets were added.

Currently, the bridge, which for a number of years has been used for vehicular traffic with a maximum gross weight of five tonnes, recently has been reduced to three tonnes.

Alan and I were really satisfied with our winter morning's expedition to find Lad Hill Packhorse Bridge, which I did not know existed, prior to my friend Sue bringing me the post card. Undoubtedly, it is a superb specimen of an historic Pennine packhorse bridge to which the people of Greenfield should be proud.

Close-up photograph showing the massive, roughly-hewn, gritstone parapets.
January 2010.

Taken from upstream, double-arched Lad Hill Packhorse Bridge. It is unfortunate the
large iron water pipes crossing in front of the structure spoil the image of this attractive,
historic bridge. January 2010.

© Christine McEwen Collection.

NORTHUMBERLAND AND COUNTY DURHAM

COAL

Lying to the north-east of the main spine of the Northern Pennines are the former Northumberland and Durham coalfields and the industrial towns of the Tyne, Wear and Tees valleys which the locally mined coal and the vast quantities of iron, lead and other minerals helped to create.

From the Tudor period, throughout the region, huge quantities of quality coal were mined from hundreds of small pits, known as bell pits, and later numerous large collieries. Trains of packhorses carried the valuable coal down to the shipping staithes at Newcastle and Sunderland. From the seventeenth century Tyneside and Wearside colliery owners had established a lucrative trade in seaborne coal which was carried to London and other south-eastern towns in colliers.

GALENA, LEAD-ORE

As in the Yorkshire Dales, the mining of lead in Northumberland and County Durham was immensely important; the high Pennine fells at the head of Weardale and at the top of the South Tyne valley were from earliest times extensively mined for galena, lead-ore, which lay in abundance beneath the surface of the wild, remote moorlands.

The lead-ore was loaded onto scores of packhorse trains which conveyed hundreds of tons on a yearly basis to smelt mills, such as Langley Lead Smelt Mill near Hexham. In the north east, the packhorses were locally called 'Caraways'; the name being derived from 'Carrier-Galloways' – alluding to the Galloway breed of small, extremely strong ponies used as packhorses. The horses were often fitted with muzzles to stop them grazing on the lead mine spoil heaps that could contain extremely toxic substances such as lead and arsenic that could poison and kill the animals.

It was the Romans who first extracted lead-ore from the high, wild moorlands around Alston on the modern County Durham/Cumbria border.

The development of the lead mining industry in the North Pennines did not seriously commence until the continuous harrying of the region by violent, bloodthirsty Scottish reivers ceased, resulting from the union of the Scottish and English thrones in 1603.

During the following two hundred years, numerous packhorse trails and rough roads that criss-crossed the Pennine summits were regularly used for the conveying of lead-ore, and also other ores, such as silver and iron. Other valuable ores extracted were: barites, fluorspar, witherite and zinc. As elsewhere, limestone was also quarried and burnt in lime kilns to make lime. As the lead-ore fields were developed, a number of important packhorse tracks ranged over the hills from Alston and Stanhope and down to the other important market towns of the North Pennines in Cumbria, County Durham and Northumberland.

The use of packhorse trains for the carrying of lead-ore, and coal rapidly became significantly important for the economies of Northumberland and County Durham. Smelted lead was manufactured into water pipes, lead sheet for weather-proofing roofs and for making musket balls etc.

Strings of up to twenty-four packhorses, their panniers bulging with lead-ore carried this mineral wealth from the lead mines high on Alston Moor and also around the head of Weardale down to Stella on the River Tyne, just to the west of Blaydon for smelting.

THE LEAD ROAD

Located in the Pennine foothills west of Gateshead is the small attractive village of Greenside which sits astride the historic 'Lead Road': the packhorse trackway that links the lead-ore and silver producing areas of the North Pennines to Stella near Blaydon on the River Tyne. In the eighteenth and nineteenth centuries many of the Jaggermen, the packhorse operators, lived in Greenside. The Jaggermen would regularly lead their packhorse trains loaded with either lead-ore or silver-ore, extracted from the mines located in the remote, desolate, high altitude moorlands, and wend their way over the crude, rough tracks to the village of Slaley, then onto the trackway known as the 'Lead Road' to Greenside and eventually to the refining or smelt mills at Stella. To the north-west the Lead Road climbs higher into the Pennines heading towards Allendale, which together with Blanchland was one of the most productive lead-mining areas hereabouts during the seventeenth and eighteenth centuries.

JAGGERMEN'S BRIDGES ON PACKHORSE TRAILS

In the middle of the twelfth century, this ancient trackway passing through Greenside, was known as 'Ledeshepeswaye' – referring, no doubt to the numerous lead mine spoil heaps that would be alongside harking back into pre-medieval times. Lead was so important, that in 1694, the Ryton Lead Company established a Lead Smelt Mill in Greenside.

THE NORTH PENNINE LEAD DISTRICTS

Between around the middle of the eighteenth century and about 1850, the mining of lead had become one of the most important industries of the North of England, with Britain being the predominant producer of lead and lead products in the world.

The extensive lead-ore districts of the North Pennines comprising the South Tyne Valley, Weardale, Teesdale and the Derwent Valley, together with the neighbouring lead mines of the Yorkshire Dales at Swaledale and Arkengarthdale, formed the most significant lead mining area in the whole of Britain.

Evidently, it was the Romans who pioneered the extraction of lead-ore within the region and the valuable ore was also mined during the early Middle-Ages. The Prince Bishops of Durham also extracted lead and some silver ores from the upper, remote reaches of Weardale. During the sixteenth century, Sir William Bower owned a great many of the lead mines in Weardale and Teesdale, including a Lead Smelt Mill.

It was not, however, until the late decades of the seventeenth century that the lead industry developed and prospered.

It is recorded that in 1684, the Blackett family, Tyneside coal magnates, owned extensive lead mines in the Allendales, near to Hexham, Northumberland. Several years later and this important coal and lead-mine owning family leased from the Bishop of Durham land rich in lead-ore in Weardale. Some of the more important lead mines owned by the Blackett's included: Burtree Pasture, Weardale; Coalcleugh at West Allen, and Allen Heads mine.

From 1696, The London Lead Company were busily engaged winning lead-ore from beneath the wild, remote Alston Moor, and in the eighteenth century were extensively extracting lead-ore from mines in the Derwent Valley, and Weardale and Teesdale. The company operated the lead mines in Teesdale until they closed in 1905.

WHAT WAS LEAD USED FOR?

The burgeoning towns and cities of Britain and Europe from earliest times and particularly so during the Industrial Revolution stimulated an ever increasing demand for lead products such as: lead sheet for weatherproofing roofs of buildings; early castles and monastic buildings used lead sheet for roofs and rainwater drain pipes and also for decorative works.

Lead could be readily cast into multifarious forms, and lead water piping could be manufactured by pouring the molten lead into moulds, or could be produced by rolling lead sheet around a cylindrical form and soldering the joint. Lead was used for the manufacture of paint, the production of lead-shot and was increasingly employed in glazing. The metal was therefore, immensely useful.

As the lead industry developed, Lead Smelt Mills were established along the River Tyne at places like Elswick, Hebborn, Blaydon, Bill Quay and Byker Bridge. Refined lead, originally mined in Teesdale and Weardale was transported by packhorse trains from Newcastle to all corners of Britain.

BASIC LEAD MINING PROCEDURES

From earliest times man has dug holes into lead-rich ground, generally known due to the distinctive shape, as 'bell-pits'. When lead-ore was found outcropping close to the surface, the lead-ore was won by 'hushing'. The hushing method involved damming nearby streams and watercourses to form large pounds.

Once a large catchment of water was established, the pound would be breached causing a significant volume of fast-flowing water to wash away the over-lying peat and sub-soil thus exposing the veins of lead-ore. Many of these hushings created huge, man-made valleys which could be several thousand yards long by over a hundred feet deep. A number of easily recognised hushings can still be seen in parts of Weardale.

The mining of lead and other metaliferous ores was also carried out by driving tunnels known as levels into steeply sloping hillsides to follow veins of ore. The miners would lay down rails made of timber in the levels, which were used for hauling small-wheeled tubs loaded with the lead-ore, out of the mines.

THE TYNESIDE AND WEARSIDE SALT INDUSTRY

Ever since the Middle Ages, and up to the mid-nineteenth century the manufacture of salt by boiling brine-laden water had been among the most important industries of Tyne and Wear. South Shields had enjoyed the distinction of being the most prominent producer of salt since 1448, but the town and its surrounding environment continually suffered due to the terrible pollution created by the salt-boiling process.

Both North and South Shields operated around two hundred salt pans in 1767, the furnaces set beneath the huge iron salt pans consumed a staggering one thousand tons of coal per year, which created horrendous, polluting smoke and highly corrosive fumes that repeatedly enveloped the town.

Salt production was also carried out at Sunderland, the earliest record being in 1511. In nearby Offerton in 1589, a coal pit was sunk for the specific purpose of fuelling the brine-boiling pans at Sunderland.

The Tyneside chemical industry's early development directly springs from when John Losh set up his brine boiling works in 1798. Losh purchased a regular supply of brine-rich water which had been pumped out of the Walker coal pits. Subsequently Losh Brothers, as the firm became, would expand overtime to ultimately manufacture over fifty per cent of the soda ash in England.

At Blyth, the official records of the Custom House mention that in the Michaelmas quarter of 1723, a prodigious quantity amounting to almost two thousand tons of locally produced salt was exported from the small harbour at Cullercoats. The salt came from extensive batteries of salt pans, all heated by coal, located along the foreshore on the north side of the bay.

SEATON BURN SALT PANS AND THE SALTER'S PETH

Salt had been produced by the boiling of seawater-filled pans made of lead on the beaches located at the mouth of Seaton Burn since the Middle Ages.

During the seventeenth century, due to high demand for salt, the local salt industry rapidly expanded. Large lead and iron pans were filled with salt water taken from the sea and boiled continuously, until the water had fully evaporated leaving behind salt; the fuel being locally mined coal.

The evaporation of sea water to produce salt died out at Seaton Burn during the nineteenth century which mainly resulted from cheaper salt being introduced into the North-East from Cheshire.

At Seaton Burn, an ancient track leading inland was known for hundreds of years as: 'Salter's Peth' – i.e. Salter's Path.

The 'Peths' as the Tynesiders and Wearsiders called the ancient pathways were regularly used by strings of between a dozen and fifteen Galloway packhorses for carrying the salt, and for centuries had been well travelled by the Jaggermen and their packhorses.

The combined carrying weight of the two salt panniers that each horse carried amounted to approximately 130 lbs. The panniers were strapped to the horses by wide leather belts. The strings of packhorses once loaded would walk along the Salter's Peth in single file due to the narrowness of the path. The leading horse, the 'Bell Horse' would be at the front, with its seven polished brass bells handing from leather straps around its neck jingling to warn oncoming packhorse trains.

SALTER'S BRIDGE AT SOUTH GOSFORTH

An intriguing thirteenth century stone bridge known as Salter's Bridge spans the Ouse Burn at South Gosforth. Its name originates from its location on the centuries old - 'Salter's Peth' - which originally ran from Hartley's salt evaporating pans up to Blanchland. This route which runs through Gosforth, would be used for several hundred years by the countless packhorse trains used to carry coal from one direction for heating the salt pans and on their return, to convey the newly produced salt to market.

Salter's Bridge, despite being widened from its original seven feet width, is in striking condition, and the majority of its thirteenth century stonework still survives.

For perhaps over three hundred years the North-East salt industry was highly productive, generating much wealth from its virtual monopoly of the salt trade. When cheaper salt of a substantially higher quality commenced its appearance into Tyneside, Wearside and Teesside due to the development of the railways, the North-East salt trade went into rapid decline.

This decline in the traditional production of salt, inevitably and moreover sadly, led to the disappearance of the strings of Jaggermen's packhorses that regularly travelled the ancient Salter's Peths.

DEEPDALE PACKHORSE BRIDGE, NEAR BARNARD CASTLE, CO. DURHAM.

Splendid Deepdale Bridge built in 1699 by William Hutchinson. June 2008.

© Christine McEwen Collection.

We were conveniently placed for locating this amazing old packhorse bridge because earlier that day we had attended the Barnard Castle Steam Traction Engine Show, therefore, following the information off a moth-eaten old map of the Deepdale area of County Durham, we found ourselves following a stony, rutted farm track leading up into the wilds of Teesdale.

Eventually, arriving in a large farmyard, our sudden appearance creating much consternation and panic amongst the chickens and geese that squawked, crowed and hissed, as well as a handful of Border collies, who's incessant barking resonated from the surrounding farm buildings.

Leaving Alan in the car, I nervously walked up to the stout front door of an eighteenth century, mullion-windowed cottage. I felt somewhat anxious due to the loud disturbance

our arrival had created amongst the farm animals. It was also a Saturday afternoon; the farmer may well have been with his feet up, mug of tea in hand, taking a well-earned rest.

The door opened to reveal a friendly young woman who turned out to be the farmer's wife. Quickly, I unreservedly apologised for the barking and squawking noises we had created, and then asked if we may park our car within the farmyard for maybe an hour while we explored the old bridge which our map informed was located in a limestone gill somewhere to the rear of the farm.

"Why aye, nae problem, you're very welcome", replied the lady in the lovely Teesdale dialect. She then directed me to position our car in a corner of the farmyard, where there was an iron gate, through which we should pass into the meadow behind the farm.

Once through the gate, we headed downhill over lush grass and yellow buttercups towards a beautiful beck flowing over a bed of huge limestone slabs. Five minutes later, with the delightful sound of busy, gurgling water and the mournful bleating of the sheep and lambs that were scattered all over the surrounding fells, we reached a remarkable specimen of an old stone packhorse bridge.

And what a truly superb little stone bridge it was, its segmental high arch spanning across beautiful Deepdale Beck in a leap of about thirty three feet. The bridge was built in 1699 of local random stone, the trackway width between the crude, yet attractive thirty inch parapets was a smidgen over five feet. Both parapets project out a few inches on either side of the front face of the arch's neatly dressed voussoir stones.

A local fellow, William Hutchinson of Melroo, who must have come from wealthy stock, played a hand in the building of this fine looking bridge, for he provided the finance for its construction. Local legend spins that when Hutchinson was a young boy, he almost drowned in the beck, which at the time was in full spate. Evidently, someone came to his aid and rescued him. To commemorate the saving of the young man's life, there is a large stone tablet set into the downstream parapet wall, onto which is a carved inscription:

> *'William Hutchinson of Melroo*
> *Esquire. Whose great charity was*
> *Most exemplary in all Respects.*
> *So likewise in the building this*
> *Bridge at Cragg, the place of his*
> *Most happy nativity, which was*
> *Built August 1699.*
> *Edward Addison fecit.'*

It is a pity that the inscription is now virtually indecipherable due to weathering.

Carefully avoiding several monster-sized clumps of ubiquitous stinging nettles that grew profusely around the bridge, both Alan and I, cameras in hand, trampled innocently through a bed of thickly growing wild garlic, causing the air to rapidly become pervaded with the delicious aroma of ramsons. As I like to use this wonderful plant during cooking, I managed to bag myself a large handful of the wild garlic.

We explored the packhorse bridge's immediate surroundings and discovered a distinct 'holloway', which probably had been worn into the surface of the ground by packhorses on the trackway leading northwest up the fell side to High Crag. After thanking the farmer's jovial wife, we set off to drive the short distance to locate another packhorse bridge close to the enigmatic ruins of twelfth century Egglestone Abbey.

The original random stones forming the trackway over the bridge. June 2008.

© Christine McEwen Collection.

JAGGERMEN'S BRIDGES ON PACKHORSE TRAILS

EGGLESTONE ABBEY PACKHORSE BRIDGE

The 17th century Egglestone Abbey Packhorse Bridge spanning Thorsgill Beck. June 2008.

© Christine McEwen Collection.

After arriving at Egglestone Abbey we parked in a convenient stony area, on aptly named Abbey Lane. The ruins of the Abbey are in a dominating position, high on a flat-topped hill with commanding views of the mighty River Tees that thunders down the rocky gorge at its feet. Nearby, was the next bridge I wished to visit, Egglestone Abbey Bridge that crosses Thorsgill Beck at the foot of the hill onto which stands the Abbey.

We found the bridge to be robustly built of dressed local stone; the almost semi-circular arch spans the beck in a leap of twenty seven feet. The width of the trackway over the top is sixty-six inches; the surface appears to be original and constructed of water-worn pebbles. The parapets are eighteen inches high and appear to have been partially reconstructed from small, random stones in place of the dressed ashlar stones that form the main part of the original abutments and voussoirs. There is also evidence of similar rebuilding work to the outer wings of the abutments, with some parts of the stonework being loose. Egglestone Abbey Bridge forms part of an ancient trackway linking historic Barnard Castle and Rokeby on the south bank of the River

Tees. This is a bonny little bridge in the historic and beautiful surroundings of Teesdale.

Because I wanted to visit yet another historic little bridge, located at West Hope, a hamlet perched high on the fells between Teesdale and Arkengarthdale, I was forced to almost physically drag Alan away from his exploration of the amazing carved, pointed stone arches, and other fascinating structures at the Abbey.

WEST HOPE BRIDGE

Shortly after leaving Egglestone Abbey we drove west along the fast, traffic-clogged A66 trunk road which links the North East to the Lake District, battling for space with the huge juggernauts, their powerful engines growling as they tackled the severe inclines of the road heading uphill towards the Cumbrian border. Turning left onto the Stang Road, we commenced climbing the narrow and winding uphill route, heading towards the huge conifer plantations of Stang Forest. With Alan driving and myself with map in hand acting as navigator, on arriving at a narrow lane supporting a sign that read West Hope, I instructed him to turn left.

Avoiding what we considered to be large numbers of 'death wish' pheasants, who repeatedly kept darting out from the dark road side conifer plantations, within a half mile, we came to the tiny secluded hamlet of West Hope.

Driving slowly forward around a large stone barn, we were suddenly delighted with the sight of a diminutive, parapet-less stone bridge, spanning a tiny gurgling beck. Surmounting the structure was a modern timber footbridge complete with handrail. I was sad to see this rather incongruous, although safe modern bridge, which unfortunately spoiled the character of the historic, tiny packhorse bridge.

The shallow segmental arched bridge built of local gritstone spans Waitgill Beck in a throw of around twelve feet. The trackway is about forty-two inches wide and is composed of the arch stones only, onto which are laid flat stone slabs. West Hope lies on a series of criss-crossing old trackways betwixt Bowes and Richmond, both important, historic market towns.

Whilst I just loved the tiny little packhorse bridge, actually, I was really pleased when we drove away from West Hope, for on the sunny, hot afternoon of our visit, there appeared to be millions of tiny biting midges, microscopic creatures with voracious appetites for gnawing at the exposed flesh of arms and faces resulting in itchy, painful lumps. These creatures came out of the conifer plantations in droves to land on Alan and me.

Thankfully, soon we were driving on the 1800 feet high road over Hope Moor, with not a tree or bush to be seen for miles, and with the sweet fragrance of the heather and a cool, comforting breeze.

Three fantastic, old packhorse bridges in one day. I was delighted.

The author standing on the wooden footbridge which surmounts historic West Hope Bridge. June 2008.

© Christine McEwen Collection.

MORE DURHAM BRIDGES, CLOW BECK, KETTON, HEADLAM

Clow Beck Packhorse Bridge near Croft-on-Tees. March 2010.

© Christine McEwen Collection.

CLOW BECK BRIDGE

On a beautiful sunny, pleasantly warm, spring morning, after driving sixty odd miles through the Yorkshire Dales towns and villages of Kettlewell, Leyburn, and Richmond, we arrived in the attractive mellow stone-built village of Croft-on-Tees near Darlington. We considered this a wonderful opportunity to view Croft Bridge which spans the River Tees, dates from 1356 and ranks amongst the oldest and grandest in Northern England being situated on the historic border between North Yorkshire and County Durham. This amazing structure built of local stone has seven striking, pointed Gothic arches which gradually increase in height to the centreline of each arch. Due to recent rapid melting of heavy snow on the high Pennine hills to the west, the river flowing beneath the bridge was severely swollen with deep, peat-coloured water that swept downstream at an alarming rate.

We drove along a pleasant, narrow lane bordered on our left by well-groomed gardens, while to our right extensive meadows swept down towards Clow Beck close to where it rushed to meet the swollen Tees. After driving around half a mile west of Croft-on-Tees, we arrived at Monk End Farm which stood on the east bank of Clow Beck. Here, almost hidden behind several massive steel doors that form a flood barrier, we discovered what we considered to be was a curious looking specimen of a two-arched packhorse bridge; Clow Beck Bridge. A few yards upstream there was a substantial modern concrete ford that was probably used by local farm traffic.

JAGGERMEN'S BRIDGES ON PACKHORSE TRAILS

On exploring the bridge, we noticed that the arches were well divided from each other, which to the casual observer could almost give the impression of there being two bridges, which in fact they once were. It is a consideration that the larger twelve foot span arch at the western side of the beck formed the original bridge, and what is now the mid-stream pier was the original buttress supporting the arch, with perhaps a stone causeway joining it to the east bank. The small seven feet span arch was evidently constructed in place of the stone causeway, perhaps much later in the bridge's history. Both arches are divided by a wide stony mound of alluvial material, now covered with grass and young trees. The whole bridge is constructed from random local sandstone with small quantities of old handmade bricks mixed into the structure, and spans the beck in a leap of about sixty-two feet.

The trackway over the bridge is surfaced with river bed pebbles and compacted earth; the width betwixt the sixteen inch high stone parapets is fifty-five inches narrowing at the west end to forty-eight inches. The pentagonal-shaped parapet copings are stapled with wrought iron. Some of the original coping stones at the east end have been replaced with concrete.

The bridge was probably used for crossing Clow Beck by packhorses transporting goods from south of the River Tees and west of Croft-on-Tees whilst journeying to Darlington. Once in Croft-on-Tees they would cross the river by using fourteenth century Croft Bridge.

As a result of our survey of this unusual historic packhorse bridge, our thoughts were that the structure is crying out for some maintenance work, mainly involving re-pointing and the rebuilding of the upstream buttress.

KETTON PACKHORSE BRIDGE, NEAR DARLINGTON

Ketton Packhorse Bridge in its strange, secluded location, 100 yards away from the river. March 2010.

© Christine McEwen Collection.

By the time we departed Croft-on-Tees, it had become quite windy. To avoid driving through busy Darlington town centre, we instead drove a circuitous route round the outskirts on a bewildering number of roads heaving with gigantic lorries. Eventually, we arrived in the small, pleasant farming hamlet of Ketton out in the countryside, to the north of the town.

Following our instructions of the bridge's location, subsequent to driving down a lengthy farm road, we stopped in front of several huge farm buildings standing on our right. Looking down a narrow, un-metalled farm track which sported a sign reading PRIVATE ROAD, and which passed between the farm buildings, Alan and I simultaneously sighted Ketton Bridge, which was located a field length past the farm house and through a steel gate at the bottom of the track. *"I think I'll go and find the farmer to obtain permission for us to drive down to the bridge,"* said Alan.

Leaving me with the car, he then disappeared into one of the huge concrete and wriggly tin barns, where the sound of a massive diesel tractor engine was noisily ticking over. Within a few minutes, Alan arrived back with a triumphant grin. *"Job's a good'un love. Eeh what a right pleasant young chap, the farmer is. He gave permission for us to drive down his farm track to the bridge."*

Once past the farmhouse, and with me struggling to open and then close the heavy metal field gate, we shortly arrived and parked the car at the side of a huge old Ash tree close to the old stone bridge. We both considered that the bridge appeared rather a strange spectacle, for there was not the merest trickle of water passing beneath the arch.

We noticed a square cast iron sign mounted upon a stone block at the foot of the bridge's trackway. Cast in bold lettering was the legend:

KETTON
ROAD
ENDS
HERE

Evidently, there are a number of these interesting and intriguing old cast iron signs hereabouts, which local legend mentions were erected by barrister, John Trotter some time during the nineteenth century to denote the limitation of responsibility of the Ketton Hall Estate regarding the maintenance of what was then, an important and busy trackway. The name Ketton harks back to the times of Durham's warlike Prince Bishops and was associated with warfare, fighting and much blood-letting. The Prior of Durham during this period maintained a Grange at Ketton for weary travellers. In the early nineteenth century, Ketton Hall was the home of the famous Ketton ox and a prize shorthorn cow named Comet, which was pride to world famous cattle breeders, the Colling Brothers. This famous shorthorn cow, Comet, died in 1815 and was buried with some pomp and ceremony at nearby Cleasby. The animal's remains were however, later exhumed and were deposited for all to see in Darlington Museum.

Ketton Packhorse Bridge is a scheduled ancient monument, and was probably constructed in the early seventeenth century. The bridge crossed the River Skerne until the river was re-routed sometime during the nineteenth century. Once this obvious major civil engineering work was completed, Ketton Packhorse Bridge was left in its secluded position on the edge of several fields and around one hundred yards from the river.

The bridge is constructed from coursed local limestone with dressed sandstone voussoir stones of the arch. The single segmental arch has a span of twenty-four feet and the overall length of the structure is around sixty feet. The cobbled trackway width betwixt the twenty-five inch parapets of rough stone blocks measures around five feet, and appears to be original. All around the bridge are extensive cattle and sheep pastures. There is also a trackway locally known as Salters Lane that once passed over the bridge. This historic title is an indicator that salt, produced in boiling pans sited on the Durham coast at South Shields and Greatham was carried by packhorses along the trackway and over Ketton Bridge. Unfortunately, in recent years the bridge sustained serious damage to the parapet nearest to the farm road by a huge delivery lorry.

**The interesting 19th century
cast iron sign.
March 2010.**

© Christine McEwen Collection.

JAGGERMEN'S BRIDGES ON PACKHORSE TRAILS

HEADLAM BRIDGE

Headlam Bridge spanning Dynance Beck. March 2010.

© Christine McEwen Collection

A short hop across the A1M motorway to the west of Darlington delivered us into the delightful surroundings of Headlam village, with sixteenth century Headlam Hall, whose frontage extensively swathed in carpets of delicate, nodding snowdrops welcomed us.

Looking across the rough grass of the village green attractively framed on the south and west sides with eighteenth century white painted, old stone cottages with orange pantiled roofs, we could see the little packhorse bridge built of local stone, its arched structure poking up through last year's lank grass.

This late seventeenth or early eighteenth century bridge spans Dynance Beck, a sluggish stream that snakes its way through marshy ground amongst stands of Grey Alders, Willows and Hawthorn. The span of the bridge is nine feet and the width of the trackway betwixt the stubby fourteen inch parapets is sixty-eight inches. A prominent feature is the large, roughly-hewn voussoir stones. On either end of the structure a stone causeway, now grass covered, leads onto the bridge.

Another lovely ancient stone bridge in a beautiful location.

CUMBRIA - AN EXCURSION INTO LAKELAND'S INDUSTRIAL PAST.

The thousands of holiday makers, fellwalkers, back-packers, and other devotees of the magnificently stunning Lake District, do not usually associate industry with this region of outstanding natural beauty.

With its shimmering lakes, its dense, ancient deciduous woodlands, historic villages, and characterful slate-built hamlets within the broad bottomed dales and the encircling towering jagged peaks of the mountains, Lakeland is undoubtedly one of the most popular holiday destinations in Britain.

In regard to the Lake District's industrial past, the fact is, that for several centuries man has farmed the abundant Lakeland pastures, coppiced and felled the trees for the production of manufactured goods; dug deep into the steep mountainous slopes for coal and minerals; dammed the numerous becks and streams to feed water-wheel powered mills for the manufacture of wooden bobbins and gun-powder; or for driving, crushing and pulping machinery in bark and logwood mills; powering the stamps on lead-ore dressing floors and providing power for sawmills, slate and limestone quarries; and for numerous iron-working sites, copper and other metaliferous mines.

Over two hundred years ago, before many adventurers and curious visitors ventured into the English Lake District, surprisingly, industrial activity was widely scattered with quarrying and mining, iron-making, charcoal production and diverse other manufacturing trades being in full swing all over the dales, mountain sides and lake shores across this beautiful region of Britain.

In the dense Birch, Alder and Oak woodlands that clothed the slopes of the south Lakeland hills, expert wood-turners produced dishes and other utilitarian domestic wares from the locally grown hardwoods, whilst basket-makers worked their magic to manufacture baskets of every size for carrying bread, apples, or even pig-swill; whilst high upon the steep Westmorland fellsides thousands of grazing sheep provided coarse wool for cloth-making: this industry originating in medieval times.

All of these diverse industries whether it be a remote mountainside quarry, a water-powered log mill, an iron-making bloomery, the stygian depths of a gassy, dangerous coal mine, have an incredibly fascinating history which typifies the dramatic story of Lakeland man's endeavours to create his workplace in the industrial world.

****

ALUM FOR DYES

An important ancillary industry to clothmaking in the Kendal area of Cumbria was that of dyeing. Locally dyed cloth known as Kendal Green, was popular in the eighteenth century, the dye being made from a mixture of yellow and blue colouring matter. Weld, or Dyer's Rocket together with Dyer's Broomweed are two plants that grow wild, and can still be seen growing today in the area between Windermere and Kendal. Both plants when mixed with alum produce a bright yellow dye. The southern British native plant known as Woad, when also mixed with alum produces a bright indigo blue colour. Alum was a mordant for dyeing, and was also used in the tanning and printing industries.

SEA-SALT EVAPORATION PANS

At Crosscanonby in Cumbria are the remains of the local early eighteenth century salt evaporation industry, used for the production of 'sea-salt' by boiling sea water in huge, coal-fired iron vessels, as similarly carried out in the North East. Nearby also, on the sea shore, west of the Maryport to Allenby road are the remains of salt washing and settling tanks. A short few yards distant from these tanks, is evidence of a number of iron salt-distilling pans, the heat for the distilling process would be generated by coal-fired reverberatory furnaces. Also set back from the road are an interesting row of old Saltworker's cottages.

PACKHORSE TRAINS

Both of these important, long established Cumbrian industries relied on the packhorse trains for the distributions of their products; the alum would be transported to Dyehouses where it was a significant ingredient for the manufacture of natural dyestuffs; whilst the sea salt would be carried to diverse industrial users, for example, Leather Tanners as well as for domestic use.

INTERESTING LESS KNOWN INDUSTRIES

KENDAL SNUFF

The manufacture of tobacco-derived snuff has been carried out in Kendal since the first snuff mill was established on the Natland Beck in 1740.

An enterprising, Kendal native, Thomas Harrison becoming increasingly aware of public interest in snuff-taking, took himself off to a snuff-making concern in Glasgow, where he then studied with some zeal all there was to learn about the manufacture of snuff. Whilst in Glasgow, Harrison on appreciating the potential of setting up his own profitable snuff-making enterprise back home in Kendal, purchased around fifty tons of redundant snuff-manufacturing plant and machinery, which he transported the 140 mile journey to Kendal on a string of packhorses.

In 1792, Thomas Harrison set himself up as a snuff-manufacturer in an old water-powered mill at Mealbank, a tiny hamlet located two miles north of Kendal on the River Mint.

Subsequent to establishing his snuff mill, in 1793, Harrison appears to have entered into a business partnership with local druggist and chemist, Thomas Brocklebank. Around this period of the late eighteenth century, chemists would sell tobacco and snuff, snuff-taking becoming increasingly popular.

During 1793, Thomas Harrison's son, also named Thomas was born, and would later inherit his father's snuff manufacturing concern at Mealbank when Thomas Harrison senior died.

By 1837, Thomas's eldest child, Jane met her future husband, a plumber and glazier named Samuel Gawith, and in the following year, 1838, on the 15th of January, Jane and Samuel got married 'over the Blacksmith's anvil' at Gretna Green.

Thomas Harrison – the Kendalian snuff-maker died in 1841, leaving his Snuff Mill, and his share in the firm of Harrison and Brocklebank to his daughters Jane and Ann. It soon followed that Samuel Gawith, on seeing a more lucrative business opportunity beckoning rather than plumbing, relinquished his trade and commenced working with the now elderly Thomas Brocklebank. In 1842, Jane gave birth to a boy, who they also named Samuel. During the mid 1840s, the elderly senior partner, Thomas Brocklebank, passed away. Later, in 1852, Jane Gawith's sister, Ann Harrison died, which resulted in Samuel Gawith owning the entire snuff manufacturing and retailing business.

Consequently, the name Samuel Gawith became renowned in the history of snuff manufacture in Kendal. The firm of Samuel Gawith & Co. is still going strong in the striking custom-built, multi-storeyed factory at Canal Head that the firm constructed out of local limestone in 1878. This long established Kendal snuff manufacturing company still operate from these historic buildings.

SNUFF MANUFACTURE

The making of snuff involves the carefully controlled roasting of the tobacco, which is then graded followed by grinding down to a fine powder in pestle grinders. Other snuff processing machinery were ball mills, mixers and riddle and shaker machines. After careful processing the finished snuff was then blended, attractively packaged and finally retailed.

Several of Cumbria's other early snuff manufacturing firms were located at the small port of Whitehaven and at Penrith. Whitehaven situated on the west Cumbrian coast enjoyed considerable imports of tobacco in the early decades of the eighteenth century.

PACKHORSE TRAINS

Packhorse trains, heavily laden with Whitehaven tobacco regularly carried the highly aromatic merchandise over the vertiginous Hardknott Pass and down into Westmorland, now in the south-eastern part of the modern county of Cumbria. Whilst being transported, due to the tobacco being continually jolted and compressed within the packhorse panniers, the resultant tobacco dust together with the broken stalks of the tobacco plants, on reaching Kendal, were possibly considered to be slightly inferior and were therefore purchased by a bargain-hunting Kendal trader, who consequently kick-started the trade of snuff manufacture, that would eventually become one of Kendal's most profitable industries.

KENDAL FELL LIMESTONE.

Extensive quarrying of limestone from quarries on Kendal Fell to the west of Kendal has been of great importance to the town and district for several hundred years. Due to the majority of the older buildings in Kendal being constructed from the local greyish-hued limestone, Kendal is locally called the 'Auld Grey Town'.

These quarries provided the town's building stone, as well as the lime mortar and the 'lime-wash' used for lime washing the walls. As a direct result of Kendal becoming connected to Britain's canal network following the opening of the Lancaster–Kendal Canal in 1819, a number of lime-burning kilns were constructed in the quarries on Kendal Fell, lime-making thereafter, becoming prominent among the town's industries.

There is a wonderfully preserved lime kiln built into the bank of the Kendal to Crossthwaite Road, and several smaller lime kilns can be seen scattered throughout the villages and hamlets of the South Lakeland district from Underbarrow to Kirkby Lonsdale. Many of these small lime kilns were used for the local manufacture of lime for mortar-making or for lime spreading on acid farm soils. On the north-eastern moorlands of the former county of Westmorland there are several extensive areas of carboniferous limestone outcroppings, and here also are a number of interesting surviving examples of small-sized lime kilns, several of these being originally constructed as a branch of the lead-mining and lead-smelting industry. The coal used for firing these moorland lime kilns was mined in small pits at Stainmore and Kaber. In the early nineteenth century there was a thin coal seam extracted from workings at Thrimby, south of Lowther also used for the firing of lime kilns.

Each individual lime kiln would be supplied with broken limestone rubble from small quarries or limestone cliff faces located closeby. There is another fine extant kiln which is built into a high rocky bank south of Levens village, near Kendal, and is typical of the local types of kilns, being around fifteen feet in height, with an arched hearth entrance and a flue at the rear.

LIME-MAKING

The Lakeland procedure for the manufacture of lime involved the burning of alternate layers of broken limestone and charcoal or dry peat. Cheap coal would be used if readily available. During the tremendous heat generated during the firing, the calcium carbonate of the limestone was converted to calcium oxide or quicklime, which was then shovelled out of the bottom of the kilns following the cooling period of between 12 and 24 hours.

PACKHORSE TRAINS

Due to ever increasing vast demand for lime as a flux for iron smelting; for mortar-making during the construction of buildings; and for the sweetening of significant acreages of acid-rich pastures, the finished lime on being removed from the kilns was then loaded into the panniers of the packhorse trains, which transported the lime within the local neighbourhood and also considerable distances all over Northern England, Southern Scotland and even further afield.

SLATE QUARRIES

Slate for roofing was one of the most important of the Lakeland industries, the massive quarries at Kirkby-in-Furness producing dark blue slates known as Burlington's from about the late seventeenth century; and by the middle of the eighteenth century a number of the slate quarries at Tilberthwaite, Coniston, Gaitswater and Walna Scar were in full swing.

Coniston, Tilberthwaite, Elterwater, Borrowdale and Honister produced quality slates of a deep green hue – the colour resulting from the ferrous oxide content, the stone being volcanic in origin.

PACKHORSE TRAINS

Until the early nineteenth century in the more remote quarries such as Honister, getting the slates out of the quarry and down to the port of Ravenglass, a distance of fifteen miles where they were loaded onto ships, was a prolonged and therefore costly business. The slates, in demand for roofing all over Britain, had to be loaded onto packhorses, that transported their heavy loads in all weathers along a high-level packhorse trail, traditionally known as Mose's Trod which went via Brandreth, the western ridge of the mountain Great Gable, and over the heights of Wasdale Head.

Towards the close of the nineteenth century, quarrying had developed into one of Cumbria's most important industries, which apart from roofing slates and limestone, included granite and polished limestone marble production.

COPPER MINING

Copper was one of the most important metals mined in the Lake District, the metallic ores occurring almost entirely in the Skiddaw slates, with the notable exception being the extensive copper mines at Coniston, whose depths reached over sixteen hundred feet: remarkable depths, with the inevitable problems of flooding.

Even in the Middle Ages, it was well known that the valuable and useful metal copper, could be found in certain areas of the Lake District. However, the serious mining of copper did not commence until around the 1560s, when German miners, expert in prospecting and mining copper, arrived in the Coniston area.

These early German copper mining operations usually commenced by the men working the copper ore out-croppings with simple iron picks and shovels. When driving levels the miners would set fire to huge stacks of dried timber heaped up against the rock face which would heat the rock to high temperatures. The men would then quench the rock with cold water, resulting in the rock disintegrating into manageable pieces.

The most productive copper mine with the richest ores around this period was named by the Germans: 'Gottesgab' – meaning 'God's Gift'; the name subsequently becoming anglicized into Goldscope. Mining had actually commenced around 1556 by cutting into a nine foot thick vein containing significant copper ore. Twelve years later in 1568, the Company of Mines Royal was formed, and consequently commenced the rapid development of copper mining on the Caldbeck Fells.

Over the next two or three decades, the Company of Mines Royal invested heavily in copper mining around the Keswick area and they also constructed a number of smelt mills.

PACKHORSE TRAILS

The Company of Mines Royal also established a considerable network of packhorse trails which enabled the transportation of the copper ores to the smelt mills, and then to despatch the refined copper all over the country. The packhorse trains transporting the vast quantities of copper along these trails would regularly consist of thirty horses. Packhorses also conveyed considerable quantities of charcoal required as fuel for the smelting of the copper ore from the scores of charcoal burners located in Borrowdale and the other wooded valleys. The production of charcoal was of profound importance, with demand sometimes outstripping supply which eventually resulted in the decimation of extensive woodlands.

Prior to the English Civil War, the copper ore was transported in panniers on the backs of packhorses along a treacherous, mountainous route to the smelt mills located close to Keswick, some twenty miles distant. The Keswick copper ore smelt mills were destroyed during the conflict.

In the 'Keswick Journal' dated 1659 mention is made of a party of Germans extracting copper ore from a mine on the western shore of Buttermere. Around the mid-seventeenth century, mining for copper was being carried out in the Newlands Valley, and also at Dalehead, Castlenook, Longwark and St. Thomas Wark.

After the Goldscope Mine, the second most prominent area mined for copper was on the Caldbeck Fells, for it was hereabouts that a number of the larger, more productive mines were located: Roughton Gill Mine, Silver Gill and Red Gill Mine and the Mexico Mine. Red Gill mine was renowned for the rare, deep azure blue crystals of linarite – a curious mixture of sulphate of lead and copper.

Between 1590 and 1600, as a result of the intensive prospecting and exploration the Company of Mines Royal discovered at Coniston a significant number of enormous, pure copper ore veins.

The outbreak of the English Civil War in 1642 forced most mining operations to cease, and very little copper mining was actually carried out until well into the eighteenth century, when in 1758, the Macclesfield Copper Company, created by Charles Roe, mined the rich Bonsor Vein at Coniston, extending the workings to over one hundred and fifty feet below the surface, this depth being considerably deeper than the old workings originally mined by the Germans.

The extraction of quality copper ore was proceeding well at the Paddy End and Tilberthwaite Mines about this time, no doubt due to the employment of Lakeland manufactured gun-powder which assisted the driving of tunnels and significantly accelerated the extraction of the copper ores.

By the end of the eighteenth century, the galleries, tunnels and headings had descended in excess of three hundred feet below the surface, and due to the copper ores becoming thinner, the Management decided to abandon the mine as they considered it being worked out. Evidently, this was a serious mistake and later events involving John Taylor, a renowned and well respected Mining Engineer would prove them wrong.

Taylor, arrived in Coniston in 1824 and was the driving force that consequently transformed these ancient mines into the most colossal, highly productive, highly profitable copper mines in Northern England. Later, Taylor drove new, larger and safer access tunnels into the rich Bonsor Vein in the Red Dell Mine, and also cut deeper tunnels to access valuable ore veins deep under the old German workings in the Paddy End Mine.

Then in 1825, Taylor commenced work at tackling his most ambitious and most expensive project he had ever undertaken at Coniston: the driving of the Deep or Horse Level – a massive undertaking which created a one and a half miles long draining adit, which eventually drained water from the many branches of the vast workings; the adit also served as a first class waggonway for the numerous horse-hauled waggons that operated throughout the mine.

During these early decades of the nineteenth century, the Lake District's numerous and extensive copper mines had once again entered into a rapid decline. Even, the once highly productive Goldscope Mine was no longer winning the rich copper ore it had been famous for producing. This famous old mine was by now only producing the considerably less valuable metal, lead. Other Lakeland copper mines such as Roughton Gill and Borrowdale's, Copperplate Mine – previously closed, were re-opened, but only meagre tonnages of copper were extracted. However, the Birkside Gill Mine situated above the impressive waterfall to the north of Dunmail Raise and two smaller mines at the northern end of Hawes Water, were in full production.

Due to the high demand for copper required for a wide range of industries, this encouraged the substantial prospecting for copper ore in Seathwaite Tarn Mine, Logan Beck Mine, Cockley Beck Mine, Hesk Fell Mine and Ulpha Copper Mine, all located in the Duddon Valley.

At the Tilberthwaite Mine at Coniston in 1850, significant effort was in progress to drive a new drainage level to a considerable depth. This drainage adit was named Barrett's Level after John Barrett, the Mine Manager, and was finally driven through the unyielding rock to a length of three thousand feet. Incredibly this massive feat of mine engineering took around ten years to achieve.

1856 was the year when copper production at the Coniston Mines peaked at over three thousand, six hundred tons; the value of the ore amounting to a figure in excess of £27,860.

The Coniston copper mines had become so productive and moreover, highly profitable that in 1858, the Company gave the green light for the construction of a branch line from the Furness Railway at Foxfield. By June 1859, the railway was completed which cancelled out the despatching of heavily laden, ponderous, horse-drawn copper ore waggons, down the severe and dangerous inclines to Coniston Water, where the ore would be loaded onto steam boats and shipped to the Ulverston Canal.

Despite the good fortune in the copper mining industry as alluded to above, by the 1860s, once again, the output of copper ore, lurched into a massive terminal decline. By 1864, copper ore output at Coniston had dipped to below two thousand tons. The once highly productive Bonsor Vein workings had become so deep, that the operating costs involving general maintenance, the hundreds of pit-props and roof timbers required, and in particularly, the continuous pumping of water was rising inexorably. Interestingly, by 1870, there were sixteen waterwheels powering ore-raising machinery and driving the water pumps.

During this period, with the mine having now reached a depth of over a thousand feet into the bowels of the earth, it was regrettably discovered that the copper ore being extracted, was becoming less pure due to it being adulterated with magnetite.

By the early 1870s with the majority of the Lake District copper mines being worked out many of them finally closed. Despite the employment of new compressed air rock drills and the increased use of dynamite for blasting, the final nail was driven into the coffin of Lakeland mined copper in the 1880s when cheap copper ore was increasingly imported from overseas resulting in the locally mined copper becoming unprofitable.

However, despite the general malaise in copper mining, the Paddy End and Red Dell copper mines carried on relentlessly drawing up quality ore, notwithstanding considerably lower quantities, until they too finally ceased mining at the start of the twentieth century. Therefore, this was the end of one of Lakeland's oldest, prominent and profitable industries.

WHISTLE STOP SURVEY OF EAST CUMBRIAN PACKHORSE BRIDGES

Built of local random limestone, Barbon Bridge, a typical narrow packhorse bridge, spans Barbon Beck. August 2007.

© Christine McEwen Collection.

Our whistle stop survey of four packhorse bridges in the Pennine, eastern part of Cumbria commenced with Alan and I standing on the magnificent, strikingly beautiful, thirteenth century, 'Devil's Bridge' at Kirkby Lonsdale, that surely must be the finest Medieval bridge in Northern England, which in a leap of one hundred and eighty feet spans the River Lune. Devil's Bridge has three ribbed arches, beautifully crafted by Medieval masons, that carry the bridge around forty-five feet above the deep waters of the Lune that hereabouts swiftly flows through a wide gorge cut into massive beds of ancient limestone.

I consider this historic, beautiful stone bridge truly fascinating, and although not originally constructed as a packhorse bridge, for maybe six hundred years, most certainly it would have been used by the Jaggermen with their packhorses.

With the awesome roar of the fast flowing Lune generated by the huge volume of swirling water being squeezed between the limestone bedrock of both banks slowly diminishing, we walked back to our car.

BARBON BRIDGE, BARBON, NEAR KIRKBY LONSDALE.

Located around two miles north of Kirkby Lonsdale is the tiny, secluded hamlet of Barbon. About a mile to the west of Barbon village spanning the beautiful, meandering, tree-lined Barbon Beck is Barbon Bridge, a fine example of a typically narrow packhorse bridge. A few yards downstream a concrete ford serves Beckfoot Farm.

My research records Barbon Bridge, built of local random limestone, harking back to either the late seventeenth or early eighteenth century. The bridge's segmental arch spans the beck in a leap of twenty-four feet. The trackway is narrow, being just twenty-seven inches betwixt the twenty-six inch parapets; the coping stones are long, rough limestone slabs fastened together with leaded-in wrought-iron staples.

Barbon Bridge: the narrow trackway betwixt stubby parapets. August 2007.

© Christine McEwen Collection.

Barbon Bridge may have served the ancient packhorse trackway and cattle drove road, known as the 'Galloway Gate', that ran down from Galloway in southwest Scotland, through Cumberland and Westmorland into Lancashire.

Our visit to this lovely old bridge was in August 2007, which I recall was a warm, pleasant day, and as we examined and photographed the structure, the air was filled with the droning sounds of many busy bees, the melodious chatter of the lovely stream flowing beneath the bridge and the distinctive call of pheasants coming from a nearby wild flower-filled meadow.

What a delightful old packhorse bridge in a beautiful, sun-kissed, tranquil part of Cumbria.

STAINTON BRIDGE, STAINTON, NEAR KENDAL

Following our most reluctant departure of delightful Barbon Bridge, we drove through Kendal en route to the next bridge, Stainton Bridge. Upon driving around four miles east, with much welcome relief from throbbing, traffic-clogged Kendal, Alan and I quietly drove into the tiny, peaceful hamlet of Stainton, where all we could hear was the delightful chatter of St. Sunday's Beck tumbling in a merry dance through the hamlet of ancient, whitewashed, limestone cottages adorned with thought-inspiring names such as: Waybend Cottage, Hawthorn Cottage and Nightingale Cottage.

Dappled sunlight forcing its way through the overhead canopy of ancient Elms, Oaks and Beeches glinted from the surface of the beck. Parking in an out-of-sight place, we approached an old stone-bottomed ford leading into a tranquil backwater. A large, variegated Holly brightly illuminated a shady spot beside a lovely mullion-windowed cottage, and from a gigantic, gnarled old clump of Hawthorn, delicious birdsong filled the air. Every Stainton cottage garden was a riot of colour with flowering shrubs and flowers.

This bonny little packhorse bridge built from roughly dressed local limestone is located in the heart of the hamlet. Its segmental arch spans the beck in a leap of around eighteen feet; the width of the narrow trackway betwixt the parapets is three feet, the latter vary in height from twenty-nine to thirty-four inches.

Stainton Bridge built from roughly-dressed local limestone spans St. Sunday's Beck in a leap of around eighteen feet. August 2007.

© Christine McEwen Collection.

From Stainton, we headed back into Kendal where again we did reluctant battle with unrelenting traffic to cross to the east side of the 'grey auld town', and to drive up the steep, zig-zagging road that climbs high over the fells to the small market town of Sedbergh in the Howgills. We thoroughly enjoyed the breathtaking scenery and welcomed the cool air blowing in through the open car windows to combat the sticky heat of the sun-kissed afternoon.

No sooner had we arrived in attractive Sedbergh, we took the scenic road through beautiful sheep and cow-filled meadows to Dent, a little grey stone town that sits at the foot of craggy, bonny Dentdale. Here, we both sat outside an attractive Dentdale pub slaking our thirst with a welcoming glass of delicious, locally brewed bitter, and admiring the splendid verdant scenery of the surrounding fells. With the ale supped, we motored slowly up the narrow, tortuous road that ascends the Dale, passing hay meadows filled with a rainbow-mix of wild flowers, whilst the bleating of young sheep high on the fells could be heard above the quiet purring of our car's diesel engine.

At the end of a wondrous climb on the road to the Dale head, we pulled onto a rough area of limestone quarry waste forming a parking area beneath the huge, dominating Dent Head viaduct of the Settle to Carlisle railway. We had reached our goal: the third packhorse bridge of the day: COWGILL BRIDGE.

COWGILL BRIDGE, DENT HEAD, UPPER DENTDALE

This enigmatic, ancient parapet-less packhorse bridge built of local stone, spans a feeder beck of the River Dee in a leap of around thirty feet. The width of the grass covered, cobbled trackway at the centre of the bridge is about fifteen feet which tapers down at either end to about eight feet.

Cowgill Bridge rises from massive limestone bedrock, is built from roughly dressed sandstone and lies beneath one of the massively constructed stone arches of the Midland Railway's Dent Head viaduct on the Settle to Carlisle railway. The voussoir stones forming the segmental arch have been cut from thin flagstones.

The bridge probably lay on the old packhorse trackway connecting Sedbergh and Dent with Horton-in-Ribblesdale via nearby Gearstones and High Birkwith, all once well frequented by the Jaggermen.

Cowgill Bridge rises from massive limestone bedrock, is constructed from roughly-dressed sandstone, and spans a feeder beck of the River Dee in Upper Dentdale. This pleasing little bridge is dominated by the high arches of the Dent Head viaduct on the Settle to Carlisle railway. August 2007.

© Christine McEwen Collection.

Built of local reddish-coloured sandstone, 16th century, double-arched, Frank's Bridge crosses the River Eden in an overall span of around sixty feet. Note the many Mallards swimming beneath the bridge. August 2007.

© Christine McEwen Collection.

FRANK'S BRIDGE, KIRKBY STEPHEN

It was around tea-time when we left peaceful Dent Head to drive the ten miles over lonely moorland roads to Hawes in Wensleydale. With no spare time to tarry in this lovely, historic market town, we cut west through Appersett on the A684 heading back towards Sedbergh. However, just before Garsdale Head, at the Moorcock Inn – once the haunt of Drovers and Jaggermen, we branched onto the B6259 that leads to Kirkby Stephen across the desolate, but wild grandeur of Mallerstang Common, dominated by the massive haunch of Wild Boar Fell; at 708 metres – or in old money 2,327 feet – one of the highest mountains hereabouts and reputedly the last place in England where a wild boar was killed.

Despite, being high summer, we nary saw another car, although we did pass a couple of huge, modern tractors hauling trailers stacked high with freshly mown hay.

Travelling through the Vale of Mallerstang we came to the thought-inspiring ruins of Pendragon Castle on the bank of the River Eden. Reputed to have been founded by Uther Pen-

dragon, father of the legendary King Arthur, Dale's legend spins that Uther Pendragon, together with around a hundred of his warriors were killed here, when invading Saxon warriors poisoned the drinking water in the well. There is also a claim that the Romans built a temporary fort on the site to link up with their forts at Brough and Bainbridge. There is however, no concrete evidence that any buildings were constructed on the site prior to the present castle, which was probably built by the Norman, Hugh de Morville in the twelfth century. Similarly to the nearby castles at Appleby and Brough, Pendragon Castle eventually came into the possession of the Clifford's of Skipton Castle in Craven. In 1341, marauding Scottish Rievers fired the castle, raising it to the ground. It was however, rebuilt around 1360. Another serious fire in 1541, caused the castle to fall into ruin, but yet again, it was fully restored in the mid-seventeenth century by Lady Ann Clifford of Skipton Castle. Following Lady Ann's death at Brougham Castle, near Penrith, Pendragon Castle overtime became ruinous.

JAGGERMEN'S BRIDGES ON PACKHORSE TRAILS

About a half hour after driving away from enigmatic Pendragon Castle, with Alan regaling me with dramatic gory tales of Scots Border warfare, we eventually reached the small, market town of Kirkby Stephen, which is attractively located at the head of the valley of the River Eden. The town was granted a market charter by Edward III circa 1353. Secreted within the town's St. Stephen's Parish Church – locally known as the 'Cathedral of the Dales' is the Loki Stone, an eighth century carved representation of the Norse god Loki, bound and heavily chained. This enigmatic carved stone is one of only two known carvings of its type found anywhere in Europe and the only one in Britain.

Graceful, two-arched, Frank's Bridge built of the local reddish-coloured sandstone, crosses the River Eden with an overall span of around sixty feet. The arch nearest the town measures a span of thirty feet, whilst the other arch is twenty-eight feet; the centre pier incorporates triangular cutwaters on the upstream and downstream sides. The large voussoir stones forming the arches are roughly dressed. The trackway over the bridge is fifty-two inches between thirty-two inch high parapets. The parapet coping stones on both sides are around three feet in length with triangular tops.

So who was Frank, thought I? Local legend mentions that the bridge built in the sixteenth century was named after local brewer Francis Birbeck whose brewery buildings originally surrounded the bridge. These old stone buildings in recent years have been tastefully converted into attractive homes.

On the right at the town end of the bridge there is Riverbank Cottage. The bridge is also known as a 'Corpse Lane Bridge', and at the far end of the structure there are several stones, where in earlier times coffins were rested by bearers bringing the dead from the nearby hamlets of Hartley or Winton, to St. Stephen's for burial.

Frank's Bridge, evidently is another haunted bridge, for it is reputedly haunted by the ghost of a woman known as 'Jangling Anna', whose ghostly spirit has been seen walking across the trackway over the bridge jangling her heavy chains that hang from her arms. Anna is said to have been imprisoned in Hartley Castle, and after escaping while still bound in her heavy chains and manacles, tragically drowned in the swollen river whilst attempting to cross the treacherous, fast flowing, deep water.

Across the river, standing on top of a small grassy hillock, afforded us both a fantastic view three miles to the west, of Nine Standards Rigg, a line of ancient dry stone cairns standing near to the 2,172 foot summit of a mountain on the Pennine watershed. We were extremely lucky to see the Riggs, for on most occasions, the mountain summit is shrouded in dense cloud. On our return to the river, we delighted in seeing a goodly number of mallards swimming near the bridge, which on our approach appeared very tame. Kirkby Stephen is locally renowned for the curious visitations of numerous brightly-hued, semi-wild parrots which are periodically released from a private aviary, and can usually be seen darting hither-thither around the town's historic buildings.

Leading from the town's marketplace down to Frank's Bridge is a narrow lane called Little Wiend, built like a number of other lanes on the outer edge of the town to protect Kirkby Stephen's towns folk from the once regular raids of Scottish Reivers.

Kirkby Stephen was an important packhorse centre, with many routes used by the Jaggermen extending from hereabouts to other northern towns: Newcastle-upon-Tyne, Stockton-on-Tees, Barnard Castle, Richmond, Sedbergh, Kirkby Lonsdale, Kendal and Lancaster. In 1770, goods carried by packhorses leaving Kirkby Stephen averaged 11d per ton, per mile. Packhorses carrying locally-made woollen stockings from Kirkby Stephen and Dent to London, a regular commodity, usually took a fortnight, and during the 1780s around a thousand pairs of stockings were carried to the capital, usually in packs of fifty dozen pairs weighing around 322 pounds, - with a value of around £50.

A packhorse route from Appleby-in-Westmorland leads through Kirkby Stephen where the river would probably be crossed by using Frank's Bridge, the route continuing down through Mallerstang to Garsdale and Wensleydale.

A TRIO OF LAKELAND PACKHORSE BRIDGES

**Ancient Stock High Bridge or Old Mill Bridge spanning Stock Ghyll in Ambleside town centre.
March 2010.**

© Christine McEwen Collection.

Before the last Ice Age of some 10,000 years ago, whose glaciers and melt waters sculptured the mountains and lake-filled valleys of the English Lake District, in the district of Ambleside, there was no human life. As the massively thick ice sheets retreated, forests rapidly grew to cover the valley bottoms and extend to around two thousand, five hundred feet to clothe the steep, rocky, mountain sides.

As the climate warmed – it was much warmer than today – Neolithic man came to hunt and live within the dense forests where there was abundance of wild animals to hunt, edible berries, roots and fungi to gather and with lakes and rivers teaming with fish.

By circa 2000 B.C. much of the forests on the valley floors and lower fell sides had been cleared by man, the soils planted and the breeding of stock was slowly developing into basic farming communities.

However, it was not until around the 1st century A.D. that archaeological evidence records the presence of man in the area, today known as Ambleside. For by this period, the Romans had built a fort named Galava on land at the head of Lake Windermere to defend Southern Lakeland from raids by marauding Picts and Scots tribesmen, as well as to protect the Roman port at Ravenglass.

Around 400 A.D., the Romans abandoned Britain and the Dark Ages begun. Eventually, Christianity developed and over the next few centuries the monks of nearby Furness Abbey cleverly controlled much of Southern Lakeland, skilfully managing farming including the introduction of hardy sheep on the fells, and the establishing of numerous small, iron-ore smelting furnaces, charcoal being the fuel, produced from the surrounding abundant woodlands.

By circa 1000 A.D., the area of what is now Ambleside was becoming increasingly prosperous, with farming, iron-making and charcoal production continuously developing. It was around this period also, that frequent, blood-thirsty raids by Irish-Norsemen took place. These Norse-speaking invaders forcibly dominated the area, but overtime gradually settled to farm the land and to marry and integrate with the indigenous people. These Irish-Norsemen also named parts of the surrounding district, which are still used in modern times. It is said that the famous Herdwick sheep, renowned for being hardy, were introduced by the settlers. Ambleside evidently owes its name to an Irish-Norse settler called Hamel who owned a farm hereabouts, his 'saetre'.

For several hundred years following this period, Ambleside gradually developed to become an important industrial Lakeland town, and by the Elizabethan era, mining activity flourished, with expert Welsh and German miners moving into the area to assist in winning the rich copper ores from the mines at nearby Coniston. Lead was also mined, and the quarrying of the distinctive Kirkstone green slate was carried out, which overtime expanded into a significant export industry.

In 1650, Ambleside was granted a market charter, and shortly thereafter, local industries involving paper manufacture, bark (for tanning), cloth, and corn milling became established. From around 1750, Britain's new 'Industrial Age' – the Industrial Revolution slowly gathered pace, and around Ambleside and South Lakeland another locally important industry, the manufacture of charcoal, now expanded. For centuries, the forestry skills of the local people had been employed to expertly manage the coppicing of Ash, Alder, Birch, Oak, and other indigenous trees used for charcoal production. Later, the burgeoning textile industries of Lancashire and the West Riding of Yorkshire would generate a significant demand for wooden bobbins, the manufacture of which became another locally important woodland industry. In the mid-to late nineteenth century at nearby Elterwater, gunpowder was manufactured for use in the mines and quarries of Lakeland.

PACKHORSES

Due to a profound lack of passable roads – most trackways around Ambleside were often muddy and deeply rutted, and therefore, unsuitable for use by horse-drawn waggons or carts. The transportation of locally manufactured goods: corn and seeds, paper, bark, charcoal, iron-ore, lead, and woven cloth was usually carried out by packhorses who carried these goods on the many trackways that criss-crossed over the high Lakeland fells, to destinations all over northern Britain.

On a chilly, overcast, yet fair morning in late March 2010, accompanied by Alan, fascinated, I stood looking down at the considerable volume of white-flecked, foaming mountain torrents thundering over the moss-covered bedrock of Stock Ghyll beneath the robustly-built slate arch of ancient Stock High Bridge in Ambleside. I felt highly elated, for I was on the downhill trod of a very lengthy journey involving the surveying, photography and research of dozens of historic packhorse bridges scattered across Northern England for the book I had been writing for the best part of seven years. This trip into glorious Lakeland, to survey and photograph a mere handful of perhaps the forty or so examples of packhorse bridges to be found all over the Lake District, would be the last one, for my manuscript had to be completed before Easter.

STOCK HIGH BRIDGE OR OLD MILL BRIDGE, AMBLESIDE

This striking historic bridge over Stock Ghyll Beck enjoys a prominent position being right in Ambleside town centre, and is best viewed from tiny Bridge Street, originally known as Rattle Gill, - no doubt due to the ever-present ferocious roar of turbulent water thundering down the narrow, rocky ravine.

The Romans probably would have built a wooden bridge for crossing the beck. History records that nearby there was an ancient crossing point known as Hallicar Ford, which, during the winter would, no doubt, be un-crossable due to severe regular flooding.

JAGGERMEN'S BRIDGES ON PACKHORSE TRAILS

From the early fourteenth century descendants of the Irish-Norse settlers, who centuries earlier had colonised the district, used the waters of Stock Ghyll Beck to turn waterwheels for grinding corn. Later, larger waterwheels provided power for the washing of wool to remove grease, for powering looms for cloth-making, and for the fulling of the finished woven cloth. During the height of the Industrial Revolution, Stock Ghyll Beck also provided the power for numerous bobbin making machinery, and also for bark crushing rollers for the production of tannin for the treatment of leather hides.

Stock High Bridge constructed from local random stone and slate has a long a fascinating history, which probably pre-dates the town itself. The span is around eighteen feet, the abutments springing from the ghyll's natural bedrock. The segmental arch's voussoir stones are fashioned from thin slates. The parapets are built from a mixture of slate and local stone, capped with copings of lengthy pieces of sandstone joined together with leaded-in, wrought-iron straps. The trackway over the top, now tarmacadamed is around fourteen feet wide, and is named North Road. During the Roman period, it was the main road leading over Kirkstone Pass, the highest Roman road in England.

Alan and I, greatly enjoyed viewing this fascinating, ancient Lakeland bridge, and following the taking of many photographs, we walked along North Road, turned right into Kirkstone Road, then first left into Sweden Bridge Lane. We were walking to our next bridge, High Sweden Bridge.

Surrounded by the breathtaking grandeur of high fells, High Sweden Packhorse Bridge spans Scandale Beck that thunders down the rocky ravine of the Scandale Valley.

By kind permission of Edward Whiteside.

JAGGERMEN'S BRIDGES ON PACKHORSE TRAILS

HIGH SWEDEN PACKHORSE BRIDGE, NEAR AMBLESIDE

The unusual name of this delightful Lakeland packhorse bridge, has no connection with Scandinavia, but is in fact a corruption of St. Swithen's Bridge, the original name for the bridge, or is derived from Old Anglo-Norse, 'swidden' meaning, 'the land cleared by burning'.

Quickly leaving the bustle of Ambleside behind, we proceeded up the steep incline of Sweden Bridge Lane until where the tarmac ended, we reached a field gate, the other side of which there was a narrow, stony track hemmed in betwixt dry stone walls.

The track was the original packhorse route leading up from Ambleside into the secluded Scandale Valley, and to our goal, High Sweden Bridge, a distance of about a mile and a half. As we climbed the old packhorse trackway, the cool, spring morning started to warm up, the light mist hanging over Ambleside was thinning, and our view west of Rydal Water and the slopes of Low Pike, – the last summit of the Fairfield Horseshoe, – was wonderfully clear with the pale sun becoming stronger for every yard of our progress.

We ascended the stony trackway for about a mile until we reached another gate which we went through. We had now reached Lower Sweden Coppice, the steeply wooded fellsides dropping vertiginously down into the bolder-strewn bottom of Scandale, where we could hear the almighty roar of a fast-flowing mountain torrent cascading over rocky ledges. We delighted also in seeing bunches of flowering wild primroses scattered among the rocks and patches of last year's heather.

Wild and lonely Scandale Valley cuts deeply into the high fells situated on the north side of Ambleside, and this location, with the Scandale Beck rushing down the valley bottom, was to both Alan and me, heavenly.

Shortly after us reaching some crumbling, old dry stone walls blanketed below huge clumps of mosses, Alan suddenly spotted High Sweden Bridge. *"By golly, Christine, Doesn't that bonny, little bridge look just spell-binding?"* Enthusiastically, he then raced across massive slabs of bedrock to reach the bridge.

In its beautiful, secluded setting with majestic, high fells on either side, High Sweden Bridge, built from a mixture of large, water-rounded stones and slates, spans Scandale Beck in a leap of around fourteen feet. The structure is without parapets, the trackway around sixty-eight inches wide, its surface consisting of slate and patches of concrete. The single arch, generally semi-elliptical in form, appears to have settled; to become distorted, although remains robust.

The old packhorse trackway linking Ambleside with Hartsopp runs up the east side of the Scandale Valley, and therefore, would not have needed to cross the bridge. However, it has been suggested by local historians, that an alternative packhorse route from Ambleside, using another bridge, Low Sweden Bridge, on the west side of the valley, probably crossed the beck via High Sweden Bridge, thereby joining the main packhorse trackway over the pass.

This highly photogenic specimen of a Lakeland packhorse bridge is now regularly used by fell walkers, hiking around the circuit of hills known as the Fairfield Horseshoe. During our photographing of High Sweden Bridge, the sun suddenly dived behind a bank of dark clouds, and within a few minutes the landscape was transformed under a blanket of sleet.

Thoroughly satisfied with viewing High Sweden Bridge, we made our way down on the old Jaggermen's trackway into bustling Ambleside where, in a delightful little tea shop, we both enjoyed tea and scones. Whilst in the tea shop, the sun burst forth again lighting up the pleasant Lakeland town, and after finishing our tea and scones, we set off in our car through Grasmere to St. John's-in-the-Vale, near Threlkeld to locate the last packhorse bridge on my list known as Sosgill Bridge.

SOSGILL BRIDGE, ST. JOHN'S-IN-THE-VALE NEAR THRELKELD

Whilst driving along the quiet B5322 in glorious Spring sunshine down the beautiful glen of John's-in-the-Vale, four miles south-east of Keswick, both of us delighted on rounding a bend in the road with the sudden appearance of the graceful, arch of Sosgill Bridge rising high above St. John's Beck. Parking beneath some Grey Alders displaying hanging catkins on a gravelly patch on the road side, we then went through an iron field gate on a track running along the east bank of the beck.

We noticed that along both banks there were extensive, deep deposits of sand and pebbles, the result of the serious flooding that had ravaged this part of Cumbria during the previous November, when considerable acres of farmland was irretrievably lost due to the retreating flood waters dumping heavy deposits of riverbed materials. Arriving at the foot of this splendid bridge, a small gate afforded us access to the trackway over the top. From here, with the sun lighting up the whole of this beautiful, quiet, green glen, from our position atop the bridge we could see to the north the dominating mass of the mountain, Skiddaw.

JAGGERMEN'S BRIDGES ON PACKHORSE TRAILS

Looking south, we took in the splendid vista of Blencathra, or the Saddleback as this magnificent mountain is sometimes called due to its shape. Further to the south we could also see the sunshine lighting up the summit of majestic Helvellyn.

Deep in thought, taking pictures, we were both so engrossed that we didn't notice a pleasant looking, dark haired woman, a young chap of around twenty and a border collie, suddenly appear at the west foot of the bridge. *"Hello, isn't it a grand sunny afternoon,"* said the woman, who, after greeting us informed us that her family farmed all the land hereabouts. The young man, whom she introduced as her son, and who spoke in a lovely Cumbrian lilt, recalled how the family were devastated when the November floods blighted their hay meadows along both banks of the beck. He pointed out the colossal 'beaches' comprising, sand, gravel and pebbles that the flooded beck had deposited onto the hay meadows owned by the family, leaving the land totally useless for grass. He also drew our attention to several thought-inspiring, crumbling remains of stone farmsteads, that perhaps, two hundred and fifty years earlier, would have been frequent customers of the Jaggermen for the delivery and transportation of lime, woollens, and a diverse range of other goods; the packhorses crossing St. John's Beck by Sosgill Bridge.

The bridge spans the beck in a leap of around thirty feet. The trackway width betwixt the twenty-four inch high parapets is around eight feet. The segmental arch consists of roughly dressed green slate, making the whole structure most attractive and pleasing to the eye. On the trackway, many of the arch stones protrude to form the surface.

Sosgill Bridge, the last of the three bridges representing the many stone bridges to be found all over the Lake District, was sadly, also the last bridge featured in this book. After the long, dark, cold winter of 2009/2010, our foray into beautiful Lakeland was not only refreshing, but was also truly unforgettable.

Sosgill Bridge gracefully rises high above St. John's Beck amidst the dazzling beauty of the glen known as St. John's-in-the-Vale. March 2010.

© Christine McEwen Collection.

OTHER QUALITY BOOKS FROM SLEDGEHAMMER

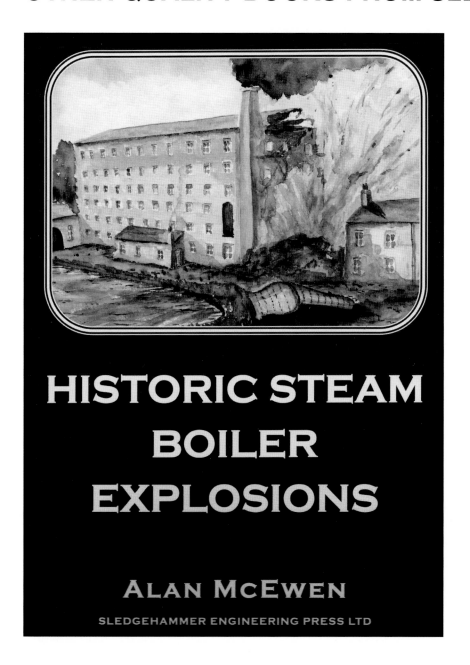

£24.95
+ Post and Packing

IMMEDIATE DESPATCH

HISTORIC STEAM BOILER EXPLOSIONS includes basic histories of early industrial boilers such as: Waggon, Rastrick Vertical, Egg-Ended, Cornish, Lancashire, Scotch Marine Return-Tube; unfired pressure vessels called Kiers, as well as Locomotive Boilers and Marine Rectangular or Box Boilers.

The writing of this book - HISTORIC STEAM BOILER EXPLOSIONS - the first modern publication for decades that authoritively chronicles early British industrial boiler explosions, has been a long time coming for author, Alan McEwen, a qualified Boiler Engineer, for he has spent well over 30 years researching and gathering material, including many rare photographs that has made the publication of this book a reality.

Within his book, Alan has chronicled 23 highly dramatic and informative stories based on his extensive research of the terrifying and devastating boiler explosions, including multiple explosions, that claimed the lives of hundreds of people whilst destroying the neighbouring buildings in Cotton Mills, Bleachworks, Collieries, Ironworks and other industries of the 19th and early 20th centuries. Included also, are 11 accounts of Traction Engine, Railway Locomotive and Marine Boiler explosions.

HISTORIC STEAM BOILER EXPLOSIONS is effectively two books in one.
Over 170 black and white illustrations.

OTHER QUALITY BOOKS FROM SLEDGEHAMMER

IMMEDIATE DESPATCH

£24.95 + Post and Packing

Author Alan McEwen, a retired Master Boilermaker and Steam Engineer well-known in the industrial heritage and steam world was a close friend of the late Master Steeplejack and Chimney Demolition Expert Fred Dibnah M.B.E. for close to 25 years, and within this beautifully produced book he has passionately and vividly chronicled 28 out of Fred's 90 amazing and often spine-tingling, dangerous chimney toppling exploits. Alan accompanied Fred on numerous extremely exciting and dangerous chimney demolition jobs all over North Western England, which enabled him to write the only authoritive account of Fred Dibnah's chimney toppling exploits.
This highly acclaimed book has received several brilliant reviews. This brilliant book chronicles 28 of Fred's amazing and often exceedingly dangerous chimney drops. Over 250 black and white and colour illustrations.

BOTH BOOKS A4 SIZE HARD BACK QUALITY PUBLICATIONS, 200 PAGES, WRITTEN BY ALAN McEWEN AND PUBLISHED BY SLEDGEHAMMER ENGINEERING PRESS LIMITED

Visit our amazing web Site: www.sledgehammerengineeringpress.co.uk

We accept payment by most credit/debit cards, cheques, cash and postal orders made out to
SLEDGEHAMMER ENGINEERING PRESS LTD